REGIONAL EXCELLENCE

Governing Together
To
Compete Globally and Flourish Locally

William R. Dodge

D1114258

NATIONAL LEAGUE OF CITIES

To
my parents, Dorothy and William,
my wife, Cynthia,
and my sons, Christopher, Matthew, and Zachary,
for nurturing, supporting and sharing
my love of community

The following newspaper story is hypothetical, but it offers a view of the future, a tale of two regions ...

National Regional Times Weekly
September 12, 2002

NEIGHBORING REGIONS
WORLDS APART
Divergent Journeys Began in Last Decade

Heather Wright is hoping that the future in suburban Fragmented will be as good as the recent past.

In 1995, when her son Ben reached school age, Heather and her family moved from Distressed, the central city in the Fragmented region. Since then, she has watched other families make the same move. Even her husband Sam's employer moved to the suburbs, unfortunately to the other side of Distressed. Now Sam's daily commute has increased from 25 to 45 minutes each way. Heather's part-time job at the Third Millennium Shop is closer, at the Nirvana Mall, but barely covers the cost of the second car they need for commuting and chauffeuring Ben and his sister Mary to their many after-school and weekend activities.

Until recently, Heather's major complaint was that every outing required a car trip on congested highways. She listens to the 24-hour traffic reports to determine which highways are passable and when. Even the private toll road that was completed last year to reduce delays is already congested and expensive to use.

Since the turn of the century, Heather and Sam have been concerned about the future. In the past year, three major factories closed and consolidated their operations in other regions. Even worse, Sam's employer also reduced the size of its operations soon after the relocation and anticipates further reductions in early 2003.

The Wrights still like their community, but they are worried. They believe that the problems of Distressed, and now some of the other inner suburbs, have finally caught up with them. They fear the growing number of "city" kids on their streets, which is one of the reasons Ben and Mary are, as Sam says, "plugged into" so many organized activities. They blame the increasing crime and drug usage on "marauding gangs" and are pleased that their local government built barricades, with beautiful floral planters, to block off all except major roads to Distressed. These same fears discourage the Wrights from visiting the museums and restaurants still located in Distressed. As a result, Mary and Ben hardly know that Distressed exists, much less ever see it, except as background in crime scenes on TV.

Some of the Wrights' neighbors are moving out, to "get further away from city problems," they say. Heather and Sam don't know what to do about these new concerns either. They are frustrated that their local government cannot deal with them, and they don't know where to go to deal with problems that seem to cut across communities and the entire region.

The Wrights wonder if they too should move, given that housing values are leveling off in their community. They have even begun talking about relocating to a small town far away from Distressed, where, as Mary says, "we can trust and get to know our neighbors."

Inner-City Distressed

Owen Moore is afraid that the future will be like the present or worse.

His neighborhood on the west side of Distressed is filled with boarded-up houses and shops. Drugs and crime make it unsafe to be on the streets, even with the youth curfew. High school dropouts, single teenage mothers, and high unemployment rates abound. His neighborhood is as poor and minority as the Wrights' is affluent and white.

Owen is glad that his children are grown, since it's hardly safe to allow kids to play in the yard, much less use the streets to visit friends. Government services have been cut back; garbage is only collected every other week, roads are potholed, and the neighborhood center has been closed since the late 1990s. Owen, and especially his wife Dolores, who is active in the neighborhood association, complain to the Distressed city government but get little response. The more affluent city neighborhoods, which became gated compounds after the riots of '99, hire their own security guards, and collect their own garbage.

The Moores rarely leave their neighborhood anymore. Without a car and living on a limited social security income, they used to take the bus downtown to walk around and sometimes visit a museum or go to a baseball game. Now, they say, it's hardly worth the trip. The last downtown department store closed in 1999; the football and baseball teams moved to the outer beltway; and the museums operate on limited schedules. The cutbacks in bus service make it difficult to travel to suburban communities, or to work. Dolores had to give up her part-time job at a dry cleaning plant when her bus route was eliminated. Many businesses, unable or unwilling to operate in such surroundings, have moved to the suburbs.

Owen's neighbors seem to move out as soon as they can afford to, leaving behind the poorest and oldest residents. Owen's friend Rodney, who lives in one of the gated compounds, wants to move to the suburbs as well, but is afraid that he will lose what's left of the investment in his house.

Fragmented's Journey

The Wrights and Moores and other citizens across the Fragmented region have a lot in common, but they don't know it.

They all feel a sense of isolation, not knowing many of their neighbors, much less citizens in the next community. They fear that social problems are beyond their control; after all, neither their local governments or other community organizations have been able to solve them. They share a great deal of economic insecurity, whether they have jobs or not, and they believe that they are losing out to other regions.

Some community organizations have offered ideas for addressing the challenges to the Fragmented region. The Distressed Area Chamber of Commerce has asked the state government to take over the Distressed government. The Mayor of Distressed has repeatedly asked suburban communities to help address the city's concerns. Community leaders and citizens, however, have few opportunities to discuss the merits of these ideas or develop their own. Not surprisingly, *Dis-*

tressed *Chronicle* surveys indicate that citizens have little confidence that they can solve their problems and believe that they will have to move somewhere else to maintain or improve their quality of life.

The Wrights' children, Ben and Mary, say there is "no way" they will stay in the Fragmented region. The Moores' children, Roger and Sherril, who are adults, have already moved, to another region, Networked.

Networked's Journey

Roger and Sherril and other citizens in the Networked region are confident that the future will be better than the present.

They started with the same problems as the Fragmented region but developed the confidence to address them before the turn of the century. They started in small ways.

Getting Started

Community officials and citizens started talking with counterparts in neighboring communities about common concerns, such as drugs and crime, traffic, and economic competitiveness. These conversations led to the creation of informal groups that explored the concerns. These informal groups approached elected officials, business executives, foundation directors, college presidents and other civic leaders, who also were beginning to think about these challenges. Together, they hosted a series of informal dialogues, called "regional confabs," that involved citizens from across the region. Roger Moore participated in one that brought together newcomers who had lived in the region for less than two years. The results of the regional confabs were reported on in a series of articles in the *Core Gazette*.

The participants in the regional confabs then launched a year-long campaign to focus attention on the region, including giving the region its name, Networked,

and adding the name to community signs. They hosted dinners and dialogues to develop personal relationships between residents of affluent suburban communities and distressed neighborhoods in Core, their central city. They established regional sections of newspapers and television newscasts and launched a new regional magazine, *The Networked Inter-Dependent*. During the year, they conducted the first regional citizenship class, to prepare individuals to participate in addressing regional challenges. They even selected the first group of individuals and organizations to be recognized as Networked Treasures for their extraordinary contributions to making the region work. Sherril Moore's employer bought a table and selected her to participate in the dinner recognizing the first year's winners.

At the end of the year-long campaign, a regional alliance, called Networked Tomorrow, was formed by representatives from all parts and sectors of the region, to design a future vision for governing the region. The vision, called Regional Excellence 2020, focuses on building the collective capacity of the region's communities to work together, empowering community leaders and citizens to be involved in addressing cross-cutting challenges, making each of the region's communities economically competitive, and providing the problem-solving and service-delivery mechanisms to address cross-cutting challenges, effectively. Participants called for creating a region of grace whose future is actively shaped by its citizens.

Each of the participants in the planning process signed a "regional pledge" to support cooperative regional decision making, negotiate proposed activities with neighboring communities, share available resources with poor communities, involve citizens in decisions that affect them, and, in general, work for the overall good of the region. Networked Tomorrow task groups monitor the implementation of the action plan to achieve the Regional Excellence 2020 vision, prepare an annual report on the state of the region, and host an annual regional excellence day to celebrate regional governance successes. Both Roger and Sherril Moore volunteered to clean up a new site for the Networked regional park system during the 2002 Regional Excellence Day.

Institutional Change

Various mechanisms have been created or redirected to address regional challenges. The Networked Regional Planning Council has negotiated agreements that define the land use, environment, and transportation policies guiding future regional development. The Networked Regional Citizens League has focused its agenda on educating and involving citizens in addressing regional challenges. The Core State University has defined itself as a metropolitan university and created the Institute of Networked Studies to assist in addressing regional challenges. Community foundations and private corporations have matched public monies and established the Networked Fund to support new governance and other regional initiatives.

In addition, pairs of city neighborhoods and suburban communities have established "sister community" relationships to share information, exchange cultural groups, and work on joint projects. A regional conflict resolution service has been established to assist communities to mediate intercommunity differences. Regional tax sharing has reduced the service inequities between rich and poor communities, often through joint delivery of services, by almost 50 percent. A regional affordable housing policy, adopted by more than 90 percent of the region's municipalities, sets aside 15 percent of new housing developments for low and moderate income residents. Most of the old public housing complexes in Core have been converted to mixed-income housing or torn down. The chambers of commerce and other business development organizations have created the Networked Regional Growth Association to coordinate regional marketing and economic development activities. A coordinating group, called Serving Networked, has been created among the organizations responsible for delivering regional services to citizens.

Facing the Future

Community leaders and citizens are continually considering additional cooperative actions, including a recent proposal by the Networked Association of Community Organizations to hold simultaneous dialogues on developing a regional transit system. Called the Regional Voice project, it would test a new approach for involving citizens regionwide in exploring a timely regional challenge.

The community leaders and citizens of Networked have not resolved all of their problems, but, by working together, have engaged the energies of the affluent communities and given hope to the distressed ones. They compare their actions to weaving a quilt — stitching people and communities together into a strong regional network.

Perhaps most important, the children of Networked have opportunities, and they want to stay around.

Contents

Chapter 6
Making Regional Governance Empowering:
Regional Citizenship and Community

Chapter 7
Making Regional Governance Institutionalized:
Regional Problem Solving and Service Delivery

Foreword

This is an important book. It is simply the best available thinking to help people who want to make things work regionally. It is relevant, practical, and focused. It is firmly grounded in a wonderful mix of experience and analysis, and it is pointed toward doing things that matter to bring about effective governance for regions that encompass multiple governments.

Dodge's approach is like ours. He gets beyond the all-too-often dead-end debate over metropolitan government. He focuses on the broader issue of governance, and this allows him to discern specific steps that can be taken to add to communities' abilities to address their regional needs.

People who have toiled in these vineyards would have expected something like this from Bill Dodge. He has worked toward a coherent view of regional challenges, in print and in practice, and here he has put it all together.

Based on NLC's work on these topics over the past few years, Dodge proposed an outline of this book to us in early 1995. We immediately saw it as a major contribution to the field, worthy of our support as part of the ongoing agenda of the National League of Cities. NLC's work has focused especially on the need for effective governance and good economic policy for the local economies that are the real basis for economic growth in what our recent report termed the "United States Common Market of Local Economic Regions." This book will certainly help city and town officials and others who seek to meet that need.

We are delighted to have worked with Bill Dodge on the preparation of this volume. We commend his good work. We are grateful to all the individuals that supported the preparation of this book — they are listed in the Preface — as well as the organizations that are collaborating with us to make it available to community leaders and citizens nationwide, including the American Chamber of Commerce Executives, International City/County Management Association, International Downtown Association, National Association of Counties, National Association of Regional Councils, and National Civic League. Thanks are especially due to Clint Page, who served as editor for the project, and Jeff Fletcher, who took the lead at NLC on printing and distribution.

Donald J. Borut
Executive Director
National League of Cities

William R. Barnes
Director
Center for Research and
Program Development.
National League of Cities

Preface

I would like to thank the National League of Cities for publishing this book and the hundreds of community leaders and citizens across regions, nationally and internationally, for providing the materials for its contents. I would also like to thank the individuals who advised me throughout the writing and editing of this book, including:

- Don Borut, Bill Barnes, and Jeff Fletcher of the National League of Cities;
- John Epling and Pat Atkins of the National Association of Regional Councils;
- Chris Gates, John Parr, and Alan Wallis of the National Civic League;
- Bill Hansell and the members of the Regionalism Task Force of the International City/County Management Association;
- Larry Naake, Ed Ferguson, and Sharon Lawrence of the National Association of Counties;
- Bill Davis and Bruce McDowell of the Advisory Commission on Intergovernmental Relations;
- Eric Stowe of the American Chamber of Commerce Executives;
- Brian Dobson and Bill Schweke of the Committee for Enterprise Development;
- Rich Bradley of the International Downtown Association;
- Scott Fosler and Dewitt John of the National Academy of Public Administration; as well as
- Bruce Adams, Jim DeAngelis, John Gardner, Ted Hershberg, Larry Ledebur, Mary Ellen Mazey, Neal Peirce, Jan Purdy, Hank Savitch, Jim Svara, John Thomas, and my brother Rick Dodge.

I would like to especially thank John Gardner for fostering my interest in excellence, Pat Atkins for reviewing my drafts from cover to cover, and Clint Page for skillfully editing my prolix profundity.

Finally, I would like to thank my wife Cynthia for providing emotional and financial support during the sometimes demanding writing process.

I am indebted to all of these individuals and organizations for participating in an effort that was as truly cooperative as any successful regional decision-making process.

Since this is one of the first attempts to provide a practical guide for improving regional governance, it has its limitations. In spite of almost three decades of laboring in the trenches of regional governance, I am certain that I have left out some excellent initiatives for its improvement, as well as overlooked some excellent examples of the application of initiatives. Moreover, I am sure that I have misstated the facts for some of the options, in spite of my attempts to corroborate them. For both the oversights and mistakes, I beg forgiveness.

The major limitation, however, is caused by the topic itself. Attempting to capture the essence of regional governance is analogous to holding a moonbeam in one's hands. Regional governance has taken a quantum leap in complexity over the past decade, enriched by more experimentation than occurred in the previous century. It gives every indication of being a — if not the — governance movement of import as we enter the third millennium.

I hope this book provides both guidance and inspiration. I also hope that you will share your experiences in strengthening regional governance with me. Or, if you need further assistance, are looking for additional information, or have ideas for strengthening regional governance, please contact me. I can be reached by telephone (412-371-8124), fax (412-371-9524) or by mail (209 North Lang Avenue, Pittsburgh, Pa. 15208).

William R. Dodge
Pittsburgh, Pennsylvania
Southwestern Pennsylvania Region

Introduction

A thousand years ago, in the late 900s, people literally feared the end of the world in some cataclysmic explosion.

Their fears caused them to consider reforms, especially of their spiritual behavior. Hoping that the end would coincide with the second coming, community leaders and citizens of the time, at least the Christian ones, dedicated themselves to a religious building campaign of colossal proportions. Their collaborative efforts resulted in constructing many of the monumental Romanesque cathedrals of Western Europe. A Cluniac monk, Raoul Glaber, observed in 1003, "It was as if the whole earth, having cast off its age by shaking itself, were clothing itself everywhere in a white robe of churches." (Sloann, 23)

Today, in the late 1900s, people fear the end of their local political worlds in some equally drastic change.

What used to be resolvable in their individual communities now defies resolution with neighbors or across entire regions. What used to be clearly the responsibility of public, private, or non-profit organizations now creates overlapping confusion. What used to be perceived as common — even American — values are increasingly contested by conflicted communities and interest groups.

Such fears have caused people to consider reforms, especially of their temporal behavior. Not depending upon divine intervention for resolving their earthly challenges, community leaders and citizens are experimenting with new approaches to intercommunity and regional decision making. These experiments have not yet reached colossal proportions, but they may preview a regional renaissance by the dawn of the 21st century.

Maybe, just maybe, our regions will be clothed with regional governance excellence in this change in millennia!

By regional governance, I mean how we bring community leaders and citizens together to address challenges that cut across communities — from crime and drugs to economic competitiveness. This usually involves defining the challenge, assigning responsibility for addressing it to an existing or new regional mechanism, involving community leaders and citizens affected by it, designing a strategy for addressing it, negotiating responsibility and implementing the strategy, and monitoring and evaluating success in addressing the challenge. By excellence, I mean doing this in a more timely, flexible, and effective manner with each new challenge, so as to take advantage of regional opportunities before they are lost and prevent regional threats from exploding into crisis.

By regional governance, I do not mean metropolitan government, the one-big-government approach to regional challenges.

The purpose of this book is to share this regional governance experimentation and assist you — community leaders and citizens — in improving the way you address each new regional challenge and building your regional governance capability and capacity to compete globally and flourish locally in the 21st century.

This book begins with a background primer on the rising importance of regional governance or decision making. Next, it provides a framework for addressing the topic and developing a vision and targeted strategy for pursuing regional governance excellence. The heart of the book is an inventory of three dozen different types of regional governance initiatives, illustrated with hundreds of examples of their application in regions in this country and around the world.

I refrain from considering the book a "tool kit" because many of these experiments have neither individually nor nationally proven themselves. Maybe it is more appropriate to consider this a "holistic regional governance catalog" since it attempts to share specific experiments as well as provide a framework for achieving regional governance excellence.

The book makes four important assumptions.

First, regional governance has risen in importance.

Regions are organic systems organized in ways surprisingly similar to flowers, fish, mammals, and humans. They have evolved out of less complex, but not necessarily lower, life forms, especially in urban areas that started with small settlements that grew into cities that, in turn, expanded into regions containing suburbs and exurbs. As a result, regions have one or more vital organs — central business and cultural districts, suburban employment centers and shopping malls, and even regional parks — tied together with the sinews of transportation, the arteries of commerce, and the protoplasm of community.

Healthy regions nurture us, their individual cells, by concentrating the resources and providing the connections to pursue a desired quality of life, locally and globally. In turn, they need our care and feeding, since, like other living beings, their health and happiness is determined by whoever or whatever shapes and controls their growth.

States and nations do not usually stir the same biological thoughts. As critical as they are to providing military security, setting uniform standards, redistributing wealth, and even supporting local and regional initiatives, they appear more to be human contrivances than living organisms.

It is not surprising, therefore, that the region has emerged again as it has repeatedly over recorded history. This time, it has become more important as the cold war, which had required *nations* to develop competitive armies, cooled off, and the global common market, which now requires *regions* to develop competitive economies, heated up.

The era of the region is already being proclaimed worldwide. In Europe, the borders between nations are dissolving in the European Community and a "Europe of Regions" is taking its place. In Asia, Hong Kong shows every sign of surviving its transfer from Great Britain to the Peoples Republic of China as a relatively independent region, one that now includes a considerable part of the Guangzhou province of China. I suspect that neither ideology nor nationalism will seriously restrict the behavior of this powerful living organism in the global ecosystem.

What might be surprising, however, is that this same Global Competitiveness, and four other major developments, or change drivers — Challenge Explosion, Citizen Withdrawal, Structure/Challenge Mismatch, and Rich/Poor Community Gap — have transformed regional governance from a nicety to a necessity, as described in Chapter 1.

Bottom line: Community leaders and citizens need to focus priority attention on the growth and development — the governance — of their own living organisms, their regions.

Second, pursuing regional governance excellence requires a guiding strategy.

We have a long history of being easy "creationists" and reluctant "evolutionists" concerning regions.

On one hand, as easy "creationists," we have all too readily bought into the idea that a metropolitan government, in the form of a single monolithic structure that directs all decision making, would eventually be created, almost overnight, and guide regional development. It, I suspect, is doomed to be the eternal will-o'-the-wisp of regional governance.

No matter how creative we become, we cannot anticipate the range of challenges or nail down the geographic scope of the region long enough to have it governed by a single structure. Even those places that have annexed extensively, such as Columbus, Ohio; consolidated city and county government, such as Unigov in the Indianapolis region; or created two-tier governments, such as Metro Toronto, continue to be confronted with irrepressible sprawl leapfrogging across their borders into the great beyond.

Unless we are willing to pursue the highly unlikely option of making each region a state, and to then redraw state boundaries every decade to conform with the changing spheres of regional influence, we will need to build a "network" of regional decision making mechanisms — processes and structures — to address emerging challenges in each region.

On the other hand, as reluctant "evolutionists," we have resisted the evolution of regional decision-making mechanisms, condemning most of them to be ineffective "footballs without laces," giving all the appearances of addressing regional challenges but being genetically flawed in their powers, participants, practices, or perseverance. Or, even worse, we have flirted with the myth that the region was divisible — that the donut (the suburbs) is not connected to the hole (the central city). To borrow a metaphor from Peter Senge, author of *The Fifth Discipline*, dividing a region into parts has no greater chance of working than dividing any other living organism, such as an elephant, into parts; all one gets is a mess.

I believe that we now need to be strategic "pragmatists" and foster a regional renaissance. We need to pursue a visionary strategy for achieving regional governance excellence in the closing years of the second millennium if we are to compete globally and flourish locally in the third. Achieving excellence, I further believe, requires launching initiatives to improve each of five components of regional governance; that is, we need to make it Prominent, Strategic, Equitable, Empowering, and Institutionalized as explored in Chapter 2.

Bottom line: The pursuit of regional governance excellence needs to be empowered by community leaders and citizens in each region and enjoy the involvement and support of state and national, governmental and non-governmental, organizations.

Third, achieving regional governance excellence will strengthen, and even save, our federal system of governance.

Regional decision making complements local, state and national decision making by providing mechanisms for addressing cross-cutting challenges that cannot be sponsored by any one of those levels alone. It does not replace, but rather enriches and helps preserve our federal system of governance.

As regions continue to evolve, they will create a new political force in state capitals and Washington. At times, communities within regions will come together in a collective voice that has the clout to drive almost any agenda through the legislative process and shift funding streams to regional initiatives. Witness the success of regional lobbying efforts in many state capitals.

At times, these same communities will agree to differ and offer a divided voice but still probably make state capitals and Washington their battleground. In the Washington, D.C., region, for example, the political dividing line has shifted to the Beltway, with those inside who feel they are experiencing a declining quality of life — traffic congestion and resulting pollution, loss of contact with nature, increasing economic and racial segregation, and higher taxes to try to fix these issues — increasingly confronting those outside who still want to carve out a new place in the virgin hinterlands. Resolving regional challenges now consumes a considerable amount of the agendas of a city, two states and even the national government.

It might not be unreasonable to speculate that achieving regional governance excellence will someday result in strengthening the federal system. There is an excellent historical precedent for the impact of such challenges.

In 1785, representatives from the states of Virginia and Maryland met with George Washington at Mount Vernon to deal with the regional challenge of "jurisdiction and navigation" on the lower Potomac River. Finding that regional cooperation would not suffice and that part of the problem stemmed from the limitations of the Articles of Confederation that governed relations among the fairly autonomous states, the delegates decided to invite representatives from all of the states to a meeting in Annapolis the following year. The delegates at the Annapolis conference decided that the issues had such gravity that they decided to call a constitutional convention in Philadelphia the following year. The rest is history. (Gutheim, 157-161)

Will the challenge of "jurisdiction and navigation" on the growth "streams" sprawling out of our regions have a similar impact on national, state, and local government two centuries later? And this time, will it result in the ceding of critical authorities to regional governance mechanisms?

Bottom line: Resolving regional challenges could redefine our federal system of governance and breathe life into regional governance mechanisms.

Fourth, community leaders and citizens need to act decisively now to achieve regional governance excellence.

Achieving regional governance excellence is more an act of the mind than the pocketbook.

The real fears of addressing challenges regionally have to do with confronting unfamiliar communities and peoples, especially those that are richer or poorer or of a different ethnicity, and unpopular challenges, especially future growth, since whoever shapes it controls regional decision making.

Not that this lack of interaction has made life better or governance cheaper for any of us. When central cities decline, when crime and drugs escalate, when impoverished school districts cannot graduate productive workers, when segregated populations cannot find jobs; or when suburban communities are paved over with highways and parking lots, when the only way to get anywhere is by personal auto, when we squander resources on inefficient services, when we mourn the loss of community — then we all suffer and pay.

Achieving regional governance excellence needs to begin decisively, now.

We have attracted the attention of community leaders and citizens and are experimenting with regional governance initiatives. That's positive, but it raises the first set of questions posed by the book: Are we handling each new regional challenge better than the last one? Are we developing individual regional decision-making mechanisms that efficiently guide community leaders and citizens through equitable and empowering processes that handle the most pressing challenges?

We have also attracted the attention of economic interests that are already jockeying for influence in each of the regional economies that constitute the global common market. That's also positive, but it raises the second set of questions posed by the book: Are we shaping regional growth and development so as to compete globally and flourish locally? If we are, are we also overcoming intercommunity disparities and building regional citizenship and a sense of regional community? And are we developing a "network" of regional decision-making mechanisms that interact seamlessly to provide regional governance excellence?

Finally, we are witnessing radical changes in the responsibilities and relationships of state and national governments. It's difficult to say whether this is positive or negative for regional governance, but it helps reinforce the need for community leaders and citizens to act decisively, now.

Community leaders and citizens in some regions are already beginning to launch their regional renaissances. They have started to consider the communities of the region in the singular, as *us,* and not just in the plural, as *you and me.* Community leaders and citizens in other regions may join them. I have no doubt that those who pursue this journey will live in the most desirable regions at the dawn of the 21st century.

Bottom line: Achieving regional governance excellence is in our hands.

Using this Book

To help get you started on the path to regional governance excellence, here are some thoughts on using the book.

Before beginning, I encourage you to put on your "regionalist" hat. It might not fit too well and probably isn't as well worn as your other government and special interest hats. Then I suggest reading (if you haven't already) the tale of two regions, at the front of the book, which presents a hypothetical snapshot of the future. Together, they will help put you in the appropriate frame of mind for perusing the book and get you used to clothing yourself in a persona that will become more familiar over the coming years.

The book is organized as follows:

- Chapter 1 describes the rise of regional governance, from a nicety to a necessity.
- Chapter 2 presents a framework for achieving regional governance excellence.
- Chapters 3 through 7 present the five components of regional governance excellence — making regional governance prominent, strategic, equitable, empowering, and institutionalized — and describe regional governance initiatives that can be pursued to strengthen each of the components. Some of these initiatives are relatively new and generally untested, and are so indicated in the descriptions.
- Chapter 8 presents options to make regional governance a priority of state and national, governmental and nongovernmental, organizations.
- Chapter 9 presents guidance on putting it all together and achieving regional governance excellence.
- The References section presents the references cited in the book as well as state and national contacts for further information on regional governance.
- The Index facilitates quickly finding information on specific regional governance topics.

First, I suggest exploring the background material on the current state and future potential of regional governance (see Chapters 1 and 2).

Then, if regional governance is a relatively new topic to you, I suggest getting together with other community leaders and citizens, and their organizations, and:

- conducting an initial exploration of regional governance or holding a symposium for community leaders and citizens (see Prominent #1 and #2 in Chapter 3) or
- experimenting with some regional governance initiatives to address specific crosscutting challenges (see Chapters 3 to 7).

If you have already experimented with improving regional governance, I suggest perusing Chapters 3 and 5 to 7 to refresh your memory of initiatives that you have taken or considered taking to improve regional governance.

Finally, whether regional governance is a new topic or you are already experienced in improving regional governance, I suggest building community leader and citizen support and developing a future vision and action plan for strengthening regional governance — a Strategy for Achieving Regional Governance Excellence or SARGE— as presented in Chapters 4 and 9. This strategy could draw upon the options for regional governance initiatives, presented in Chapters 3 to 7, as well as, it is hoped, new initiatives you develop for strengthening regional governance.

If you are a state or national, government or non-government, official, I suggest especially reviewing Chapter 8 for options for state and national actions to support pursuing regional governance excellence.

May you achieve the regional excellence to which you aspire!

Chapter 1
The Rise of Regional Governance: From Nicety to Necessity

Men stumble over the truth from time to time, but most pick themselves up and hurry off as if nothing happened.
— *Winston Churchill*

Five types of trends, events, and developments — change-drivers — are collectively raising the importance of regional governance from an incidental nicety to a critical necessity:

- **Challenge Explosion,** the increasing frequency and intensity of crosscutting challenges that is overwhelming community leaders and citizens;
- **Citizen Withdrawal,** the withdrawal of citizens from public involvement just as they are needed to shape regional strategies;
- **Structure/Challenge Mismatch,** the mismatch of governance structures with regional challenges;
- **Rich/Poor Community Gap,** the widening fiscal, economic, and racial gaps across communities regionwide; and
- **Global Competitiveness,** which is requiring us to address regional challenges effectively if we are to compete successfully in the global economy.

Before reviewing these change-drivers, I encourage you to review "The Language of Regional Governance," which begins on page 38 and presents the regional governance terms used in this book. Some of the terms have acquired multiple definitions, an almost inevitable fate in the development of any new governance topic.

Change-Driver #1:
Challenge Explosion

We probably have been dealing with challenges that cut across regions and threaten our livelihood and quality of life since we started walking upright.

Our regional awareness was probably piqued by the time we were living in caves. Crosscutting opportunities, such as an approaching mammoth herd, or threats, such as a forest fire, spurred interaction and resulted in some cooperative "inter-cave" strategies, maybe even as well-designed and implemented as some of the current ones.

Regional forms of governance have been evident throughout recorded history. City-states appeared as early as 3000 BC to provide security for peasants and warriors for kings to wage war. (Peirce, 7) Over the succeeding millennia, city-states have experimented with most of the forms of regional governance; the Greek city-states molded the principles of democracy, ancient Rome temporarily amassed an empire that influenced our language and customs, the feudal fiefdoms of the middle ages introduced more hierarchical lord-serf governance. The renaissance spurred new democratic forms of governance — the merchant and artisan guilds, universities, mutual-aid societies and communes — that contributed to the development of nation states and continue to influence regional governance today.

National forms of governance have only been predominant for the last few hundred years. Nation-states displaced city-states during the Renaissance as "the age of colonial exploration and exploitation, the rise of capitalism, and the breakdown of medieval society" led to "the decline of monarchies and the rise of broadly based nationalism," according to Neal Peirce, the syndicated columnist popularizing the importance of regionalism. (Peirce, 7)

The reemergence of regional challenges over the past few decades has refocused attention on regional governance. Not that regional forms of governance are even new in this country; such challenges spurred the consolidations of the cities and counties of Philadelphia and San Francisco and the merger of multiple counties into New York City in the last century. By 1899, at the turn of the last century, reformers were calling for central city annexation of suburban communities to "bring about the adjustment which lay in the wider and larger interests of all." (James, 14-5)

Today, crosscutting challenges are emerging with increasing frequency and intensity; challenges that appear local or even national usually require regional responses.

The major challenges of the 1990s include exponential increases in drug use and related violent crime, undereducated current and future workers, congested roads and bridges, polluted air and water, unrestrained urban sprawl, widening fiscal disparities and continued ethnic segregation of communities, and uncertain economic competitiveness.

Almost any challenge requiring serious attention by community leaders and citizens cuts across communities and requires an intercommunity, if not a regional, response. Air and water pollution do not wait for visas at community boundaries. Crime waves often begin in distressed communities but quickly surge into more lucrative neighboring areas. Roads and transit lines have to meet at community borders. Regional cooperation is even needed to secure a major league baseball franchise, as St. Petersburg and Tampa, Florida, discovered.

Similarly, economic competitiveness, seen by many as the major national challenge, requires regional responses. With the thawing of the cold war, international competition has become more economic, requiring the capacities found at the regional, not the state or national, level. Regions are "large enough to take on the cross-jurisdictional challenges of work force preparedness, education, physical infrastructure, environmental quality and economic positioning. Yet a citistate (region) is generally small enough to allow a measure of personal interaction between citizens and institutions." (Peirce, 13)

In sum, the exploding emergence of regional challenges creates a decision overload.

Change-Driver #2:
Citizen Withdrawal

We have probably always been suspicious about dealing with regional challenges, especially if they involve the sharing of power.

Bruce McDowell, the regional guru at the U.S. Advisory Commission on Intergovernmental Relations, suggests that we have made attempts to deal with challenges at the regional level, but they usually dissipate into local jurisdiction-by-jurisdiction responses. He attributes this in part to the fact that few regional challenges have yet caused the crises needed to foster conversions to regional governance. "In conflicts between real cities [regions] and real governments [municipalities, counties and states], the real governments win," he says. (Committee for Enterprise Development)

Our reluctance to cooperate regionally has also been attributed to the lack of regional leadership. Few are elected to regional offices, except to the governing bodies of counties in single-county regions, or to the regional planning and service district in the Portland, Oregon, region. As a result, few Americans identify themselves as regional leaders or citizens.

This reluctance has also been ascribed to our lack of experience in working with our peers. We are conditioned to work vertically in hierarchical organizations or between local, state, and national governments, and we have difficulty in taking off our local "blinders" and cooperating across communities horizontally.

But maybe it is all the product of biology. Scientists now speculate that the brain operates like a committee without a chair, in which rogue members may sometimes act alone or fail to show up for meetings. If so, can we be expected to behave any differently in regional decision making?

In any case, we seem to be reluctant regional stewards, even when there is some evidence of the benefits of cooperation. Sometimes it seems as if we are playing Prisoner's Dilemma, that classic of games theory. In this game, one can earn the most points by winning a round, but one can also win some points (as does one's opponent) by cooperating. Robert Axelrod confirmed that the most successful winning strategy for playing the game repeatedly with the same players is "tit-for-tat." In following this strategy, one starts off by cooperating and after that does exactly what one's opponent did on the last move. Given that interactions between communities resemble a regional version of this game, we should be encouraged to follow a strategy of cooperating until others are not, especially if we expect to have to continue interacting with the same players, or communities, in the future. (Axelrod, Preface)

Cooperating until others don't appears to be the best policy for building cooperation: Confucius said "Repay kindness with kindness, but evil with justice." Instead, we all too easily believe that we follow the golden rule, "do unto others as you would have them do unto you," and all too quickly practice the iron rule, "an eye for an eye and a tooth for a tooth."

Now, when we need to expand our horizons and become regional citizens, we are withdrawing from exercising even our local citizenship.

In 1990, James Patterson and Peter Kim reported on their 1,800-question survey of 2,000 people nationwide in *The Day America Told the Truth*. It revealed some disturbing indicators of the health of community and citizenship:

- Two-thirds of us have never given any time at all to community activities or to the solving of community problems. Not surprisingly, more that two-thirds of us cannot name our local representative in Congress.
- More than half believe they have no influence on the decisions made by local government.
- One-fourth admitted that they don't really give a damn about any of their neighborhood's problems. (Patterson/Kim, 171)

Similarly, Robert Putnam, Harvard University professor and author of *Making Democracy Work,* has found a distressing decline in citizen involvement, and especially civic engagement with fellow citizens, over the past three decades. This includes a:

- 25 percent decline in voting,

- 40 percent decline in attending municipal or school meetings,
- 20 to 25 percent decline in religious service attendance,
- 60 percent decline in labor union membership,
- 50 percent decline in parent-teacher organization membership,
- 20 percent decline in men's groups, such as the Elks,
- 50 percent decline in women's groups, and
- even a 40 percent decline in bowling league membership, although there has been a 10 to 15 percent increase in bowling.

Overall, he concludes that the average number of "association" memberships has fallen about one-quarter over the last quarter of a century. (Putnam, 1995)

Putnam found growth only in organizations where membership requires no personal interaction, only "moving a pen" to make a contribution, such as paying annual dues to the American Association of Retired Persons. He doesn't attribute blame, but he suggests that some of the factors might be the explosive growth of working women, the increasing geographic mobility of citizens, and the isolation of technology, especially by television and even computers. (Putnam, 1995)

Most important, citizens' trust in government, the media, and each other has declined precipitously and could even undermine our economic competitiveness.

In the late 1970s, 75 percent of the public trusted government to do the right thing most of the time. By the mid-1990s, only 19 percent had that degree of trust in government. (Putnam, 1995) Henry Cisneros, the Secretary of the U.S. Department of Housing and Urban Development, suggests that the public sector, which often provides the forum for resolving pressing challenges, contributes to these results: "Programs that treat citizens as passive consumers of services rather than engaged co-producers of solutions merely perpetuate dependency, as well as disillusionment and hopelessness." (Cisneros, 1994, 383)

Trust in newspapers has declined as well. A couple of decades ago, 80 percent of the public trusted them. By 1988, only 58 percent said they trusted newspapers, and today, only 25 percent do. More than 70 percent of the public now believe that journalists stand in the way of resolving problems. The paradox is that citizens have access to more information sources, including a whole new world of electronic databases, but appear to be less well-informed. (Merritt)

Trust in other people has declined from almost two-thirds (58 percent) of the public responding *positively* to the question "Do you trust most other people?" to almost two-thirds (63 percent) responding *negatively* during the same period. (Putnam, 1995) According to Haynes Johnson, the syndicated columnist, Americans are forsaking community and retreating into private worlds. "The only way to maintain some quality of life is by creating a kind of private wealth you can put inside the walls of your little house," says a married couple in Oakland, California. "Step out the front door and [you can] be blown away by random violence on the street." (Johnson)

Finally, trust is critical to economic competitiveness. Francis Fukayama of the Rand Corporation has written a compelling book, entitled *Trust,* that concludes:

> Although there are other factors accounting for firm size, including tax policy, antitrust, and other forms of regulatory law, there is a relationship between high trust societies with plentiful social capital* — Germany, Japan and the United States — and the ability to create large, private business organizations. The economies of relatively low-trust societies like Taiwan, Hong Kong, France and Italy, by contrast, have traditionally been populated by family businesses. In these countries, the reluctance of non-kin to trust one another delayed and in some cases prevented the emergence of modern, professionally managed corporations.
>
> The prevalence of trust does not simply facilitate the growth of large scale organizations. If large hierarchies are able to evolve into networks of smaller companies through modern information technology, trust will help in their transition as well. Societies well supplied with social capital will be able to adopt new organizational forms more readily that those with less, as technology and markets change.

* Societies that have the capacity to spontaneously develop voluntary associations outside of family ties and government institu-

tions, such as sports clubs, singing societies, and religious groups. (Fukuyama, 30)

As Daniel Kemmis, the philosophic mayor of Missoula, Montana, and author of *The Good City and The Good Life,* observes, we are so disconnected from the political process that we don't even call ourselves citizens, but taxpayers so as to separate ourselves from government; me taxpayer, you government. Or we refer to ourselves as private citizens, which he compares to the civic equivalent of dry water. (Kemmis, 1995, 10) At least one government, Montgomery County, Maryland, found the word "government" to be so disliked by residents that it dropped it from its letterhead.

E.J. Dionne, the author of *Why Americans Hate Politics,* offers the most disturbing observation: "A nation that hates politics will not lost long as a democracy." (Dionne, 355)

At a time when many of us are withdrawing from acting like local citizens, few of us have ever behaved like regional citizens, or felt like members of a regional community. We have not encountered regional challenges threatening enough to our jobs and quality of life to lead us to make "deathbed conversions" to regional citizenship.

Thoughts of our citizenship in the regional community are bound to increase, however, as regional challenges invade our consciousness, more often and more personally.

A recent example of that phenomena occurred in the Washington, D.C., region during the rise and fall of the proposed Disney America theme park, amongst the Civil War battlegrounds of Northern Virginia. On the day that the Disney Corporation announced its decision to stop the park project, probably everyone within that enormous region thought of the implications on their lives. In fact, given the follow-up dialogue in the media and on talk shows, their thoughts have continued, like the after shocks following an earthquake. Similar regional thoughts probably occur, at least momentarily, when professional sports teams win a national championship.

These incidents of regional consciousness, like the emergence of regional challenges, will occur with greater frequency, but we are still unsure about how to interpret them, much less what to do about them, and about how to begin to behave like regional citizens, and leaders, in the regional community. But once we do, we might find one of the critical paths out of the wilderness of citizen withdrawal.

Finally, and more positively, Francis Lappé and Paul DuBois, authors of *The Quickening of America,* are beginning to see broad evidence of positive changes in citizen involvement. They have found that people across the country are letting go of their despair, cynicism and feelings of powerlessness and are rethinking their self-interest, redefining power, and exploring new opportunities in public life. (Lappé, 8)

In sum, citizen distrust undermines our fledgling sense of regional community.

Change-Driver #3:
Structure/Challenge Mismatch

We are organized to respond to challenges at municipal-county, state, and national levels, but the major ones are emerging at neighborhood, regional, and international levels.

This government-governance mismatch has become more dramatic over the past few decades and created a regional conundrum.

In part, it is a result of governments not expanding with population. In the 1950s, 70 percent of the population of the 168 major metropolitan areas lived in 193 central cities. By 1990, more than 60 percent of the population of the 320 major metropolitan areas lived in the suburbs. (Rusk, 1993, 8). In 1970, 23 percent of the nation's offices were in the suburbs; now closer to 60 percent are. (Peirce, 1993, 28) Most central cities have been unable to expand by annexing growth areas, resulting in a plethora of suburban municipalities in most regions.

It is not surprising that it has become increasingly difficult for individual units of government to respond to challenges. To address neighborhood challenges, central city governments have developed ties with neighborhood organizations and even established neighborhood-based citizen advisory committees. Moreover, state and national, government and non-government, organizations have supported community-based organizations, such as community development corporations. To address international challenges, the United Nations has received expanded authority from its member nations, especially to address threats to world peace.

Various approaches have been tried to address regional challenges in most regions, resulting in an array of regional problem-solving and service-delivery mechanisms. Most of these mechanisms are of an ad hoc variety, so that the basic powers of governments are not threatened, but all too often they fall short of successfully addressing current challenges, much less surviving long enough to address the next round of challenges.

Today, existing problem-solving and service-delivery mechanisms are being overwhelmed by regional challenges; most of these mechanisms lack timeliness, flexibility, inclusiveness, stability, or clout.

All too often, we have gone through the following steps to address a regional challenge:

- First, we often deny we have a threat or, even worse, an opportunity: "We don't have a crime problem, that only exists in the central city."
- Second, we accept that we have a challenge, but deny that it's our problem: "We have a crime problem, but it is the county/state/national government's responsibility to resolve."
- Third, we eventually accept that it's our problem, but try to solve only "our" part of it: "We will deal with our part of the crime problem, and let others deal with the rest of the problem."
- Fourth, we finally conclude that the problem is regional and agree to work cooperatively with our neighbors: "We share the crime problem with our neighbors and need to work together to address it successfully."

At times, we turn to an existing regional problem-solving mechanism to take the lead in addressing the challenge. Often there is neither an appropriate nor acceptable mechanism, so we create a new one. Whatever the case, we usually invite the wrong people to at least the first few meetings. If we are lucky, we finally get the participation right and design an acceptable strategy for addressing the challenge. If we are luckier still, and not distracted by the next round of regional challenges, we successfully negotiate the implementation of the strategy with the usual suspects, the array of generally local service-delivery mechanisms across the region.

By now, however, the regional opportunity might already be lost to another region and the regional threat has probably already exploded into a crisis. Then, whether the problem-solving mechanism is successful or not, it is often ad hoc. So we abolish it, forcing us to reinvent the wheel when the next regional challenge emerges.

We seem to have a propensity for creating flawed regional decision-making mechanisms. Like a football without laces (try passing or kicking one), they have one or more critical defects that prevent them from effectively addressing regional challenges. They are either too late to shape the challenge, too restrictive to include the public and other interests, too inflexible to try new tactics, or too weak to command the participation of key decision makers. Finally, they are often too ad hoc to be applied to new challenges. Like some lower order of species that passes nothing on from generation to generation, we often act as if we are genetically impaired when it comes to regional decision making.

John Mutz, formerly with the Lilly Endowment, compares regional governance mechanisms to the corpse at an Irish wake — expected to be present but not expected to do much.

Worst of all, addressing the most immediate challenges, such as drugs and related violence, usually consumes the energies of community leaders and citizens, thus precluding their addressing underlying and often more pervasive challenges, such as the widening service inequities between rich and poor communities.

The good news, however, is that we have learned from the frustrations of earlier experiences and have been putting "laces" in some of the more recent regional problem-solving and service-delivery mechanisms. This more recent experimentation is presented in detail in Chapters 3 through 7.

We have been poorly served by the existing models of regional governance: Balkanization and Metropolitanism have offered unappealing options for responding to regional challenges.

"Balkanization" refers to the almost always maligned scattershot pattern of independent government jurisdictions practicing fend-for-yourself behavior and interacting infrequently and often under some duress. Relationships among local governments or with other sectors of the community and residents usually receive little consideration under this model.

Balkanization, however, has provided a governance model supportive of the low-density sprawl development of the past few decades. Populations have grown somewhat, but they have spread out dramatically.

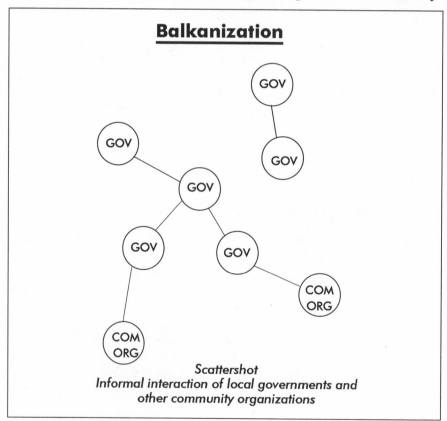

Balkanization

Scattershot
Informal interaction of local governments and
other community organizations

Metropolitan New York City grew by only 5 percent in the past 25 years, but consumed 61 percent more land; Los Angeles grew four-fold, but land growth grew twenty times. One measure of this change: during the 1980s, 22 million more people drove to work — more than the increase in jobs — while car pooling and transit use declined. (Peirce, 1993, 28)

At the same time, central cities have declined. For the 44 largest regions in the 1980s, almost all (42) of the suburban areas grew, and almost half (18) of the cities shrunk. Central cities went from having a majority to a minority of jobs over the same time period. (Downs, 45–46)

Over time, the region has become an expanding organism — a giant amoeba with a shrinking nucleus as the core becomes weaker and further away. Development leapfrogs into areas that require roads and bridges, sewer and water lines, and other amenities to catch up, creating new nuclei. Over time, some of the regional organisms spread out so far that they bump up against others, resulting in new, but not necessarily higher, life forms — "megalopoli."

In the absence of any single center, every household develops its own unique patterns for work, shopping, and entertainment. Access to the center becomes more difficult but less necessary, as activities and services are duplicated along every major highway or in "edge" or "magnet" cities — those new employment centers that have sprung up in the past few decades and rival the central cities. Complexes such as Tysons Corner in the Washington, D.C., region have turned beltways and other major highways into the main streets of urban America. (Downs, 211–217; Garreau, 1991, 6–7; Coffey, 10)

New development areas have tended to set up their own local governments, except in regions where central cities have been able to annex aggressively thanks to favorable state legislation or control of water supplies. Small local governments fit into the low-density sprawl vision of "unrestrained individualism:" "ownership of detached single-family homes on spacious lots, ownership of automotive vehicles, low-rise workplaces and an environment free from signs of poverty," according to Anthony Downs, the thoughtful regional analyst and author of *New Visions for Urban America*. (Downs, 6)

This unrestrained form of development soon creates numerous problems, such as longer commutes to work, lack of affordable housing, duplicative infrastructure, difficulties in siting locally undesirable land uses (LULUs), and absorbing accessible open space. According to David Davis at the University of Toledo, it creates "urban deserts in the old industrial land" and forces "new industrial users onto virgin land." (Davis) Those receiving benefits do not want to give them up and seem to prefer Balkanized governance that borders on gridlock, becoming "the voice of unbridled self-interest," according to Syracuse University professor Astrid Merget. (Downs, 15)

Unfortunately, neither central cities nor suburbs know how to broaden decision making, once crosscutting challenges begin to occur. Nor do they know how to stop wasteful spending as the American Dream often turns into the American Nightmare. (Cisneros, 3) An editorial in the *Philadelphia Inquirer* summarized the consequences: "One reason the money isn't there (to address regional challenges) is that the region squanders so much of its treasure on prideful but pointless duplication of services, on parochial decisions that only shove problems onto the folks next door." (*Philadelphia Inquirer*)

Collectively, we continue to pursue a latter day guns-and-butter approach to regional spending by constructing new underutilized infrastructure in suburban areas while supporting existing underutilized infrastructure in central cities.

We continue to repeat past behaviors. We build highways to cure congestion, which has been compared to loosening one's belt to cure obesity. We discard existing development, even older suburban employment centers and shopping malls, especially those that are overwhelmed by congestion or crime or lack any "soul" or sense of community. (Lockwood; Garreau, 1995) We have been reluctant to consider, much less implement, strategies to provide for the balanced growth of regions, such as the European practice of building "greenbelts" to discourage suburban sprawl. (Senge, 67)

A recent study conducted by Rutgers University for the New Jersey state government puts the tradeoffs in terms that can be understood by community leaders and citizens. It concluded that New Jersey state government would save more than $400 million annually — $8 billion over twenty years — and another $1.3 billion in capital investments if it could channel future growth into existing development areas. The tradeoff, and potential public cost, for these savings: $355 million in the lost equity of affected urban fringe land owners. (Richmond, 9) A similar study by the Bank of America documented the costs of sprawl for Californians, including the loss of 95 percent of the state's wetlands and air pollution controls that cost approximately $600 per resident annually in the Los Angeles region. (Bank of America, 8)

It is not surprising, then, that Balkanization has been used over this century as a straw person against which to showcase the merits of Metropolitanism.

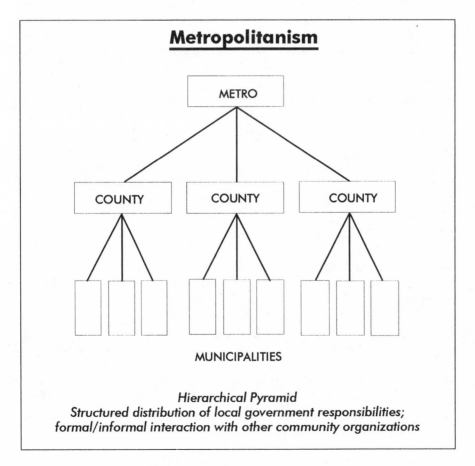

Metropolitanism

METRO

COUNTY   COUNTY   COUNTY

MUNICIPALITIES

Hierarchical Pyramid
Structured distribution of local government responsibilities;
formal/informal interaction with other community organizations

"Metropolitanism" refers to the never-achieved hierarchical pattern of local government jurisdictions, with service-delivery responsibilities defined and differentiated for municipal, county, and anticipated general purpose region level governments or even consolidated and carried out by a single all-powerful metropolitan government. As with Balkanization, little consideration is given to nongovernmental and citizen interactions. While no region has subscribed to this model, smaller ones contained within the parameters of a single urban county and multi-county ones that have established a directly elected regional planning and service district (only in the Portland, Oregon, region) mimic some of the multi-tier characteristics of this model.

In addition to politically threatening local governments, "Metropolitanism" struggles with the conceptual difficulty of defining the geographic scope of its authorities. In ever expanding regions, or in those that intersect with other regions, it is difficult to create a metropolitan government that won't be quickly outdistanced by new development or demands.

It's no wonder that elected and other community officials have been reluctant to engage in regional decision making when the models for addressing crosscutting challenges are so distasteful. It is as suicidal for elected officials to challenge the sacred rights of individual communities under Balkanization as it is for them to support general purpose metropolitan governments. Moreover, neither provides a very positive regional vision nor suggests a sense of regional community — a marketplace connecting people, resources and ideas — that might appeal to other community leaders and citizens.

In spite of the flaws of regional governance, community leaders and citizens rarely give its improvement a high priority.

There have been all too few efforts to address directly the topic of regional governance or to examine systematically how we address regional challenges and design future visions and action plans for achieving excellence.

Even when we agree to address crosscutting challenges, we like to set up ad hoc problem-solving processes so we don't have to worry about their powers and longevity. We put off discussing how we are going to implement strategies for addressing these challenges as long as possible, and all too often prepare strategies that just assume that the usual suspects — existing local governments and other private, academic, nonprofit and civic organizations — will oversee their implementation. Not surprisingly, they often don't address, or even jointly agree not to address, the systemic impediments to effective implementation.

Conversations with community leaders and citizens suggest that we are ready to strengthen regional governance, in part because of the historic frustrations related above and the topics to be raised in the next two sections — the gap between rich and poor communities and global competitiveness. Raising regional governance to the same prominence as the particular challenges being addressed would represent significant progress.

In sum, the mismatch of governance structures and regional challenges fosters interest in experimenting with new regional decision-making mechanisms.

Change-Driver #4:
Rich/Poor Community Gap

Widening economic disparities and racial segregation are creating almost insurmountable obstacles to bringing rich and poor communities together in regional problem solving and service delivery.

Economic disparities have created a nation of haves and have-nots that tend to live in separate communities, and continued ethnic and racial segregation has further divided these communities. The combination has resulted in regions of widening extremes: Rich and usually white communities get richer and whiter with the fiscal capacity to do anything, while poor and usually minority communities get poorer and more African-American, Hispanic, and Asian with the fiscal capacity to do very little.

This widening gap in the capacity of communities has become the Achilles heel of regional decision making. Cooperative decision making is most successfully conducted among relatively equal partners, each of which has something to bring to the table to address common challenges and each of which will benefit in their resolution. It is very difficult to bring extremely different communities together into regional decision-making processes, much less negotiate cooperative agreements as equal partners, without narrowing this widening inter-community gap.

There is plenty of evidence of economic and income disparity.

Personal income disparities narrowed during World War II but have widened over the past two decades. According to Doris Kearns Goodwin, the noted historian and author of *No Ordinary Time,* the "middle class emerged" during World War II. Incomes doubled for the half of Americans at the lower end of the income scale, while they only increased 50 percent for the upper half. Moreover, the wealth shared by the bottom half of Americans increased 16 percent, while that of the richest Americans declined 6 percent. The "barriers to social and economic equality which had stood for decades were either much reduced or entirely overthrown." (Goodwin, 625)

For the early years of the post-World War II period, the richest 20 percent of households received about 43 percent of pre-tax income; by 1993, they accounted for 48 percent, or approximately $10,000 more per household annually. Through the middle 1970s, all households enjoyed average annual income growth rates of approximately 2.5 percent. Since then, only the affluent have continued to see any growth in household income; the poorest households have seen household income decline. (Cassidy) As a result, the poorest 20 percent of households went from receiving 4.2 percent of pre-tax income to 3.6 percent, or approximately $1200 less per household annually.

One measure of this change is the declining income of high school graduates; since 1980, their average income has declined $7,000, from $28,000 to $21,000. By the mid-1980s, the ratio between the richest and poorest 10 percent of families was approximately 6 to 1, greater than in other major industrial nations. (Phillips, 9; Pearlstein, 7)

Not surprisingly, the number of millionaires (by assets) doubled between the late 1970s and late 1980s to approximately 1.3 million, even adjusted for income; the number of billionaires went from a handful to almost 50 in the same period. Moreover, corporate executives went from making less than 30 to 40 times as much as their average employees to more than 190 times as much. (Cassidy) According to Kevin Phillips, syndicated columnist and author of *The Politics of Rich and Poor,* "No parallel upsurge in riches has been seen since the late nineteenth century, the era of the Vanderbilts, Morgans and Rockefellers." (Phillips, 10)

Regional income disparities between central cities and suburbs have widened over the past two decades. Per capita income in the central cities of regions went from slightly above parity with suburban per capita income in 1960 (105 percent) to slightly below parity in 1973 (96 percent), but fell precipitously to only 84 percent of suburban per capita income by 1989, according to Larry Ledbur and Bill Barnes, the provocative analysts examining the economic aspects of regionalism. (Ledebur and Barnes, 1992, 2) Ironically, a substantial amount of the disparity is being financed by central city jobs held by suburban residents; for example, in the New York City, Washington, D.C., and St. Louis regions, more than half of the income earned goes to the suburbs. (Savitch, 1995, 6)

In many regions, the income disparity between inner and outer suburbs has also been widening. In the Minneapolis/St. Paul region, for example, the central city has a median family income of about $26,000, about 70 percent of that in inner ring suburbs ($37,000) but only 55 to 60 percent of that in the outer ring suburbs ($43,000–47,000), according to Myron Orfield, the Minnesota state legislator with an active regional agenda. (Orfield)

Inelastic central cities have larger income disparities with their suburbs than elastic ones. Inelastic central cities, in the view of David Rusk, former mayor of Albuquerque and a thoughtful urban professional, are those that have not been able to expand by annexing newly developing areas, as opposed to elastic ones, which have. For example, residents of Detroit and Cleveland, two inelastic cities, have on average only 53 percent of the per capita incomes of their suburban neighbors. Compare them to residents of Houston, Nashville, Raleigh, and Albuquerque, four elastic cities, who have 89 percent, 98 percent, 103 percent and 118 percent, respectively, of the per capita incomes of suburban residents. Overall, residents of the inelastic cities have only 68 percent of the per capita income of suburban residents, and residents of elastic cities almost have parity with their suburban counterparts, 96 percent of per capita income. (Rusk, 1993, 32)

Poverty and other indicators of urban hardship are concentrated in central cities and especially in inelastic cities. It is no surprise that poverty is more concentrated in inelastic central cities (25 percent of population in poverty) than elastic ones (15 percent). (Rusk, 1993, 42) Only half of the suburban communities in the Minneapolis/St. Paul region have more than 10 percent of their children living in poverty, but the central city has over one third living in poverty. (Orfield) Richard Nathan, Director of the Rockefeller Institute of Government, found a similar increase in other indicators of hardship — unemployment, dependency, education, and crowded housing — between 1970 and 1987. (Nathan, 484)

Much of this concentrated poverty is found in public housing, the public sector's "dirty secret," according to Sal Sarabella, deputy mayor of Pittsburgh, Pennsylvania. For example, 40 percent of the minority population of the city lives in public housing, including 90 percent of all single mothers, a total of over 40,000 residents in 13,000 units. He contends that you cannot create reservations in central cities and expect the region to work. In the Atlanta region, sixteen out of twenty of the poorest neighborhoods have major concentrations of public housing, from almost 40 percent to all of the dwelling units. (Rusk, Atlanta Regional Commission)

There is also no lack of evidence of ethnic and racial segregation.

Residential racial segregation continues across all income levels. Racial dissimilarity indexes indicate the percentage of African-Americans who would have to move from one census tract to another in order to produce a uniform percentage of African-American residents in all tracts. Zero percent represents a distribution equal to the population regionwide; 100 percent represents racial apartheid. In the thirty metropolitan areas with the largest African-American populations in 1990, the index has shown some improvement but confirms the persistence of segregation. In 1970 the index was 75.3, in 1980 it was 68.3, and in 1990 it was still 66.5. Racial segregation also persists at all income levels. In the same thirty metropolitan areas in 1990, the index was 74.4 percent for households with incomes of less than $25,000, 66.6 percent for $25,000 to $27,500, and 72.8 percent for those with incomes over $50,000. (Downs, 25)

White flight continues to be a dominant practice in regions. While those moving out of central cities talk about the "love of newness," to be "near to nature," and "individualism," (Wallis, 1994, 5) they also seem to be fleeing minorities, since sprawl tends to segregate by race and class in suburban communities. In the Pittsburgh region, a recent survey shows that white flight occurs in suburban communities once they become approximately 20 percent minority. Most African-Americans would prefer to live in neighborhoods that are racially balanced (50 percent each); most whites do not want to live in neighborhoods that are over 33 percent African-American and a majority would move out once they became 50 percent African-American. (Downs, 26) Now the flight is even out of regions. According to Joel Kotkin of the Pepperdine Institute for Public Policy:

> After losing population for decades, rural areas are now adding people at three times their 1980s growth rate. Between 1990 and 1994, more than 1.1 million net migrants moved into rural areas and small towns, most of them from suburban or urban locations. (Kotkin)

Minorities are a growing part of the population and are more likely to live in poor communities. "Over the 1980s, white America grew by 6 per cent, compared with 53 percent for Hispanics, 108 percent for Asians, 13 percent for blacks, 39 percent for Native Americans. Already, the nation is one fourth black, Hispanic, Asian and Native American." (Peirce, 303) Three times as many African-Americans live in poverty as whites and they have an average family income $13,000 below that of whites, a U.S. assistant attorney general told the U.S. House of Representatives. (Patrick) In the Atlanta region, nine out of ten poor whites live in middle class communities, but two out of three African-Americans live in poor communities. (Rusk, Atlanta Regional Commission)

The evidence of resulting extremes in the fiscal or service capacity of rich and poor communities includes:

Central city governments spend $1.50 for every dollar spent by suburban governments (1987), up from $1.40 for every dollar in 1981. In 1987, central city residents' taxes were about 25 percent higher, and as a percentage of income, about 44 percent higher than those of suburban residents. (Bahl) In the central county in the Pittsburgh region, Allegheny County, during the 1980s, the tax capacity (tax yield divided by tax effort) of the 32 most fiscally distressed communities *decreased* by 5 percent; the tax capacity of the 32 most fiscally affluent *increased* by more than 40 percent. In 1980, the average tax capacity of the most fiscally affluent communities was 3.2 times as great as the most fiscally distressed. The gap grew to 4.8 times as great by 1990. (Pennsylvania Economy League, *Pressing Regional and Community Problems,* 1992)

Central city school districts spend $440 less per student annually than suburban school districts. (Strauss) Again Allegheny County provides an example. The widest fiscal extremes are between the abandoned mill towns and suburban residential communities. For example, the local tax base provides only $2,035 per school child in the Duquesne school district versus $6,713 in the Fox Chapel school district; Duquesne has only $40,700 in local operating funds per classroom contrasted with $134,260 in Fox Chapel (Thomas, 1994, 3 & 9) Some of the mill towns are not even able to afford their own police departments, depending instead on irregular state police patrols, and lack the equipment to clear streets after snowstorms. (Belko)

The consequences of intercommunity fiscal disparity on economic competitiveness and quality of life echo through the recent literature.

Hank Savitch, of the University of Louisville, tells us that "Suburbanites may feel that they can shield themselves from urban decline, but like a hole wearing at the center of a rubber raft, everybody is likely to ride a little lower in the water. Those at the center may be in the lowest incline, but hanging onto the periphery is not a sufficient defense. The challenge of repair is as much for those outside the center as for those in it." (Savitch, 1992)

Joe Gyourko, at the University of Pennsylvania, points out that "A 10 percent decline in the value of real estate in just our nine largest cities would mean losses of nearly $160 billion.... A great many suburbanites

— share holders in the banks, insurance companies, and pension funds that own these urban properties — would be among the losers." (Quoted in Hershberg, 1994)

David Rusk notes that "In highly segregated urban areas — no matter how wealthy areawide — concentrated poverty, welfare dependency, and crime compound each other and inner cities are failing. In more integrated urban areas — even when poorer areawide — poverty, dependency and crime lack critical mass, and the cities are surviving." (Rusk, 1993, 2)

The most succinct view comes from an editorial in the *Philadelphia Inquirer:* "The city's [Philadelphia's] pitch [to suburbs] should not be: Without us, you die. Instead: With us, you will thrive far more than you will alone." (*Philadelphia Inquirer*)

Shrinking national, state, and local resources, and sometimes regional populations, are also compounding the difficulty of developing collaborative strategies.

Community leaders and citizens fear that they are playing a zero sum game, or worse, that they will not have the resources to address economic distress, ethnic segregation, intercommunity service inequities and other regional challenges. They are afraid that they will be compelled to create a level playing field that is below everyone's expectations.

First, community officials and citizens see state and national government assistance declining. Many fear that they are reliving the 1980s nightmare of shrinking national government largess, this time at the state government level. They further fear that fiscally constrained state legislatures will step up the pace of enacting mandates on local governments and leave the major responsibility for implementing — and funding — them in local hands.

Second, community officials and citizens in some regions are afraid of losing the population needed to finance regional initiatives. One out of every five metropolitan statistical areas lost population during the 1980s, and another one out of three grew more slowly than the 10 percent average population growth for the nation. (Schwartz) Regions with flat or, especially, negative population growth, cannot turn to newcomers to help finance responses to emerging intercommunity challenges or readily raise resources from existing city dwellers, suburbanites and exurbanites.

In sum, growing intercommunity economic disparities, ethnic segregation, and service inequities compromise regional decision making.

Change-Driver #5:
Global Competitiveness

Economic competitiveness is demanding improved responses to regional challenges.

The anxiety of community leaders and citizens about addressing regional challenges is being especially heightened, however, by the fear of becoming less economically competitive.

Just as community leaders and citizens realize that only world class businesses will be competitive and thrive, they also realize that excellence will determine their communities' fates. Just as businesses need to have access to the best ideas (concepts), skills (competence), and "Rolodexes" (connections) to become cosmopolitans and prosper, according to Harvard professor Rosabeth Moss Kanter, so community leaders and citizens need to become regionalists and address crosscutting challenges. (Kanter)

Community leaders and citizens also see their regional economies becoming more global. For example, one out of six of our manufacturing jobs is linked to exports to regions outside the country. Approximately 5 million of us work for foreign-owned businesses located in this country. International tourism has become the largest earner of foreign exchange, higher than the export of aircraft or agriculture.

To respond to the globalization of economic development, state governments spend approximately $100 million annually on international trade and tourism programs and have created approximately 160 offices overseas to promote export and investment activity. Likewise, local governments and chambers of commerce have created regional marketing programs, sponsored trade fairs, and sent delegations to other regions, internationally. (National League of Cities, 5)

Our counterparts on other continents have drawn similar conclusions about the globalization of their regional economies. For example, the national boundaries in the European Community are being replaced by "....a 'Europe of Regions' in which regions, not nation-states, are seen as the basic building blocks of Europe. The European Commission has explicitly set out to identify regions as the basic unit for economic development initiatives...." (Blais, 18)

Community leaders and citizens have concluded that the region has emerged as the basic unit of competitiveness in the global economy. Collectively, regions have become the individual stalls in the farmers market of global economic opportunities. Neither central cities nor suburban communities alone can usually compete for world class businesses.

Community leaders and citizens are also concluding that their communities are competing with other regions, not with their central city or suburban neighbors, and must learn to cooperate to compete successfully. Cities and suburbs need each other to compete in the global economy. As summed up by Neal Peirce, suburbs need healthy central cities for positive global image, trained labor force, social stability, personal safety, efficient use of infrastructure and economic growth; central cities need suburbs for customers, workers, jobs, political clout and "oomph" in the local economy. (Pierce, 130) Community leaders and citizens in almost any region can tell stories about how intercommunity competition led to losing one business prospect or intercommunity cooperation led to attracting another.

If the growing gap between rich and poor communities tends to drive them apart, global competitiveness has the potential to bring them back together. (Savitch, 1995, 15)

Finally, community leaders and citizens are concluding that although businesses, both profit and nonprofit, still drive the regional economic engines and create jobs, their economic competitiveness increasingly depends on their own performance in addressing regional challenges. This especially includes providing critical transportation facilities, maintaining air and water quality standards, educating and reeducating the work force, and marketing their regions internationally.

Business development and governance performance are becoming more regional and interdependent.

Both business development and regional governance require investment strategies to achieve our desired quality of life.

Business development and regional governance could be visualized as the opposite sides of a regional excellence investment coin. Our investments in competitiveness must take both faces of that coin into account.

One face of the coin represents the investment that needs to be made in the financing, training, and marketing activities needed to create jobs and grow businesses. Increasingly, community leaders and citizens are concerned that this investment results in balanced growth, reducing disparities between communities, and sustainable growth, meeting "the development needs of the present but (does) not compromise the ability of future generations to meet their own needs." (National Association of Counties)

The other face of the coin represents the investment that needs to be made in improving regional decision making — in designing visions for achieving regional governance excellence and implementing strategies that will improve the capacities and capabilities of community leaders and citizens to address regional challenges in a timely, flexible, and effective manner and achieve a desired quality of life.

The definition of competitiveness developed by the Partnership for Urban Virginia, a statewide coalition of regional public and private leaders, incorporates both sides of the investment coin; competitiveness is "…. the ability of a metropolitan area to achieve higher rates of income and job growth, and lower economic disparity between its central and suburban sectors than its major competitors, by providing an attractive business climate and quality of life." (Richman and Oliver, 9)

In sum, global economic competitiveness requires regional governance excellence.

Conclusion: The State of Regional Governance Is a "Merry-Go-Sorry"

"Thou has told me of such a merry-go-sorry, as I have not often heard of; I am sorry for thy ill fortune, but am glad to see thee alive."
                    — Nicholas Breton, Chance, Chance, 1606

The state of regional governance is aptly described by the old English term "merry-go-sorry," roughly translated "I have some good news and some bad news."

On one hand, we have begun to understand and accept the rising importance of regional governance, its emergence as a necessity from a tradition of being only a nicety. Moreover, we have begun to become involved in and experiment with promising regional governance initiatives, shared in Chapters 3 through 7. We have learned the wisdom of Benjamin Franklin's observation at the signing of the Declaration of Independence: "We must all hang together or assuredly we shall all hang separately."

On the other hand, we still consider regional governance on an ad hoc basis. We seldom think about future visions for governing our regions. Equally rarely do we design and implement collaborative strategies for achieving them.

We need to raise our sights from accepting ad hoc expediency to demanding systemic regional excellence.

The Language of Regional Governance

Regional decision making or governance: the interactions of community officials and citizens, and the organizations they represent, as they design strategies for addressing challenges that cut across communities and deliver services for meeting common needs.

Regionalism is commonly used as a more general term to refer to anything regional; *regional cooperation* is commonly used as a more restrictive term to refer to the anticipated or realized positive results of regional decision making.

Region: a central core city and its contiguous suburbs and future growth areas or a rural area that is commonly influenced or impacted by crosscutting economic, physical, and social development challenges.

Areas ranging in size from a couple of neighborhoods in a central city to adjoining states and nations have been called regions. In this book, the term is reserved for those areas that fall within a common or integrated development area that has a separate identity in the national and international marketplace; a regional economic commons as defined by Larry Ledebur and Bill Barnes, (Barnes and Ledebur, 1995), or a cititstate as defined by Neal Peirce, (Peirce, 1993, preface).

Urban regions usually contain a central core city, or sometimes two or three nearby cities, a suburban ring with various municipalities and employment centers engulfing one or more counties, and the areas in which future growth is envisioned to occur. Rural regions usually contain a number of small cities and scattered development spread over often large geographic areas. Some urban regions have expanded so far that they now bump up against adjoining regions, creating *megalopoli,* especially along the East and West coasts.

Governance: once a close synonym with government and referring primarily to government institutions responsible for delivering services; now evolved into a more inclusive term to encompass: (1) all community interests affected by challenges and necessary to their resolution, not just government institutions, and (2) the collaborative problem-solving mechanisms needed to design timely strategies as well as the government institutions and other service-delivery mechanisms needed to implement them.

Decision making and *governance* are used as synonyms in this book, both referring to the designing of strategies and delivery of services to address challenges.

Intercommunity: a more general term than *regional* to refer to any interactions between two or more communities, such as between neighboring communities, city neighborhoods and suburban communities, across the communities within a county, or across an entire region.

Intergovernmental: a more restrictive term than *intercommunity* to refer to the relationships between units of government, as opposed to interactions across all sectors (public, private, academic, nonprofit, civic, etc.) of communities; such as among adjoining municipal governments to jointly deliver services or adjoining counties to provide a solid waste disposal facility.

Community: two usages: first, for a geographic area, most commonly a central city neighborhood or a suburban jurisdiction; and second, for a racial or ethnic group, such as the African-American or Hispanic community. At times, community is used in refer to the entire region, especially to emphasize the need to develop regional citizenship and a sense of regional community.

A *community leader* represents the interests of *citizens* or residents of the community.

Regional problem-solving (RPS) mechanisms: informal arrangements and formal entities that (1) focus on designing strategies to handle regional challenges, (2) tend to exercise planning and policy-development authority, and (3) often are experimental and difficult to sustain, much less replicate. Regional problem-solving mechanisms range from the regional planning councils established in the 1960s and 1970s to the experimental regional alliances of the 1980s and 1990s.

Regional service-delivery (RSD) mechanisms: informal arrangements and formal entities that (1) focus on delivering services to meet common regional needs, (2) tend to exercise operational authority, and (3) usually are relatively well-defined and, at least for the public ones, difficult to change, much less eliminate. Regional service-delivery mechanisms range from intergovernmental agreements to single and multiple service authorities.

Regional problem-solving/service-delivery (RPS/SD) mechanisms: formal entities that both design strategies for addressing cross-cutting challenges and deliver services to meet common regional needs. Regional problem-solving/service-delivery mechanisms range from county governments and central city-county government federations and consolidations in single county regions to regional planning and service districts in multi-county regions.

Metropolitan government: a separately chartered, general purpose unit of government that conducts or at least guides all major regional decision making and its interrelationships with county and municipal government problem solving and service delivery; repeatedly proposed, but never implemented in this country, a governance "will-o'-the-wisp."

Chapter 2
A Future for Regional Governance: A Regional Renaissance

In the opening scene of Winnie-the-Pooh, Christopher Robin drags Winnie down the stairs behind him, "bump, bump, bump on the back of his head..." It is, as far as he knows, the only way of coming downstairs, but sometimes he feels there really is another way, if only he could stop bumping for a moment and think about it.

— Bruce Adams

Community leaders and citizens in all regions are already laying the groundwork for a regional governance renaissance. The actions they are taking now will determine the degree of regional governance excellence each will achieve.

At the heart of this renaissance, we find community leaders and involved citizens dispelling old myths, adopting new truths, and pursuing regional governance excellence.

Old Regional Governance Myths

The old myths about regional governance that are being dispelled by the experiences of community leaders and citizens include:
- We can divide up crosscutting challenges and deal with them community by community.
- We can continue to afford endless flight to the hinterlands.

- We are too rich to have to worry about economic distress, too much of a melting pot to have to worry about ethnic and racial segregation.
- The answer to governing regions is structural; if desperate, we can always create an all-powerful metropolitan government.
- We can address regional governance challenges successfully with ad hoc approaches. And, worst of all,
- Regional governance is not that important; it is more of an intermittent nuisance than an ongoing necessity.

There is another myth, suggested thirty years ago, by Jane Jacobs in her classic work *The Death and Life of Great American Cities,* that community leaders and citizens were not ready to govern regions, that they should practice "metropolitan administration" first in our central cities.

Workable metropolitan administration has to be learned and used, first, within big cities, where no fixed political boundaries prevent its use. This is where we must experiment with methods for solving big common problems without, as a corollary, wreaking gratuitous mayhem on localities and on the processes of self-government.... If great cities can learn to administer, coordinate and plan in terms of administrative districts at understandable scale, we may become competent, as a society, to deal too with those crazy quilts of government and administration in the greater metropolitan areas. Today we are not competent to do so. (Jacobs, 427)

That final old myth — that community leaders and citizens are not up to the task of regional governance excellence — has haunted us for decades and might be the most critical to dispel as our regions hurtle into the 21st century.

Emerging Regional Governance Truths

As the myths are being dispelled, community leaders and citizens are beginning to perceive some important truths about regional governance.

We are beginning to ask the right questions. We are at a stage in the evolution of regional governance at which we can begin to ask the right questions. We need to engage in a great deal more experimentation before we get the right answers.

One question, for example, is the one raised by George Latimer, the former mayor of St. Paul, Minnesota, at a National Civic League Conference: "How can we make government and economic forces support people where they live and derive values, how can we bring love of community back into the life of the region?" Another is one that I raised with the Annie E. Casey Foundation in the design of a new jobs initiative: "Is this to be another central city attempt to deal with a distressed community concern, with some regional involvement, or a new type of regional initiative to address a disparity challenge that cuts across poor and rich communities regionwide?"

We are beginning to develop a regional governance capability and capacity. Ongoing experimentation in regional problem solving and service delivery is strengthening community leaders' and citizens' capabilities to recognize workable and unworkable approaches. On bad days, this experimentation looks like the most confused polyglot of processes and mechanisms; on good days, one can begin to see a glimmer of governance in the 21st century. The essence of this experimentation is presented in the following chapters of this book.

This experimentation is also developing a cadre of regional governance "pioneers," individuals and organizations who are willing to assist in designing strategies and supporting initiatives to address regional challenges. These include the "regional entrepreneurs," who take the lead in addressing regional challenges; the "regional wizards," who guide regional problem solving and manage regional service delivery; and the "regional champions," who provide financial, political, moral, and other support for improving regional governance.

We are beginning to explore some working guidelines and new models for improving regional governance. John Kirlin, a University of Southern California professor and dedicated regionalist, has suggested "ten emerging ideas that are likely to evolve, and perhaps be combined, into a framework for guiding creation of regional institutions." They are:

- Responses must be developed within regions, not imposed from a state capital or Washington, D.C.
- Functional fragmentation must be overcome.
- Political accountability must be to the region.
- Regional and neighborhood governance both must be strengthened.
- Plans and ordinances are limited tools.
- Greater use should be made of decision rules and private market mechanisms in governance.
- The public and private sectors must be harnessed together.
- Equitable access and mobility must be provided for those currently disadvantaged.
- Vision is critical.
- Effective governance requires sustained effort. (Kirlin, 124)

Examples of new models for regional governance include David Rusk's elastic cities, Allan Wallis' cross-sectoral alliances or my Strategic Intercommunity Governance Network (SIGNET), all of which are explored in Chapter 4.

We appear to be ready to modify existing traditions of local governance and make new investments in rebuilding community, locally and regionally. Stanford University's John Gardner, former foundation and government official and the founder of Common Cause and the Independent Sector, leads the Alliance for National Renewal movement, designed by the National Civic League, to deal with the "social disintegration" of community. He stresses that community is a regional concern: "It must not be thought, however, that the rebuilding of community is necessary only in economically distressed areas. The sense of community may be wholly absent in the privileged family, in the affluent congregation, in the well heeled suburb, with clear consequences in terms of white-collar crime, substance abuse, child neglect and so on." (Gardner, 1994, 377-9)

Gardner is concerned with turning around the mood of the country and creating a "lend a hand attitude" that results in communities that have "wholeness incorporating diversity." He also has one of the potentially right questions: "How can the American people be awakened to a new sense of purpose, a new vision and a new resolve?" (Gardner, 1994, 377-9)

We might even be conceding that regional governance needs a legitimacy of its own. Regional stewardship is being seen as an expression of our collective self-interest, reflected in the comments of many experts. "Today, national goals are being undercut because the fragmented form of government in metropolitan regions is inherently incapable of approving development patterns which meet the needs of the entire region," according to Henry Richmond of the National Growth Management Leadership Project. (Richmond, 7) Community leaders and citizens "must balance threatening excessive centralization on one pole and ineffective decentralization or narrow specialization on the other," according to Allan Wallis, research director for the National Civic League. (Wallis, 1994, 34) They need to forge "strong bonds of community and social solidarity" that "link the residents of metropolitan areas," according to Anthony Downs. (Wallis, 1994, 44)

The challenge is to "reinvent regionalism"; to nurture, amplify and institutionalize efforts to improve regional governance. (Wallis, 1994, 44) A new constitutional convention, such as was triggered by regional issues in the 1780s, might not be needed, but it might be timely to convene "regional confabs," possibly modeled after a proposal of a few years ago by the National Association of Counties to conduct a county governance congress for all levels of government.

We might finally have the confidence to pursue excellence in regional governance. Alexis de Tocqueville confirmed Americans' "can do" attitude on matters of governance in 1831. While traveling by steamboat down the Ohio River from Pittsburgh to Cincinnati, he wrote:

> There is one thing that America demonstrates invincibly of which I was hitherto doubtful. This is that the middle classes are capable of governing a state. I don't know if they would come off honorably from really difficult political situations, but they are adequate for the ordinary conduct of society, despite their petty passions, their incomplete education, their vulgar manners. Clearly they can supply practical intelligence, and that is sufficient. (de Tocqueville)

Perhaps community leaders and citizens finally believe they have the "practical intelligence," the "covenant of strength," to pursue regional governance excellence, according to Howard Grossman of the Economic Development Council of Northeastern Pennsylvania. "Substate regionalism needs the same fervor, trust, and recognition that the Ark of the Covenant has received over time ... From a 21st century perspective, the most ambitious and audacious program may be the considerable expansion of substate regionalism, causing public and private sector investments to be truly homogenized." (Grossman, 29)

Even earlier, in one of the first city-states, the citizens of ancient Athens took an oath that stated "I will transmit my city not diminished but greater and better than before." Today, many community leaders and citizens are developing the confidence to take a similar oath for their regions.

The final, emerging truth is that we need a regional renaissance to achieve regional governance excellence.

A Regional Renaissance

To transcend the current regional "merry-go-sorry" experience, I believe we need a regional renaissance, region by region, nationally. The original Renaissance, between the middle ages and the industrial revolution, energized a revival of arts and literature, the beginnings of modern science, and the emergence of the nation-state. A regional renaissance, between now and the dawn of the third millennium, would energize community leaders and citizens in each region, inspire the best thinking of academic and other experts, and attract priority national and state as well as local resources.

Most important, a regional renaissance would raise our sights from treating regional governance as an ad hoc *expediency*, challenge-by-challenge, to pursuing regional governance *excellence*, holisticly. Instead of responding to each new challenge with still another decision-making mechanism, community leaders and citizens could create a network of mechanisms to address emerging challenges consistent with a vision for making their region work.

Achieving regional governance excellence, I further believe, requires pursuing initiatives to strengthen regional governance in five ways.

Collectively, efforts to improve regional governance need to make it:

- **Prominent — Visible and Important:** How can we make regional governance as important, and visible, as the challenges that it is addressing?

- **Strategic — Future Regional Governance Vision and Action Plan:** How can we develop a consensus future vision for regional governance excellence and collectively pursue strategies of priority initiatives for achieving it?

- **Equitable — Economically, Racially, and Fiscally:** How can we overcome economic disparities and ethnic segregation and the resulting widening gap between rich and poor communities and develop an "equal opportunity playing field" for all citizens and communities regionwide?

- **Empowering — Regional Citizenship and Community:** How can we develop our individual regional citizenship and create an overall sense of regional community that enables us to govern together regionwide?

- **Institutionalized — Regional Problem Solving and Service Delivery:** How can we foster experimentation that results in institutionalizing a regional decision-making capacity to address emerging challenges? How can we experiment with existing and probably many new regional problem-solving mechanisms, until known and unforeseen crosscutting challenges are addressed in a timely manner? How can we redistribute responsibilities among existing and probably few new regional service-delivery mechanisms, until strategies for addressing crosscutting issues are implemented flexibly?

These five components of regional governance excellence can be thought of as the five points of a regional governance star.

Finally, I suggest two hypotheses concerning launching a regional renaissance.

The first is that the five components need to be considered in approximately the order presented, reversing the all too frequently used process of jumping to institutionalizing some new regional governance mechanism and then picking up the pieces, or even finessing, making it prominent, strategic, equitable, and empowering.

- First, we need to raise the stature of regional governance — its visibility and importance — to attract the attention and resources of community leaders and citizens. We cannot achieve regional governance excellence if it has "second class" status.

- Second, we need to understand emerging regional challenges and our ability to address them and develop a future vision and strategies to guide our efforts to strengthen regional governance. Moreover, we need to assess our performance to determine whether regional decision making improves with each new challenge. Otherwise, we do not know whether our individual efforts contribute to, or detract from, achieving regional governance excellence. We cannot ad hoc our way to regional governance excellence.

The Five Points
of
Regional Governance Excellence

Prominent

Strategic

Equitable

Empowering

Institutionalized

- Third, we need to address overcoming intercommunity disparities; otherwise the widening economic, racial and fiscal gap between rich and poor communities will be an Achilles heel undermining our collaborative initiatives to strengthen regional governance. We need to create an "equal opportunity playing field" for communities within a region.

- Fourth, we need to build regional citizenship and a sense of regional community; otherwise community leaders and citizens will not support, or breathe life into, initiatives to strengthen regional governance. We need the support of regional citizens to pursue priority initiatives for achieving regional governance excellence.

- Fifth and finally, we need to redirect existing problem-solving and service-delivery mechanisms, create new ones, and tie them together in a network that can address any regional challenge in a timely, flexible, effective manner. We need to institutionalize our capacity to achieve regional governance excellence.

In sum, we need to raise the *status,* design a *strategy,* balance the *scales* and find the *soul* of regional governance, before we tinker with its *structure.*

I am cautioned by John Gardner's advice that no matter how sound a strategy is for strengthening regional governance, implementation of priority initiatives will depend on taking advantage of the convergence of conditions beyond one's control. This sage prophet suggests in a letter:

> In a lifetime of watching a wide range of social problem solving, I've concluded that such problems rarely get solved by an orderly attack at the most logical point. I think one sees a lot of actions on a long ragged front with breakthroughs at often unsuspected spots. There are partial victories, and, with luck, enough to result in an overall victory. But it's untidy.

The second hypothesis is that any region that designs a consensus vision for the future of regional governance and aggressively pursues initiatives for addressing all five components can improve its regional governance performance and begin to achieve excellence by the turn of the millennium.

Many of the regional governance initiatives selected will probably build upon existing activities. Some of the initiatives will probably simultaneously address two or more of the components. All of the initiatives need to proactively pursue the unique future visions for regional governance excellence developed by community leaders and citizens in each region.

Initiatives for Pursuing Regional Governance Excellence

The next five chapters present regional governance initiative options to consider in a regional renaissance, one set for each component. Collectively, the three dozen initiatives, and hundreds of examples of their application, provide a "cafeteria of ideas" for community leaders and citizens to consider in strategies for achieving regional governance excellence. Each chapter presents

- background information on each component, and
- detailed explanations of initiative options, including a general description, specific examples of its application, accomplishments, strengths and shortcomings, future potential and contacts for additional information.

The final pages of this chapter present brief summaries of the regional governance initiatives. Each initiative is cross-referenced to the page on which it is more fully described. Detailed descriptions and discussions can be found in the sections identified in the cross-references.

Initiatives for Making Regional Governance Prominent (Chapter 3)

How do we make regional governance as important, and visible, as the challenges it is addressing?

- **Prominent #1: Conduct initial regional governance explorations (new) (Page 69)**

  General explorations of regionalism are often one of the first activities undertaken to make community leaders and citizens aware of the importance of addressing regional challenges and have been undertaken in most regions, nationally.

  Community leaders and citizens could conduct more-targeted initial explorations of regional governance to improve their understanding of the roles, responsibilities, and relationships of regional problem-solving and service-delivery mechanisms and the actions taken, or considered, to strengthen regional decision making.

- **Prominent #2: Hold regional governance symposia (new) (Page 73)**

  General symposia on regionalism are also often one of the first activities undertaken to make community leaders and citizens aware of the importance of addressing regional challenges and have been undertaken in most regions, nationally.

  Community leaders and citizens could conduct more-targeted symposia on regional governance to improve their understanding of the roles, responsibilities, and relationships of regional problem-solving and service-delivery mechanisms and the actions taken, or considered, to strengthen regional governance.

- **Prominent #3: Foster regional civic journalism (Page 76)**

  Newspapers and other media can foster understanding, debate and even collective action on regional challenges by community leaders and citizens. These activities include converting local sections of newspapers to region sections and local radio and TV news broadcasts to regional broadcasts, hosting town meetings and public forums on regional challenges, fostering citizen/candidate interactions on campaign issues, and publishing newspaper or magazine series on regionalism.

Community leaders and citizens could sponsor newspaper or television series on regional governance and other civic journalism activities.

- **Prominent #4: Celebrate regional governance success (new) (Page 81)**

Community leaders and citizens in all regions could sponsor recognition programs for the regional governance accomplishments of individuals and organizations so as to celebrate regional successes and encourage the launching of new initiatives to strengthen regional governance.

- **Prominent #5: Launch a regional prominence campaign (Page 84)**

A regional prominence campaign offers the opportunity to pursue an array of activities to make the region and regional governance more visible and important for community leaders and citizens, such as the combination of articles, editorials, talk shows, reports and conferences undertaken in the Year of the Region campaign in the Philadelphia region.

Community leaders and citizens in other regions could launch a regional prominence campaign, such as a Year of the Region or annual Regional Excellence Day.

Initiatives for
Making Regional Governance Strategic
(Chapter 4)

How can we develop a consensus future vision for regional governance excellence and collectively pursue strategies of priority initiatives for achieving it?

- **Strategic #1: Explore regional governance models (new) (Page 95)**

   Understanding the existing ("Balkanization" and "Metropolitanism") and emerging ("Network") models of regional governance can help community leaders and citizens to design a future vision of regional governance excellence for their region or even inspire the development of a new model for regional governance.

- **Strategic #2: Develop a Strategy for Achieving Regional Governance Excellence (SARGE) (new) (Page 109)**

   Community leaders and citizens could, or should, conduct a broad examination of regional governance to design a consensus future vision for regional governance excellence and a collaborative action plan for achieving it.

- **Strategic #3: Adopt a pledge to strengthen regional decision making (new) (Page 133)**

   Community leaders and citizens could encourage the adoption of a regional renaissance pledge to secure commitments for improving regional governance as well as begin to establish guidelines for addressing cross-cutting challenges.

- **Strategic #4: Report on the state of regional governance (new) (Page 136)**

   Community leaders and citizens could prepare periodic reports and hold conferences on progress made and initiatives still to be undertaken to improve regional governance.

- **Strategic #5: Create a regional governance fund or foundation (new) (Page 139)**

   Community leaders and citizens could create a regional governance fund or foundation to provide a predictable source of financing for launching initiatives to strengthen regional governance.

Initiatives for
Making Regional Governance Equitable
(Chapter 5)

How can we overcome economic disparities and racial segregation and the resulting widening gap between rich and poor communities and develop an "equal opportunity playing field" for all citizens and communities regionwide?

- **Equitable #1: Heighten regional interdependence awareness (new) (Page 151)**

  Community leaders and citizens could develop regional interdependence awareness programs to sensitize their communities to the threats of economic, racial, and fiscal disparities and motivate them to take advantage of the opportunities offered by diversity and interdependence. Such programs could draw upon existing efforts, such as The Atlanta Project and various local programs to build relationships across racial lines, such as the Cleveland Roundtable.

- **Equitable #2: Share regional revenues (Page 158)**

  Existing activities include:
  - targeting service support to distressed communities,
  - transferring functions to higher levels of government,
  - reforming local tax systems,
  - sharing the revenues from regional developments,
  - establishing new revenue sources for regional infrastructure and assets, and
  - sharing general tax revenues to redress intercommunity inequities and achieve other purposes, such as commuter taxes, redistributed sales taxes and property and income tax sharing programs.

  Community leaders and citizens could:
  - provide targeted general assistance to distressed communities,
  - finance more public services regionally,
  - establish enhanced boundary or service equalization commissions, and
  - establish combination tax sharing programs.

- **Equitable #3: Target regional development (Page 171)**

  Existing activities include:
  - targeting economic development support to distressed individuals and communities,

- linking jobs and development activities of rich and poor communities,
- developing arrangements for mediating and resolving intercommunity conflicts over development decisions, and
- managing growth to sustain development regionwide.

Community leaders and citizens could pursue a combination of:
- fostering the development of rich/poor community linkage projects,
- providing the benefits of projects of regional significance to distressed communities, and
- shaping future growth to balance development of all communities regionwide.

- **Equitable #4: Integrate communities regionwide (Page 180)**

Existing activities include:
- sharing leadership in regional decision making mechanisms,
- providing regional fair share housing, and
- maintaining community integration.

Community leaders and citizens could:
- institutionalize existing activities, regionally, by establishing regionwide housing commissions, authorities and coalitions,
- require and provide affordable housing in all communities, mostly as part of new construction,
- offer open school enrollments across school district lines,
- monitor racial change and provide low interest mortgages and pursue strategies to maintain racial balance, and
- provide regional interdependence awareness education programs for fellow community leaders and citizens.

Initiatives for Making Regional Governance Empowering (Chapter 6)

How can we develop our individual regional citizenship and create an overall sense of regional community that enables us to govern together regionwide?

- **Empowering #1: Develop regional citizenship skills (Page 198)**

  Community leaders and citizens could develop their leadership, followership, and overall citizenship skills so as to prepare for becoming effectively involved in regional decision making. This initiative could build on existing community leadership and visitation programs, such as by:
  - expanding the curriculum of regional leadership programs to include followership and citizenship,
  - offering regional citizenship skills programs to a broader audience, and
  - providing follow-up training and support to develop the skills of regional governance "pioneers", such as regional mentoring programs, user groups, and exchange or service corps.

- **Empowering #2: Disseminate regional governance information (Page 206)**

  Regional governance information is critical to graduates of regional citizenship programs as well as community leaders and citizens participating in activities to strengthen regional governance, such as the combination of a Metropolitan Clearinghouse, Metropolitan Briefing Book, Metroscape newsletter, and electronic Metropolitan Newsnet being sponsored by the Institute of Metropolitan Studies at Portland State University.

  Community leaders and citizens in other regions could pursue similar combinations of regional governance information activities.

- **Empowering #3: Establish regional community identity (Page 212)**

  Regional identity programs are directed at making the region better known and appreciated by community leaders and citizens, such as selecting a regional name, obtaining a regional post mark, installing community signs with regional logos, arranging for regional logos on license plates, distributing a regional newsletter and other activities undertaken by the Piedmont Triad Partnership in the Winston-Salem/Greensboro/High Point region of North Carolina.

Community leaders and citizens in other regions could establish similar regional identify programs.

- **Empowering #4: Forge a city/suburb regional constituency (new) (Page 215)**

  Community leaders and citizens could forge a regional constituency among city and suburban citizens, especially one that cuts across the communities with the widest fiscal, economic and racial disparities, to address regional challenges. This initiative could build upon the Regional Unity Program of the North Texas Commission (Dallas/Fort Worth) and combine a number of activities under a "Sister Communities" program.

- **Empowering #5: Empower citizen standing in regional decision making (Page 220)**

  Existing efforts include:
  - creating citizen advisory committees for regional decision making mechanisms,
  - appointing citizen representatives to governing bodies of regional decision making mechanisms, and
  - electing citizen boards to participate in central city decision making.

  Community leaders and citizens could:
  - create regional citizen advisory committees for individual regional decision making mechanisms,
  - appoint or elect citizen board members of regional decision making mechanisms,
  - create an elected regional citizens board to advise regional decision making mechanisms,
  - create regional coalitions of citizen-based organizations, and
  - foster use of citizen initiative and referenda on regional topics.

- **Empowering #6: Establish regional problem-solving centers (new) (Page 231)**

  Community leaders and citizens could establish regional problem-solving centers in which they have access to facilitators and regional experts, decision making electronic software, and best practices from other regions. This initiative could build upon the Collaboration Center established by The Atlanta Project or the Team Technology Center of the Federal Aviation Administration.

- **Empowering #7: Develop a regional citizens charter (new) (Page 235)**

  Community leaders and citizens could develop a citizens charter that presents the rights and responsibilities of regional citizens, the opportunities for citizen involvement in regional decision making and the standards for services provided by regional organizations. This initiative builds upon the Citizens Charter of the John Major administration in Great Britain.

Initiatives for
Making Regional Governance Institutionalized
(Chapter 7)

How can we foster experimentation that results in institutionalizing a regional decision-making capacity to address emerging challenges? How can we experiment with existing and probably many new regional problem-solving mechanisms, until known and unforeseen cross-cutting challenges are addressed in a timely manner? How can we redistribute responsibilities among existing and probably few new regional service-delivery mechanisms, until strategies for addressing cross-cutting issues can be implemented flexibly?

Regional Problem Solving

- **Problem-Solving #1: Public regional problem-solving mechanisms (Page 249)**

  The most common examples of regional problem-solving mechanisms over the past few decades have been ad hoc intercommunity problem-solving groups and regional planning councils. Ad hoc intercommunity problem-solving groups work best for addressing sub-regional challenges, such as those primarily affecting neighboring municipalities or counties. Regional planning councils are associations of local governments, usually state and national government mandated and supported, that oversee regional transportation, air and water quality, land use and other planning activities and foster cooperative approaches to addressing regional challenges.

  Community leaders and citizens could create new regional planning councils and strengthen existing ones by clarifying their roles and responsibilities, including empowering them; and diversifying their membership, including adding non-public members to their governing boards, exchanging members with other sector organizations, or directly electing citizen representatives.

- **Problem-Solving #2: Private regional problem-solving mechanisms (Page 260)**

  Regional chambers of commerce and growth associations and other business leadership groups often take the lead in conducting regional economic development and related problem-solving and planning activities.

Community leaders and citizens could create new private regional problem-solving mechanisms and strengthen existing ones by:
- broadening citizen involvement in their planning processes,
- adding representatives of other regional problem-solving mechanisms to their governing boards, and
- fostering the creation of academic and other research institutes to advise them on addressing regional challenges.

- **Problem-Solving #3: Academic regional problem-solving mechanisms (Page 265)**

College or university research institutes and public service programs conduct neutral, professional research on regional challenges and often provide information and staff support for regional problem-solving processes, such as regional strategic planning processes or annual leadership symposia.

Community leaders and citizens could create new academic regional problem-solving mechanisms and strengthen existing ones by focusing more of their attention on regionwide challenges and formalizing their relationships with and support for other regional problem-solving mechanisms.

- **Problem-Solving #4: Citizen regional problem-solving mechanisms (Page 270)**

Regional civic organizations, such as citizens leagues, forums and councils, are non-partisan, independent and open membership organizations that conduct studies of emerging regional challenges and educate and encourage citizens and community leaders to address them.

Community leaders and citizens could create new citizen regional problem-solving mechanisms and strengthen existing ones with professional staff and adequate budgets so as to take the lead in addressing regional challenges, especially developing regional citizenship skills and the other Empowering and Equitable initiatives, or even take the lead in developing Strategies for Achieving Regional Governance Excellence.

- **Problem-Solving #5: Multi-sector regional problem-solving mechanisms (Page 275)**

Multi-sector or regional alliances or partnerships have been the focus of the greatest experimentation in regional decision-making over the past decade, from involving affected interests in addressing a particular challenge to developing regional leadership networks for involving community leaders and citizens regionwide in developing regional visions and economic competitiveness strategies.

Community leaders and citizens could create new multi-sector regional alliances and strengthen existing ones by:
- broadening the membership of single sector regional problem-solving mechanisms,
- providing predictable funding sources for multi-sector regional alliances,
- recycling temporary multi-sector regional alliances to address related regional challenges, and
- expanding multi-sector alliances in single counties to multi-sector regional alliances.

Regional Service Delivery

- **Service-Delivery #1: Intergovernmental service-delivery arrangements (Page 285)**

  Voluntary Informal and formal arrangements among groups of municipalities, counties and even school districts for the delivery of services have grown over the past few decades, and can be found for almost any service in most regions of the country. Most of these arrangements are sub-regional, but some involve the major local governments in the region, such as between central cities and counties, to sort out their respective service-delivery responsibilities, or for county government delivery of municipal services.

  Community leaders and citizens could develop new intergovernmental service-delivery arrangements, primarily for the delivery of sub-regional services.

- **Service-Delivery #2: Other than public regional services (Page 292)**

  In some cases, private, academic, non-profit and civic organizations deliver intercommunity and regional services, at least on a piecemeal basis, often as part of publicly-financed privatization efforts. For example, private firms often offer some or all of the solid waste collection and disposal services and other public works services or deliver water, sewer, cable television, electric and other public franchise services. Colleges and universities sometimes offer regional data collection and processing services and provide a home for small business development centers. Nonprofit organizations operate regional cultural facilities, such as art museums and history centers, and offer the majority of social services in many regions. Most recently, multi-sector partnerships have been developed, such as to construct and operate fiber-optic communications networks and toll roads and bridges.

Community leaders and citizens could expand private, academic, non-profit and especially multi-sector delivery of regional services; it might even be more flexible than public service-delivery as long as it meets the needs of distressed communities and is coordinated regionwide.

- **Service-Delivery #3: Regional single-service authorities (Page 295)**

Regional single-service authorities — delivering water treatment and supply, air pollution control, solid waste disposal, transportation, industrial development and other regional services — are the most common form of regional service-delivery mechanisms in most regions.

Community leaders and citizens could modify regional single-service delivery mechanisms, including:
- consolidating like authorities into larger entities,
- consolidating special purpose districts into multi-purpose ones,
- abolishing special districts with obsolete functions,
- merging special districts with counties and other general purpose units of government, and
- transforming independent special districts to more closely resemble dependent public agencies.

- **Service-Delivery #4: Regional multiple-service authorities (Page 299)**

Regional multiple-service authorities are much rarer; their most common form is regional port and development authorities which generally provide transportation, economic development and other services in addition to providing port facilities.

Community leaders and citizens could create new regional multiple-service authorities, such as for multi-modal transportation services and facilities.

- **Service-Delivery #5: Regional service-delivery coordinating groups (new) (Page 304)**

Community leaders and citizens could create regional service-delivery coordinating groups, composed of members and staff of regional service-delivery mechanisms, to foster dialogue among providers, coordinate the delivery of existing services, and help implement strategies for delivering new regional services.

Regional Problem-Solving/Service-Delivery

- **Problem-Solving/Service-Delivery #1: Empowered counties and central cities (Page 307)**

  Counties have emerged as the major units of local government in many regions, empowered to provide a mixture of state-mandated, locally demanded, and regionally needed problem solving and service delivery. Central cities that have been empowered to annex surrounding growth areas also serve as regional problem-solving and service-delivery mechanisms.

  The future potential of counties and central cities as regional problem-solving and service-delivery mechanisms is being compromised by development patterns. As growth expands beyond county boundaries and central city annexation, the ability of either to influence growth or other regional challenges is diminished; however, community leaders and citizens could encourage either to address the county or central city level aspects of regional challenges, such as intercommunity or interneighborhood disparities.

- **Problem-Solving/Service-Delivery #2: Municipal/county government modifications, federations, and consolidations (Page 312)**

  The relative structure of municipal and county governments has provided almost endless opportunities for strengthening, and weakening, regional problem solving and service delivery. Municipalities can be incorporated, combined, and even disincorporated; central cities can actively annex their surrounding communities; and central cities and urban counties can create federated or consolidated governments. All of these options change the relationships among local governments and, thereby, have an impact on regional decision making.

  Municipal modifications will probably continue to make few contributions to regional decision making, except increase its complexity with each new municipal incorporation. Central city-county consolidations or federations could continue to have an impact on regional decision making, by bringing together the two major local governments.

  Community leaders and citizens could pursue the opportunities for municipal modifications, federations, and consolidations that strengthen regional governance.

- **Problem-Solving/Service-Delivery #3: Regional planning and service districts (Page 326)**

  A few examples of regional districts exist that combine regional planning councils and the delivery of regional sewer, transit or other services. The most touted examples in this country are the Metropolitan Council in the Minneapolis/St. Paul region and the Metropolitan Service District, or Metro, in the Portland, Oregon, region. A similar example is the Greater Vancouver Regional District in the Vancouver, British Columbia, region of Canada.

  Community leaders and citizens in other regions could create regional planning and service districts.

Chapter 3
Making Regional Governance Prominent: Visible and Important

Everyone is ignorant only on different subjects.

— *Will Rogers*

The region has invaded our consciousness, as community leaders and citizens, with increasing frequency over the past few decades.

We have been witnesses to the suburbanization of our regions for more than half a century. We have learned to live, work and play in different parts of the region. We have fought with other communities in the region over the siting of highways, airports, land fills, and other public facilities. We have also competed with them for economic development opportunities, often by offering expensive incentives. We have seen problems often follow a perverse "domino" theory as they spread across communities. We might even have given some thought to a proposal developed by a business, academic, or citizens group to create a new regional alliance for addressing an emerging challenge or a new authority for delivering a service regionwide.

We have probably also seen the growing interdependence of communities across the region. This is obvious when we travel, especially when we travel by air. The lines that so prominently divide us on a map are invisible from the air. The most striking features are the natural ones, such as the rivers, lakes and mountains. Among the ones we have made, it is difficult to pick out anything beyond "downtown" in the central city and a few highways and suburban employment centers or shopping malls. No wonder that we often use the name of the central city to identify where we live, even if we live in one of its suburbs.

Sports teams reinforce this awareness. Everybody in the region roots for the home team, even if it is in some other part of the region. Everybody in the region feels as if they're a participant when the mayor of the central city backs the home team in a bet against a counterpart in another region. We are equally affected by the outcomes of economic competitions — proud when a desirable foreign manufacturing prospect locates in the region, disappointed when another prospect goes somewhere else.

We're probably also proud when our region ranks high in a national survey of livability or the quality of education or cultural facilities or some aspect of our economic competitiveness. We're probably disappointed, even angry, at a low ranking that results from crime or infant mortality rates. Maybe our sense of interdependence was reinforced, along with some trepidation, when that same business, academic or citizens group proposed a bolder initiative to consolidate the central city and county governments or establish a directly elected regional planning council.

To begin the regional renaissance process, we need to build upon this informal growing awareness and pursue initiatives to make the region more understandable to fellow community leaders and citizens. We need to educate them on current and emerging regional challenges and the processes and mechanisms we use to address them. We need to provide them with the information to assess the importance of regional governance, to grapple with the implications of regional governance excellence for the money in their pockets (their livelihoods) and the amenities in their communities (the quality of their lives).

We need to capture the attention of community leaders and citizens and convince them that we all need to improve regional governance; to invest time and resources in developing a future vision and action plan for improving regional governance so as to deal effectively with particular regional economic, social, and physical challenges.

We need to pursue making regional governance prominent with some of the same fervor, but maybe different tactics, as private industry uses to sell cars and cereal, if we are to educate community leaders and citizens and convince them of the importance of regional governance. If we do not make regional governance visible and important — prominent — for community leaders and citizens, we cannot start down the path of achieving regional governance excellence.

Initiatives for Making Regional Governance Prominent

How can we make regional governance as important, and visible, as the challenges that it is addressing?

Most of the applications to date of the initiatives for making regional governance prominent have actually played down governance. They have focused instead on educating community leaders and citizens on pressing regional challenges, identifying the subject of a symposium as regionalism or regional cooperation but not as regional governance.

This has probably been a sensible marketing strategy for attracting the attention of community leaders and citizens. Focusing on pressing regional challenges probably provides a strong inducement to review a report or participate in an event. At the same time, putting too much emphasis on governance could raise fears of losing local control or the threat of a metropolitan government, either of which would discourage the participation of citizens and especially community leaders.

Now, however, community leaders and citizens realize that one of the major obstacles to dealing with these challenges is our reluctance to make regional decision making — governance — work. It is difficult, if not impossible, to wrestle with how to address economic, social, and physical challenges cooperatively if we are ignorant of the roles, responsibilities, and relationships of existing regional problem-solving and service-delivery mechanisms. It is almost as difficult to convene follow-up meetings of symposia participants unless we know who could convene these meetings and who should be invited to participate.

All of the Making Regional Governance Prominent initiatives now need to focus on regional governance, to make it important enough to attract community leader and citizen involvement in conducting examinations for achieving regional governance excellence (see Strategic #2 in Chapter 4).

The initiatives for Making Regional Governance Prominent are:
- Prominent #1: Conduct initial regional governance explorations (new)
- Prominent #2: Hold regional governance symposia (new)

   In addition, Empowering #2 in Chapter 6 (Disseminate regional governance information) complements Prominent #1 and 2.
- Prominent #3: Foster regional civic journalism
- Prominent #4: Celebrate regional governance success (new)
- Prominent #5: Launch a regional prominence campaign

   In addition, Empowering #3 in Chapter 6 (Establish regional community identity) complements Prominent #3 to 5.

Community leaders and citizens could begin the process for making regional governance prominent by conducting an initial regional governance exploration (Prominent #1) or holding a regional governance symposium (Prominent #2) to begin educating community leaders and citizens. Then they could launch one or more of the last three initiatives — fostering regional civic journalism (Prominent #3), celebrating regional governance success (Prominent #4) and especially launching a regional prominence campaign (Prominent #5) — to make regional governance prominent.

The performance of the Prominent initiatives in pursuing regional governance excellence can be assessed by answering two questions. Does implementing the Prominent initiatives result in:
- making regional governance as visible and important as the regional challenges it is addressing?
- making intercommunity and regional problem-solving and service-delivery mechanisms as visible and important as their local counterparts?

Prominent #1
Conduct Initial Regional Governance Explorations (new)

General explorations of regionalism are often one of the first activities undertaken to make community leaders and citizens aware of the importance of addressing regional challenges. They have been undertaken in most regions across the country. While these explorations are usually conducted to educate and motivate involvement in regional efforts in general, they often provide information on regional problem-solving and service-delivery mechanisms and might even compare them to mechanisms in other regions.

The reports of these initial explorations of regionalism are usually descriptive, not prescriptive. However, they might offer some suggestions for involving community leaders and citizens in addressing regional challenges and improving regional decision making. Most important, they often explore the merits of organizing follow-up activities, such as sponsoring a symposium on regionalism (see Prominent #2) or even launching a regional strategic planning or visioning process to develop a strategy for addressing a particular challenge or developing a future vision for the region. Sometimes they are even prepared to spur public action, for example, through a series of articles in local newspapers or analyses by community foundations. As a result, the reports on these explorations can vary in length from an eye-catching brochure to longer tomes to guide follow-up efforts.

Explorations of regionalism have been sponsored by regional planning councils; central city, county, and state governments; chambers of commerce and other business organizations; citizens leagues; college and university research institutes and public service programs; community foundations; and newspapers. They often are prepared by committees of community leaders and citizens, usually with the assistance of staff and consultants.

Accomplishments

Explorations of regionalism often have provided community leaders and citizens with their first organized introduction to regional challenges. They provide a common background for individuals who are usually only partially informed about the range of decision-making mechanisms that exist throughout the region and the regional challenges that they are addressing. Moreover, they can stimulate a dialogue that leads to organized efforts to improve regional governance.

Strengths and Shortcomings

While these initial explorations are beneficial to their sponsors and recipients of reports, and can provoke the first organized region-wide thinking on regional governance, they often fail to engage the involvement of more than a few community leaders and citizens. Moreover, they rarely focus on the governance of regional challenges, either because governance does not generate the same excitement as pressing challenges or because it is too threatening to those concerned that regionalism is only a "front" for metropolitan government. Finally, since they are only initial explorations, they usually do not analyze the options for action to address particular regional challenges or improve regional decision making.

Potential

For regions that have already conducted initial explorations of regionalism, and many have, the next step could be to conduct a more targeted initial exploration of regional governance. This initial exploration could inform community leaders and citizens on actions that have been taken, or considered, to make regional governance prominent, strategic, equitable, empowering, and institutionalized, and on the roles, responsibilities, and relationships of existing regional decision-making mechanisms.

Moreover, an initial exploration of regional governance could assess the merits of conducting a more rigorous regional governance examination (see Strategic #2, Chapter V). It could address such questions as:

- What are the attitudes of community leaders and citizens towards such an examination?
- What has been the recent experience in managing regional challenges?

- What topics should be addressed, or have priority, in such an examination?
- Who are the likely sponsors of such an examination?
- What should be the products of such an examination?

These initial explorations of regional governance could be conducted by coalitions of sponsors to help assure the distribution of their reports to the widest range of community leaders and citizens.

Moreover, complementary activities could be conducted in conjunction with explorations of regional governance. For example, slide shows or videotapes could be prepared to visually convey the range and activities of regional decision-making mechanisms, which could be used in follow-up public meetings and television videoconferences to educate and motivate community leaders and citizens to become involved in improving regional decision making (see Prominent #5). Or delegations of community leaders and citizens could make visits to other regions to observe their regional decision-making processes and compare them to their own. Such regional visitations (see Empowering #1, Chapter 6) could be modeled on the annual treks of leaders in some regions to "steal" good ideas from other regions. Or regular newsletters could be prepared on new developments in regional governance.

Contacts

Explorations of regionalism have been sponsored by some organization in almost all regions, such as a regional planning council, central city, county and state government, chamber of commerce or business organization, college or university, citizens league, foundation or newspaper. The best contacts for examples might be found through contacting a sample of these organizations in your region or in others comparable to your region. A few examples:

- Regional planning organization explorations: Regional Unity, Vic Suhm, North Texas Commission, Dallas, Texas, 214-328-5001
- Central city, county and state government explorations: Strategic Choices, City of Austin, 512-499-2200
- Chambers of commerce/business organizations: The Strength of Maryland Depends on The State of Baltimore, Greater Baltimore Committee, Baltimore, Maryland, 410-727-2820

- College and university explorations: Monographs on Economic Competitiveness and Tax Sharing, Ohio Urban University Program, Cleveland, Ohio, 216-687-6941
- Citizen league explorations: Regional Problem Solving in Greater Cleveland: A New Strategy, Citizens League of Greater Cleveland, 216-241-5340
- Newspaper explorations (see Prominent #3)
- Regional visitations: Community leaders in Denver, Nashville, Portland, Oregon, and Seattle conduct regular visitations to other regions.
- Regional newsletters and magazines: *region*wise,* Center for Greater Philadelphia, University of Pennsylvania, Philadelphia, Pennsylvania, 215-898-8713; *Regional Directions,* Allegheny Conference on Community Development, Pittsburgh, Pennsylvania, 412-281-1890; *Metroscape,* Institute of Portland Metropolitan Studies, Portland State University, Portland, Oregon, 503-725-5170

Prominent #2
Hold Regional Governance Symposia (new)

General symposia on regionalism are also often one of the first activities undertaken to make community leaders and citizens aware of the importance of addressing regional challenges, and they too have been undertaken in most regions. Like initial explorations of regionalism (see Prominent #1), they are usually intended to educate and motivate involvement in regional efforts. They often provide information on regional problem-solving and service-delivery mechanisms and might even compare them to mechanisms in other regions.

These symposia on regionalism are often preceded by the preparation of a brief report on regionalism (see Prominent #1) as well as a complementary videotape or slide show to be presented at the opening of the symposium.

These symposia vary in length. Half-day symposia primarily involve presentations by regional experts, often from other regions, and questions and comments from the audience. Full-day symposia add conducting small group discussions to identify regional challenges, surveying participant attitudes on follow-up activities, or even developing policy statements or organizing task groups for addressing the challenges. Sometimes symposia begin with a reception, dinner, or presentations the night before to prod the thinking of participants prior to the following day's discussion.

Finally, some symposia are held in conjunction with regional planning and visioning processes. For example, Governors State University recently sponsored an Idea Fair to introduce community leaders and citizens in the southern suburbs of the Chicago region to initiatives being pursued in other regions. Videoconferencing has been used in some of the symposia to facilitate interaction among remote parts of the region as well as to provide television access for home audiences; a good example is the multi-region Regional Dialogue, also sponsored by Governors' State University.

Some organizations are beginning to hold symposia on a periodic basis. The Triangle J Council of Governments has sponsored World Class Region conferences every few years, the most recent one leading to the creation of the Greater Triangle Regional Council, a regional alliance (see Problem-Solving #5, Chapter 7). Similarly, the Institute of Portland Metropolitan Studies at Portland (Oregon) State University sponsors an annual symposium to introduce community leaders to new ideas, to give them an opportunity to interact informally, and to seek their guidance on the Institute's research program (see Problem-Solving #3, Chapter 7).

Symposia on regionalism are sponsored by the same wide range of organizations sponsoring explorations of regionalism, including regional planning councils; central city, county and state governments; chambers of commerce and other business organizations; citizens leagues; college and university research institutes and public service programs; local government and professional associations; or some combination of these organizations. Participation is usually open to community leaders and the public, either for a fee or free. At times, participation from particular groups, such as business leaders or local government officials, is especially encouraged.

Accomplishments

Symposia on regionalism, like explorations of regionalism, often provide community leaders and citizens with their first organized introduction to regional governance and other aspects of regionalism. In addition, they often provide the first opportunities for community leaders and citizens to share their perceptions about the range of decision-making mechanisms that exist throughout the region and the regional challenges that they are addressing.

Strengths and Shortcomings

Symposia on regionalism are beneficial to the participants, but they usually only involve a few dozen to a couple of hundred community leaders and citizens. Shorter symposia usually only provide a general overview on regional governance and the range of regional decision-making mechanisms. Longer symposia can provide an opportunity to share perceptions on these mechanisms as well as raise suggestions for strengthening regional decision making.

Potential

Symposia on regionalism have already been conducted in many regions. The next step could be to conduct a more targeted symposium on regional governance, to improve community leader and citizen understanding of regional decision making and the actions that have been taken, or considered, to make it more prominent, strategic, equitable, empowering, and institutionalized. Moreover, the participants in such a symposium could assess the feasibility of conducting a more rigorous regional governance examination or addressing a particular regional governance challenge, such as the future of a regional planning council (see Strategic #2, Chapter 4).

Similar to explorations of regionalism, complementary activities could be undertaken, including preparing slide shows or videotapes on regional decision-making mechanisms, conducting follow-up radio talk shows and television videoconferences, sponsoring regional visitations, and publishing a regional governance newsletter.

Contacts

Symposia on regionalism have been conducted in almost all regions by some organization, such as a regional planning council; a central city, county, or state government; chamber of commerce or business organization; a college or university; a foundation; or a newspaper. The best contacts for examples might be found through contacting a sample of these organizations in your region or in others that you consider to be comparable to or a model for your region. A few examples are:

- "Collaboration and Regionalism: Securing Stark County's Future," Canton, Ohio, Regional Chamber of Commerce, 216-456-7253
- World Class Region Conferences, Triangle J Council of Governments, Research Triangle, North Carolina, 919-549-0551
- Regional Issues Conference, Austin, Texas, Area Research Organization, Inc., 512-477-4000
- IdeaFair and Regional Dialogue, Governors State University, Chicago, Illinois, 708-534-6970
- Call to Action Forum, Tri-County Regional Planning Commission, Lansing, Michigan, 517-393-0342

Prominent #3
Foster Regional Civic Journalism

Newspapers and other media can foster understanding, debate, and even collective action on emerging regional challenges on the part of community leaders and citizens. This sense of civic journalism suggests a media role that goes beyond simply reporting the news, but stops short of making the news. One newspaper executive described it as "coming down out of the press box and getting on the field — not as players, but as referees." (Fouhy, 260) Another suggests that it requires journalists to sort out information and make it useful to citizens, re-engage citizens in deliberation and provide public space for such discussion, and overcome detachment from issues and learn to incorporate community improvement values into journalistic efforts. (Merritt, 265) Yet another suggests that it's about treating people as citizens: to help them be actors rather than spectators. (Jay Rosen, *Doing Democracy,* Winter, 1995)

Many news media are taking steps to involve community leaders and citizens in addressing regional challenges, including:

Converting local sections of newspapers to regional sections and local news broadcasts to regional broadcasts and providing regional weather, traffic, and air quality reports. A large number of central city newspapers and radio and television newscasts have already made this transition to help them relate to their expanding markets. In the process, they have helped create an identity for the region and introduced community leaders and citizens to regionwide news stories. Some television newscasts also have developed news partnerships with daily and weekly newspapers throughout the region.

Hosting town meetings and public forums in conjunction with a series on regional challenges. The *Charlotte Observer,* in conjunction with local radio and television stations, hosted town meetings in five neighborhoods in conjunction with a series of articles on crime and violence. The results of the town meetings were reported by all media partners, followed by special newspaper reports on the concerns and actions being considered to address this crosscutting challenge.

The *Tallahassee Democrat,* in conjunction with local universities and radio and television stations, held "living room conversations" and conducted citizen surveys to "set the stage for a public dialogue on issues that citizens say are important to them." (Fouhy, 263)

Fostering citizen/candidate interactions on campaign issues. Before a recent election, *The Boston Globe* ran extensive stories on citizen-identified campaign issues and carried public questions and candidate answers in the newspaper. It also published critiques of campaign ads by individual citizens. In addition, citizens were selected to raise questions at candidate forums and debates.

At similar forums sponsored by *The Dallas Morning News,* citizens, not candidates, made the closing statements, expressing their expectations directly to the candidates. *The Wichita Eagle* conducted a similar process to encourage gubernatorial candidates to address public concerns, based on newspaper surveys. Its efforts contributed to increased voter turnouts compared with other regions of the state.

Publishing a newspaper or magazine series on regionalism. Neal Peirce, along with Curt Johnson, John Stewart Hall, and various colleagues, has prepared regionalism series for a number of newspapers. Their approach involves:

- flying over the region to assess its physical configurations,
- setting up a "kitchen cabinet" of individuals familiar with the region,
- interviewing over a hundred individuals recommended by the "kitchen cabinet" and other representatives of the region,
- holding informal interviews with groups of community leaders and citizens, such as over pizza purchased by the newspaper,
- reviewing questionnaires provided in the newspaper and filled out by individuals,
- drawing maps displaying boundaries of interest for particular challenges,
- developing story lines for major regional themes in a working session with the newspaper and sponsors, and
- preparing a report to be serialized over a few days or inserted in a Sunday newspaper edition.

Curt Johnson identifies three hallmarks of the process; sophisticated listening; searching for the right story; and provocative, catalytic, agenda-pushing writing.

Community magazines, either of general interest or focused on some aspect of community life, such as business, are also featuring more regional stories. Even some state and national magazines now have regional sections: *Connecticut Town and City,* for example, includes a section on intermunicipal and regional cooperation.

Accomplishments

Civic journalism can "infuse community governance with both information and judgment" in a way that almost any other approach cannot, especially for regional challenges that often cut across an ever expanding landscape and impact huge numbers of citizens. (Fouhy, 266)

Regional sections of newspapers and regional newscasts have played a major role in making regional challenges prominent, because of the repeated impact of their daily message on so many community leaders and citizens, compared to the more limited impact of an exploration or symposium on regionalism (see Prominent #1 and #2). However, since most of the stories refer to single, often disastrous events, such as fires, accidents or crimes, they do not necessarily create a balanced view of individual communities, much less the entire region. A special regionalism series might provide a broader perspective, but it might only be read by a few community leaders and citizens and be displaced by more immediate stories within a few days.

Strengths and Shortcomings

A major strength of regional civic journalism is its capacity to bring regionalism to the immediate attention of large numbers of community leaders and citizens. A major shortcoming is its difficulty in conveying a balanced understanding of the importance of regional topics. Special regionalism series address this shortcoming, but they are often difficult to sell; one newspaper's response to doing such a series was that it was not sufficiently contentious, "no fights, no politics, no series."

Potential

Advocates of regional civic journalism have so far tried only a few strategies. Newspapers are now beginning to experiment with columns devoted to regional topics, such as "Dr. Gridlock" and "Intrepid Commuter," who comment on transportation issues in the Washington, D.C., and Baltimore, Maryland, regions, respectively. Similarly, little experimentation has been done on regional challenges on television, except for electronic town meetings in conjunction with regional strategic planning and visioning processes.

A potential next step could be to sponsor newspaper or television series on regional governance to reach large numbers of community leaders and citizens. The range and relationships of regional decision-making mechanisms could be described in the context of how the region dealt with recent crosscutting challenges. Electronic town meetings could be held during the series to foster discussion in meeting places or homes on regional governance. Videoconferences on regional governance could be held with groups of community leaders and citizens in other regions and also televised to meeting places or home audiences. Follow-up activities could engage interested community leaders and citizens in efforts to improve regional decision making.

Similarly, adding analyses and columns on regional topics, especially regional governance, to newspapers and radio and television newscasts could give residents a more balanced understanding of regional governance. Similar analyses and columns in professional and other publications could reinforce the importance and visibility of regional governance. Finally, a regional governance news service could be established to share news stories across regions, possibly modeled on the American News Services demonstration of the Center for Living Democracy.

Contacts

- Newspaper series on regionalism: Peirce Reports, presented in Peirce, Neal, Johnson, Curtis, & Hall, John Stuart, *Citistates: How Urban America Can Prosper in a Competitive World,* Seven Locks Press, Washington, DC, 1993
- Dr. Gridlock, *The Washington Post,* 202-334-6000

- Intrepid Commuter, *Baltimore Sun,* 410-783-1800
- Examples of engaging in civic journalism: Fouhy, Ed, "The Dawn of Public Journalism," *National Civic Review,* Summer–Fall, 1994 and the entire Winter-Spring 1996 issue of *National Civic Review,* titled "Rethinking Journalism: Rebuilding Civic Life"
- Center for Living Democracy, Brattleboro, Vermont; 802-254-1234.

Prominent #4
Celebrate Regional Governance Success (new)

Woefully little is being done in most regions to celebrate regional governance successes. Sometimes regional successes or their sponsors are recognized in more general community recognition programs, but few awards programs have been established specifically to recognize successful regional governance mechanisms or the pioneers, those individual regional entrepreneurs, wizards, and champions who contributed to their success.

Some programs do exist for recognizing intergovernmental successes, especially among neighboring communities. The Greater Pittsburgh Chamber of Commerce sponsors an Intergovernmental Cooperation recognition program; winners are recognized with appropriate ceremony at the annual meeting of the Allegheny League of Municipalities. Similarly, the Pennsylvania State Department of Community Affairs has a municipal recognition program that also recognizes intergovernmental successes. Several national organizations, among them the American Society of Public Administration, American Planning Association, International City/County Management Association, and National Association of Counties, award special recognition for successes in intergovernmental cooperation.

Some regional recognition programs are being developed. The Piedmont Triad Partnership awards "Stars" to individuals and organizations that have made significant contributions in three categories: Regional Leadership, Quality of Life, and Economic Development. (Piedmont Triad Partnership, Partnership Spotlight, 1995) The Atlanta Regional Commission presents Golden Glasses Awards that "recognize an individual, company or organization, or collaborative effort which exemplify the forward-thinking leadership needed to drive our community's vision forward. Criteria are based on the ability to focus and implement long-term goals as well as short-term solutions, enhance the quality of life for residents of the Atlanta region, and represent innovative leadership and serve as a catalyst for others." (Atlanta Regional Commission, 1995)

State and national recognition programs also often recognize the successes of individual communities or community leaders, but few, if any, focus on regional successes or pioneers. Some programs have consciously broadened their guidelines in recent years to include regional applications. One example is the All America City program of the National Civic League. The program has even been renamed as the All America City and Community program to encourage community, including regional community, applications. Some professional organizations provide recognition for their members. The Regional Achievement Awards of the National Association of Regional Councils, for example, honor outstanding regional councils and their executive directors, but such awards are often little known to community leaders and citizens in their regions.

Accomplishments

Given the dearth of regional recognition programs, it is hard to determine their accomplishments. The Intergovernmental Cooperation Awards of the Greater Pittsburgh Chamber of Commerce have had a significant impact on local government officials in the Pittsburgh, Pennsylvania, region, helping to make a previously suspect activity a more sought-after recognition.

Strengths and Shortcomings

Except for the labor of judges and the cost of awards and awards ceremonies, regional recognition programs offer mostly benefits. Obviously, winners must be selected carefully to make sure that the reality of their successes measures up to the rhetoric of their applications.

Potential

The potential for sponsoring regional, and especially regional governance, recognition programs is almost unlimited. Such a program could acknowledge activities to make regional governance prominent, strategic, equitable, empowering, and institutionalized and the community leaders and citizens, professional experts, and problem-solving and service-delivery mechanisms that designed and implemented them.

Given the efforts required to address regional challenges, it is surprising that community leaders and citizens have not already established such recognition programs. Regional governance recognition programs would express community appreciation and even help reenergize the organizations and individuals who achieved the successes. Moreover, they might even encourage other skeptical community leaders and citizens to become involved in addressing regional challenges with the incentive of a bit of immortality.

Any community organization could sponsor a regional governance recognition program. To avoid any appearance of being self-serving, a selection committee representing all sectors of the regional community could be created. Or the program could be sponsored by a coalition of community organizations to provide balance and stature for the program. Or various organizations could offer recognition awards for different kinds of applicants, such as local governments or school districts, or different types of regional initiatives, such as economic development or transportation.

To defray the costs, as well as generate the greatest media coverage, an annual fund-raising event, such as an awards ceremony or banquet to recognize winners, could be held. Follow-up descriptions of the winners could be presented in newspaper or community magazine articles or on radio and television newscasts.

Contacts

- Intergovernmental Cooperation Awards: Greater Pittsburgh Chamber of Commerce, Pittsburgh, Pennsylvania, 412-392-4500
- All America City and Community Award: National Civic League, Denver, Colorado, 303-571-4343
- Regional Achievement Awards: National Association of Regional Councils, Washington, D.C., 202-457-0710

Prominent #5
Launch a Regional Prominence Campaign

A regional prominence campaign offers the opportunity to develop an array of initiatives to make the region and regional governance more prominent for community leaders and citizens.

The Center for Greater Philadelphia recently coordinated such a campaign, called the Year of the Region, which included an integrated set of activities to make the region prominent and develop an agenda of regional initiatives. These initiatives included:

- a full-page editorial in the *Philadelphia Inquirer* and a two-hour radio call-in show on regional cooperation to launch the campaign on September 11, 1994;
- public forums co-sponsored over the fall by League of Women Voters chapters and chambers of commerce throughout the region "to begin a dialogue on what the suburbs and city expect from each other and what they are prepared to do for each other in return;"
- a Pierce Report on regional cooperation published as a special section of the Philadelphia Inquirer;
- Peirce Report follow-up events, including a series of forums and meetings sponsored by a broad array of organizations and extending through the end of April 1995;
- Greater Philadelphia First's Regional Economic Development Strategy, which articulated the business organization's vision for the region and identified priorities and developed implementation plans for community leader and citizen response;
- a "Call to Action Conference" sponsored by the Greater Philadelphia Chamber of Commerce in May 1995, to transform the Peirce Report recommendations into 85 specific action-oriented initiatives, called the Greater Philadelphia Investment Portfolio;
- the Tenth Annual Southeastern Pennsylvania State Legislators' Conference organized by the Center for Greater Philadelphia, in conjunction with the "Call to Action Conference," to follow up on specific legislative initiatives; and
- a Municipalities Conference, sponsored by various public, business, and academic organizations in the fall of 1995.

The Philadelphia Year of the Region project depended upon two critical ingredients, according to Ted Hershberg, its primary designer:

- a broad-based and sustained level of coverage from newspapers, radio, and television in order to generate interest and advance the debate throughout the region, and

- the active involvement of a large number of individuals and organizations to carry out the many programs and events that embody true regional cooperation.

One of the recommendations of the Year of the Region campaign is to create a fund to support regional arts and cultural organizations, such as through a dedicated 1/10 percent sales tax that would generate approximately $25 million annually regionwide.

Financial support for the Year of the Region campaign was provided by each of the participating organizations. Private business and community foundation contributions supported the coordinating activities of the Center for Greater Philadelphia.

Accomplishments

It is too early to measure the results of the Year of the Region, but it already has had an impact on community leaders and citizens. Ted Hershberg suggests that there has been more coverage by suburban newspapers and more discussion of regional challenges by more people in the initial months of the campaign than was collectively generated by the isolated activities of the past decade. The Call to Action Conference spurred the creation of task groups on particular regional challenges; each task group has been asked to design a specific regional initiative that could be launched as a follow-up to the Year of the Region.

Strengths and Shortcomings

While it is too early to assess the results of the Year of the Region project, it is possible to speculate on a couple of major strengths and shortcomings.

The potential major strength of a regional prominence campaign could be to coordinate the efforts directed at making the region, especially regional decision making, prominent so as to attract community leader and citizen interest in understanding and improving it. The major shortcoming could be the difficulty in developing sufficient interest and support for launching the campaign and sustaining it beyond its initial set of activities.

Potential

Based on the early accomplishments of the Year of the Region program, community leaders and citizens in other regions could consider launching a regional prominence campaign.

As in the Philadelphia region, the campaign could start with a year-long program. Or it could start with something that could be called a Regional Excellence Day. In one day, A Regional Excellence Day could package a whole series of activities to educate community leaders and citizens. The activities could include a series on regional challenges in the newspaper or on radio and television, a state of the region report or conference, the presentation of regional recognition awards, open houses at regional problem-solving and service-delivery mechanisms, and opportunities for community leaders and citizens to volunteer on regional improvement projects. These special days could be held annually to continue to educate community leaders and citizens. In fact, Regional Excellence Days would be a natural follow-up to a year-long program, to continue to reinforce the importance of addressing regional challenges.

Either a year- or day-long regional prominence campaign could focus on regional challenges in general, or on a particular topic, such as regional governance, or on building support for a specific activity, such as conducting a regional governance examination (see Strategic #2, Chapter 4) and launching initiatives for improving regional decision making.

If the underlying premise of the Year of the Region is correct, an exploration here, a symposium there, a recognition award later might not be enough to make the region, and especially regional governance, visible enough to move community leaders and citizens to action. To succeed, an integrated set of activities needs to be pursued over at least a year, and probably longer, especially for improving regional governance, given the obstacles to quickly modifying regional decision making.

Another model for a regional prominence campaign might be the Piedmont Triad Partnership, launched as a campaign to improve the identity of the Piedmont Triad (Greensboro/High Point/Winston-Salem, North Carolina) region. (see Empowering #3, Chapter 6) If the same type of innovative thinking were applied to improving the identity of regional decision making and the array of regional problem-solving and service-delivery mechanisms, it could promote understanding of, participation in, and support for improving regional governance.

Activities of the regional prominence campaign could be any of those identified in the Prominent initiatives and others in the following chapters. Such a campaign could marshal partners to take on tasks that no one of the groups could undertake alone, including sponsoring a television series on regional governance or recognition awards for regional governance excellence. A regional prominence campaign could be instigated by any of the organizations launching the other Prominent initiatives, most likely as a collaborative effort to help guarantee the participation and support of all sectors of the region. Moreover, it could be financed on a collaborative basis as well.

Contacts

- Center for Greater Philadelphia, University of Pennsylvania, 215-898-8713; also, Hershberg, Theodore, Magidson, Pam & Wernecke, Mary Lou, "Promoting Cooperation in Southeastern Pennsylvania," *National Civic Review,* Denver, Colorado, Fall–Winter, 1992 and Hershberg, Ted, "Regionalism," *Philadelphia Inquirer,* September 11, 1994

Chapter 4
Making Regional Governance Strategic: Future Regional Governance Vision and Action Plan

Greater Vancouver can become the first urban region in the world to combine in one place the things to which humanity aspires on a global basis; a place where human activities enhance rather than degrade the natural environment, where the quality of the built environment approaches that of a natural setting, where the diversity of origins and religions is a source of social strength rather than strife, where people control the destiny of their community, and where the basics of food, clothing, shelter, security and useful activity are accessible to all.

> — *Livable Region Strategic Plan,*
> *Greater Vancouver Regional District, 1990*

Pressing regional challenges have consumed our present, as community leaders and citizens, leaving little time to contemplate the future of regional governance.

We have been overwhelmed by the exploding regional agenda of the last decade. One moment, we are worried about channeling the energies of various economic development organizations into pursuing a new business prospect. The next moment, our attention shifts to coordinating disparate efforts for combating the leapfrogging of violence and gangs from community to community. And a moment after that we are attending our umpteenth meeting in the past few years to deal with congestion on the Interstate highway and there is still no resolution in sight.

Only during rare interludes do we have the luxury to be reflective, to consider the region in its entirety, maybe even to contemplate the future of the region — its people, its institutions, its development and even its governance.

We tend to address each new crosscutting opportunity or threat individually. Even when we discover critical interconnections, we rarely have time to bring the participants in related efforts together for more than informal interaction. All too often, new regional challenges have already precluded such collaboration.

Finally, we have little opportunity to consider how well we make decisions on regional challenges. When are effective decisions made and why? Or ineffective ones made and how are they different? Is regional decision making improving or worsening over time and why? For better or worse, we tend to keep repeating decision-making processes with only informal musing on their success.

We almost never think about how we want the region to work or what we want regional decision making to look like in the future. Even if the thought passes through our minds, we are all too easily scared off by the existing models of regional decision making — Balkanization and Metropolitanism. Only now are new models beginning to be developed that carve out acceptable middle ground between these unattractive extremes.

Part of the problem is that the basic ideologies undergirding the governance of societies and reform of governments have been in considerable turmoil for the past few decades.

In 1980, George Lodge suggested that the Lockean ideology, which has dominated our thinking about governing societies since the middle ages, is not working and is being replaced by a new American ideology. The Lockean ideology has been characterized by the principles of individualism (individuality and contract), property rights, competition (consumer desire), the limited state and specific specialization. Lodge's new American ideology was characterized by the principles of communitarianism (adapting to inequality and consensus), right of membership, community need, the state as planner and coordinator, and holism. (Lodge)

Others have suggested that the progressive reform model, which has dominated our thinking about governance since the last turn of a century, also needs to be replaced by one that is more responsive to the realities of the 21st century. The progressive reform model has emphasized the principles of entrepreneurism, executive control, competition and market intelligence. Jack Dustin, at Wright State University, recommends a new civic governance model that emphasizes the principles of ethics, citizenship, diversity and interdependency. He defines these principles as follows:

> Ethics acts as an internal gyroscope for urban government and demonstrates 'doing what is right' for citizens and business. Citizenship guides policy and government. It is the intelligence of political actions. Without it democratic governance is lost. Diversity forms the culture of community, and without culture government can only act as a brute. Finally, interdependency comprises reunion of politics and economics. (Dustin, 1994, 20; also John, Halley, Fosler and Svara)

Whatever the relative merits of these ideologies and general governance models, they have sparked a tempestuous debate on governance, and especially the respective roles of government and the other sectors of society, all of which have implications for regional governance.

Some have suggested "shrinking" the national government to a limited agenda, such as national defense, international relations, and interstate commerce responsibilities, leaving state and local governments to address regional challenges. Others have suggested that state governments more actively shape regional governance, through the regional packaging of their school aid and other assistance, for instance, or the reassignment of land use, transportation, and environmental authorities to regional mechanisms.

Some have suggested that local governments, with the involvement of other sectors, pursue "bottom-up regionalism," such as by creating voluntary regional alliances of community leaders and citizens to address crosscutting challenges. Moreover, some have suggested empowering neighborhood organizations and school parent-teacher councils to govern themselves, subject only to general oversight of city councils and boards of education. Others have suggested turning more governmental responsibilities over to private and nonprofit sectors, "privatizing" public services.

This debate complicates the roles, responsibilities, and relationships of already established national, state and local levels of government, but it presents even more severe challenges to shaping regional governance.

We are increasingly aware, however, that we need to examine alternative models for regional governance, to get beyond developing ad hoc approaches for dealing with regional challenges. Moreover, we are realizing that we need a compelling consensus vision for the future of regional governance and a dynamic collaborative action plan that lays out the priority strategic initiatives for beginning to achieve it.

Neal Peirce raises the types of questions that could be addressed in such an examination.

> ... how can a citistate [region] make rational plans for its economic positioning, critically needed capital facilities, quality job training and continuing education? ...how can one be certain that plans for economic development can be brought on-line and in balance with conservation, quality land use, and the goal of compact, cost-effective growth? ... how can one expect any kind of equitable distribution of social burdens and expenses, so that older cities and suburbs are not made paupers of the region, a constant drag and deep moral blemish on the citistate?...who can bargain, cajole, lobby effectively before the federal and state governments for the interests of the entire citistate? (Peirce, 316-7)

Developing visions and action plans is about as close as we come to making a "research and development" investment in the future of our communities, local or regional. If private firms invested as little in research and development as we do in charting the future of our communities, few would survive. Making such an investment in the future of regional governance can not only shape our own futures, but provide a "foreign policy" for interacting with other regions, according to Tim Honey, city manager of Boulder, Colorado.

These regional governance visions and action plans could be called Strategies for Achieving Regional Governance Excellence (or SARGEs). Perhaps, like sergeants-at-arms, they will help "preserve order" and "execute commands" in the implementation of priority initiatives for improving regional decision making.

Initiatives for Making Regional Governance Strategic

How can we develop a consensus future vision for regional governance excellence and collectively pursue strategies of priority initiatives for achieving it?

The initiatives for Making Regional Governance Strategic are:
- Strategic #1: Explore regional governance models (new)
- Strategic #2: Develop a Strategy for Achieving Regional Governance Excellence (SARGE)(new)
- Strategic #3: Adopt a pledge to strengthen regional decision making (new)
- Strategic #4: Report on the state of regional governance (new)
- Strategic #5: Create a regional governance fund or foundation (new)

The primary initiative for making regional governance strategic — as well as the most important initiative across all five components — is to design a future vision and develop an action plan for strengthening regional governance (Strategic #2). However, to prepare for this initiative, community leaders and citizens could explore the existing models and consider some of the emerging new models for regional governance (Strategic #1). Moreover, to develop the capacity to implement priority regional governance initiatives, community leaders and citizens could consider the last three initiatives — adopt a regional excellence pledge, prepare periodic reports or hold conferences on the state of regional governance, and create regional governance funds (Strategic #3, #4, and #5) — to make regional governance strategic.

The performance of the Strategic initiatives in pursuing regional governance excellence can be assessed by answering several questions. Does implementing the Strategic initiatives result in:

- designing a consensus vision for the future of regional governance and developing a collaborative action plan for achieving regional governance excellence; a Strategy for Achieving Regional Governance Excellence?
- implementing priority regional governance initiatives in the action plan?
- preparing periodic reports and holding conferences on the state of regional governance?
- regularly updating future visions and action plans for regional governance excellence?
- developing and experimenting with new models for regional governance?

Strategic #1
Explore Regional Governance Models (new)

Understanding the existing and emerging models for regional govern-ance can help community leaders and citizens to design a vision for the future of regional governance excellence in their region. Although no model has been developed that perfectly meets the desires of any region, exploring alternative models will help to identify the characteristics that fit particular regions. Such an exploration might even result in developing new models for regional governance and providing more options for community leader and citizen consideration.

First and foremost, any model of regional governance has to demon-strate to community leaders and citizens that it can address emerging regional challenges in a timely, flexible and effective manner in design-ing strategies for addressing them (that is, regional problem solving) and implementing those strategies (that is, regional service delivery).

The "Balkanization" and "Metropolitanism" models have focused al-most exclusively on regional service delivery and have given little consideration to regional problem solving. To overcome this shortcom-ing, variations on these models have been developed such as defining "rules" for establishing new local governments and clarifying their respective roles in regional decision making. Moreover, these models have primarily focused on public sector decision making and have given little consideration to the values and contributions of the entire region — private, academic, nonprofit, foundation, civic and other sectors and citizens as well as the public sector. To overcome this shortcoming, new multi-sector "Network" models are being developed.

This initiative briefly describes and notes the contributions of alterna-tive models for regional governance. Each of the models is measured against the following four general criteria; that is, whether it:

- results in addressing emerging regional challenges effectively and designing and implementing strategies in a timely manner,
- facilitates establishing and enforcing "rules" of regional decision making, such as through defining the roles, responsibilities and relationships of regional decision-making mechanisms,

- engages and empowers all regional interests, equitably, and respects the "values" of community leaders and citizens, in addressing regional challenges, and
- can flexibly change over time to address new types of emerging challenges.

These criteria could be modified and others added that meet the desires of community leaders and citizens in particular regions.

The pure "Balkanization" model has been modified to accommodate voluntary "bottom-up" cooperation in developing the "rules" of regional decision making.

"Southwestern Pennsylvania is a collection of otherwise independent communities tied together by the Steelers, Pirates and Penguins."
— Allegheny County, Pennsylvania, resident

As Chapter 1 explains, "Balkanization" is characterized by the "scattershot" pattern of independent local government jurisdictions practicing "fend-for-yourself" behavior and interacting infrequently and often under some duress. Nongovernmental sectors and citizens usually receive little consideration under this model. As also described, the "unlimited low-density sprawl" vision guiding the development of most urban regions over this century has enshrined this model of fragmented governance, resulting "in traffic congestion, air pollution, loss of open space, higher taxes to pay for additional infrastructure, and a lack of affordable housing" (Downs, 3).

Sometimes this model is called, less pejoratively, the *life-style values* model. This view recognizes that the family is not just an economic unit but a social unit, as well, and makes locational decisions to maximize positive and minimize negative messages, consistent with what they can afford. Multiple local government jurisdictions facilitate such decisions. Under this model, challenges that are neutral in controlling social access can be dealt with on a regional basis, such as sewage, water supply, health facilities and solid waste disposal; those that control social access must be dealt with on a local level, such as school busing and affordable housing. (Goodman, 201-2; Williams, 93)

Another less pejorative label is the *public choice* model. This view perceives "fragmentation" as "differentiation" and "multiple local government jurisdictions" as the "local public economies" needed to be responsive to growth opportunities and citizen preferences. Public choice advocates argue that if the *provision* of public goods (taxing and spending decisions, determinations of service standards, the monitoring of service delivery, and the securing of accountability to standards) is arranged and coordinated, the *production* of public goods (process of commingling resource inputs to make a product or render a service) can and should be numerous to prevent the formation of public monopolies. (Advisory Commission on Intergovernmental Relations, 1987, iii & 3) "...the presence of competing municipalities need not result in waste, duplication and overlap, as is often argued, but rather in choice, specialization and efficiency." (France St-Hilaire in Sancton, Editors Introduction)

Andrew Sancton, of the University of Western Ontario, in his excellent study of regional governance in Canada, *Governing Canada's City-Regions,* suggests that public choice has helped move the prevailing mindset away from structural solutions to regional challenges in Canada. But he argues that governance is more efficient in Canadian regions with single regional governments than ones with multiple regional and municipal governments: "If anything, it would appear, on the basis of flimsy evidence (four regions), that municipal efficiency in Canada is indeed promoted through clear political accountability rather than through the discipline of the marketplace." Moreover, he argues that some central regulation or fiscal equalization is needed to make the public choice "marketplace" work. (Sancton, 53)

Again, the application of these life-style values or public choice models has resulted in regions with an abundance of small homogeneous communities, protected by zoning to reinforce positive values. Conflicts arise in regions because the communities are so specialized (rich-poor, white-minority, urban-suburban, residential-commercial-industrial), and disparities so wide, that local governments have difficulty interacting and resolving intercommunity and especially regional concerns. (Goodman, 201)

One widely practiced variation on the Balkanization model, to make it more effective in intercommunity decision making, is the addition of

voluntary intergovernmental cooperation or multi-community cooperation (MC2) as it is referred to by Beverly Cigler of Penn State University.
(Cigler)

Independent local governments have found the need to develop cooperative arrangements to address crosscutting challenges or to improve
the effectiveness of service delivery. Such voluntary cooperation has
been developed extensively in all regions and ranges from informal
service-delivery connections, such as joint purchasing of equipment and
supplies, to sophisticated joint programs, such as in parks and recreation.

An Advisory Commission on Intergovernmental Relations (ACIR) study
on St. Louis County, Missouri, makes the case for voluntary intergovernmental cooperation. It "suggests that a set of relatively small local
governments, when embedded in a structure of overlapping jurisdictions and coordinated service-delivery arrangements, is a viable alternative for organizing large metropolitan communities" (Parks, 11).

For the most part, however, voluntary intergovernmental cooperation
approaches only work among a few governments, not the dozens or even
hundreds found in most regions. Moreover, they work best for fashion-
ing already well accepted service-delivery arrangements. They are
usually overwhelmed by controversial challenges, such as the siting of
a regional facility, or even orchestrating nongovernmental community
leader and citizen involvement in problem-solving processes.

Another theoretical variation on the Balkanization model, to make it
more effective in regional decision making, is the addition of a *local
government constitution.*

Another ACIR report suggests that relationships between local public
economies could be governed by a regionwide "local government constitution" that complemented state and national government regulations
and established "enabling rules for municipal incorporation, annexation, consolidation, and disincorporation, plus similar rules pertaining
to the formation of special purpose governments, school districts and
other local units....The essential consideration with respect to governance is...constitutional in nature — how to design a rule structure that
allows citizens to make optimal choices." (ACIR, 1987, 50)

These variations on Balkanization are sometimes referred to as *diplomatic* or *polycentric* models of regional governance.

Under a diplomatic model, the region resembles an international marketplace, with the local governments in a region resembling a diplomatic community whose interactions are governed by intergovernmental "treaties" or even a "United Nations" type organization. (Goodman, 205)

Under a polycentric model, the region is an arrangement of multiple independent governments, each capable of making mutual adjustments for organizing their relationships within a general system of rule. The region resembles an economic market, offering public and private goods. To discourage the selfish behavior offered by choice, arrangements are needed to resolve conflicts, either for reconstituting local governments, such as through annexation, consolidation or creating special purpose districts, or for appeal to a higher level of government, such as to state government. (Goodman, 197)

The pure "Metropolitanism" model has been modified to accommodate multi-tiered government that differentiates municipal, county, regional and even state government responsibilities.

What is metropolitan government? Metropolitan government is something that will never happen because it would lump together people who are different, thus exposing people of means to riffraff in a low-income tax bracket. It would also deprive many communities of their inalienable right to have their own sewer cleaners and volunteer fire departments as well as the right to pay more than they can afford for run-of-the-mill municipal services.

— Peter Leo, Pittsburgh Post Gazette, 2/15/91

As Chapter 1 explains, "Metropolitanism" is characterized by either a *unitary* metropolitan general purpose government combining and carrying out all municipal, county, and regional service-delivery responsibilities regionwide or by a *hierarchy* of regional, county and municipal governments with exclusive and shared service-delivery responsibilities. As with the "Balkanization" model, little consideration is given to nongovernmental and citizen participation and regional problem-solving processes.

No region has fully subscribed to either the unitary or hierarchal version of the model. A few regions have reduced the number of local governments to a handful, at least for a while, but none have achieved full consolidation into a unitary metropolitan government.

For example, the Jacksonville, Florida region has consolidated the central city of Jacksonville and Duval County, leaving only a school district and a few municipalities in the central county in a five-county region. Some of the consolidated cities and counties in Virginia have reduced the number of general purpose governments in a region to an equally small number. New York City, which consolidated five counties into boroughs of a single city, could serve as a model for a unitary regional government in almost any other multi-county region in the nation. (Rusk, 1993, 91) In addition, special purpose governments, such as single- or multiple-service authorities (see Service-Delivery #3 and #4, Chapter 7), also exist and deliver particular services in these regions.

In the 1950s, Robert Wood advocated for single areawide governments as the best alternative to Balkanization. He argued that suburbs camouflage their selfishness as free choice and recommended a metropolitan "gargantuan city" that could provide an uniform rule of law, openly deal with conflicts instead of being shut out by artificial boundaries, and foster what he called "urbanity, the anonymity and freedom to achieve at the top of one's potential, to be civil in the face of diversity and to support unique cultural and economic enterprises." (Goodman, 197)

> The conditions of urbanity are the basic reasons for supporting the ideal of a single metropolitan government, and they seem more logically persuasive than the customary arguments of efficiency and administrative tidiness. A single local government comprehending an entire metropolitan area is likely not only to be better managed in the professional sense but more democratically managed as well....The handicaps the city operates under, the loss of its middle-class citizens, the poverty of public finances, the absence of space and of solid residential sections would be removed....By

making the metropolis a true metropolitan political entity, a different type of blending of urban and suburban becomes possible. It would be less comfortable, perhaps, but it would be more defensible in terms of the values the nation has accepted. (Wood, 298)

Recently, David Rusk has argued for elastic central cities that could annex suburban areas as they developed, creating a de facto "unitary" metropolitan government across a substantial part of the region. (Rusk, 1993, 95)

The political challenges to creating such unitary metropolitan governments have been overwhelming, from the life style values or public choice advocates on one side, who fear the loss of unfettered choice, and the community power advocates on the other, who fear the loss of minority voting power. (Wallis, 1994, 14) Many of the regions also cross state lines, adding the complexities of conflicting approval processes for metropolitan governments. It might be easier to realign existing states or create new ones in multi-state regions (creating a state of the Greater Washington Metropolitan Region in the Washington, D.C., region, for example) than to create regional general purpose governments. (Lewis, Roger, 46)

In spite of the merits of reducing the number of competing local governments involved in addressing regional challenges, the odds of creating unitary metropolitan governments are probably declining over time. In many of the regions that have enjoyed small numbers of local governments, their continuing expansion into adjoining counties, and states, is rapidly increasing the number of impacted governments as well. Even regions in which central city-county consolidation has created a de facto type of metropolitan government are now experiencing the leapfrogging of development into the outlying counties, making their consolidated governments into sub-regional governments.

The hierarchy or multi-tier version of Metropolitanism has enjoyed more support in recent decades.

Many smaller regions that are still contained within the parameters of a single county or consolidated central city-county government come closest to achieving a de facto two-tier — county-municipal government — version of metropolitan government. At least one multi-county region, Portland, Oregon, has established a directly elected regional planning and service district, the Metropolitan Service District, (see Problem-Solving/Service-Delivery #3, Chapter 7)and has come closest to achieving a de facto three-tier — regional, county, and municipal government — version of metropolitan government.

The Committee for Economic Development (CED), which had originally recommended a single, areawide government as the best solution to fragmentation and problem-solving inefficiency, modified its position in the 1970s, in response to the almost insurmountable challenges of establishing "unitary" metropolitan governments. It began to advocate two-tier government in single-county regions, with exclusive and shared functions for county and municipal governments, and a third regional tier in multi-county regions, with similar exclusive and shared functions. CED touted the benefits of defining the respective responsibilities of each level of government but also bemoaned the difficulties in reaching initial agreement on dividing up responsibilities among government levels, much less being able to modify these agreements to respond to new crosscutting challenges.

The multi-tier governments that build upon existing county and municipal governments are also limited by the state statutory or home rule charter authorities of those governments. For example, even though counties might cover most of the appropriate geography in some smaller regions, they still lack the legal and taxing authorities to address crosscutting challenges or even the mechanisms to work cooperatively with the municipalities and other nongovernmental institutions in their midsts. Even where central cities and counties have created consolidated or federated governments, they often leave key functions in a vague shared category and have little latitude in addressing new types of crosscutting challenges.

One of the most closely examined recent examples of creating regional general purpose governments is the experimentation in Italy, a tale that Robert Putnam shares, with all its death-defying obstacles and potential rewards, in his excellent book *Making Democracy Work*.

The Italian constitution of 1948 called for directly elected regional governments in addition to national and local governments. Compared to the federal system of the United States, the regions fill the state niche, but in Italy's case were fashioned to include areas with common economic and social histories. Vested interests blocked their consideration until the 1960s, when "an emergent interest in regional planning" among other factors resulted in enabling legislation and the first elections for regional councils in 1970.

Each regional council then elected a regional president and cabinet and wrote a regional "statute," spelling out the organization and procedures of regional government and specifying areas of regional jurisdiction. It then took two years to transfer powers, funds, and personnel to regions from the national government, so that the regional governments did not open for business until 1972.

In their early years, the regional governments operated under severe political, legal and fiscal constraints, including having more than one-fourth of the early laws of regional councils vetoed by the national government. They also enjoyed no growth in their regional budgets for the first three years even though the national government budget grew 20 percent.

Then a number of the regional councils came together to develop a "regional front," with media and public support, resulting in the passage of new laws in 1975 calling for more decentralization of important functions. It wasn't until 1977, however, that an "all-on-one" initiative led to an agreement to transfer most of the domestic central government authorities — health, housing, urban planning, agriculture, public works and some aspects of education — to the regional governments along with approximately one-fourth to one-third of the national budget. Again, interregional solidarity and grassroots mobilization were used to gain support.

Regional government budgets grew to more than $22 billion by 1979, approximately one-tenth of Italy's domestic national product, more than could be reasonably spent in most regions, according to some critics. By 1981, the regional government bureaucracies grew to approximately 100,000 employees.

During the 1980s, relations between the national and regional governments improved, in part because the regions now had the authorities and budgets to perform. But their deficiencies became more apparent to their protagonists and intergovernmental struggles became three-party fights as local governments, over which the regional governments have some authority, engaged in debates over shared national, regional, and local government responsibilities. As one observed, "The protest marches now go to the regional headquarters instead of the (local government) prefecture." (Putnam, *Making Democracy Work,* 47)

The overall impact of regional governments, according to Putnam, is to have substantially changed grassroots politics in Italy, including the types of debates, the debaters, the career paths to higher office, and the protests. Subnational government became more important and institutions were brought closer to the people. But administrative efficiency has not materialized and regional reform might be exacerbating rather than mitigating the historical disparities between the north and the south of Italy. (Putnam, *Making Democracy Work,* 61)

Not surprisingly, the regions have had mixed results in their experiences with regional governments and efforts to foster economic development over the past two decades. The reasons for these differences are surprising, Putnam says:

> Despite this whirl of change, however, the regions characterized by civic involvement in the late twentieth century are almost precisely the same regions where cooperatives and cultural associations and mutual aid societies were most abundant in the 19th century, and where neighborhood associations and religious confraternities and guilds had contributed to flourishing communal republics of the twelfth century. And although these civic regions were not especially advanced economically a century ago, they have steadily outpaced the less civic regions both in economic performance and in quality of government. The astonishing tensile strength of civic traditions testifies to the power of the past.... (Putnam, *Making Democracy Work,* 162)

> Of two equally poor Italian regions a century ago, both very backward, but one with more civic engagement, and the other a more hierarchal structure, the one with more choral societies and soccer clubs has grown steadily wealthier. The more civic region has prospered because trust and reciprocity were woven into its social fabric ages ago. None of this would appear in standard

economics textbooks, of course, but our evidence suggests that wealth is the consequence, not the cause, of a healthy civics. (Putnam, "What Makes Democracy Work," 106)

New network models are emerging that focus equal attention on regional problem solving and service delivery and on involving community leaders from all sectors and citizens in regional decision making.

The frustration with Balkanization and Metropolitanism is spurring the interest of community leaders and citizens in new models for regional governance, especially ones that foster the civic engagement Robert Putnam found critical to the success of Italian regions.

Their concerns are being echoed by observers of domestic and international governance. Michael Maccoby, in a meeting of futurists on the future of governance, suggested the need for a new paradigm for organizations, or communities and regions, one that is interactive, rather than hierarchal, and brings all stakeholders together to make systemic change. Such organizations, or regions, need to create a culture in which people can take responsibility and be responsive "from the outside in and inside out." Harland Cleveland suggests that we need an "uncentralized" world, not a "decentralized" world, in which we have the pooling of sovereignties rather than less sovereignty for nation states. He asks one of the important regional governance questions, "How do you get everyone in on the action and still get some action?" (Wagner) Finally, Howard Grossman, Director of the Economic Development Council of Northeastern Pennsylvania, argues that we need new regional partnerships for the 21st century that supplement, not supplant, other governance; that reinforce and complement existing governments, not be new governments. (Grossman, 24)

New multi-sector network models are responding to the concerns of community leaders and citizens and observers of domestic and international governance.

For example, I recently advanced the Strategic Intercommunity Governance Network, or SIGNET, model in the National Civic Review (April 1992) to foster interest in developing new regional governance models. It hypothesizes that intercommunity governance evolves out of, or is the product of, the formal and informal interactions between intercommunity problem-solving and service-delivery processes and mechanisms. Intercommunity governance includes the interactions between adjoining communities as well as those that cut across entire regions.

The nature of these interactions range from informal planning and sharing of personnel and equipment to cooperative plans for addressing crosscutting challenges and joint agreements or compacts for delivering services and responding to state and national government mandates. Collectively, the interactions tie together the problem-solving and service-delivery mechanisms in a "network" pattern.

The shape of the network is determined by the numbers and types of intercommunity decision-making mechanisms. The strength of the network is determined by the capabilities and capacities of the individual mechanisms and the nature of their interactions, which can be both cooperative and competitive. (Skok, 330) It is also determined by the civic infrastructure or social capital of the region, the "features of social organization, such as networks, norms, and trust, that facilitate coordination and cooperation for mutual benefit." (Wallis, 1993, 132)

Intercommunity problem-solving (IPS) mechanisms focus on designing strategies for addressing crosscutting challenges, tend to exercise planning and policy development authority, and often are experimental and difficult to sustain, much less replicate. At the regional level, they range from the traditional regional planning councils established in the 1960s and 1970s to the experimental regional alliances of the 1980s and 1990s. These include such alliances as the Community Cooperation Task Force in the Dayton, Ohio, area which designed the first voluntary economic development/tax-sharing program, and Build Up Greater Cleveland, which has developed cooperative strategies for generating more than $1 billion in new public works investments for the Cleveland area.

Intercommunity service-delivery (ISD) mechanisms focus on delivering services to meet common needs, tend to exercise administrative authority and usually are relatively well defined and, at least for the public ones, difficult to change, much less eliminate. Almost any unit of local government — township, municipal, county, single or multiple purpose service authority, or central city-county federation or consolidation, as

Strategic Intercommunity Governance Network
(SIGNET)

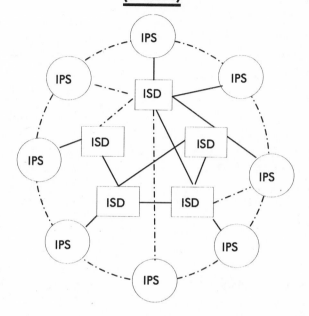

Honeycomb Network
Formal/informal interaction of intercommunity problem-solving (IPS)
and intercommunity service-delivery (ISD) organizations.

well as some state government and other private, academic, nonprofit or civic organizations — could qualify as intercommunity service-delivery mechanisms, either by exclusively delivering intercommunity services, such as a regional transit system, or delivering them on a piecemeal basis, such as community-by-community solid waste collection and disposal.

The SIGNET model hypothesizes that:

- the experimentation with existing and, almost certainly, new intercommunity problem-solving mechanisms will continue through the dawn of the 21st century;

- the redistribution of service-delivery responsibilities among existing, and probably few, new intercommunity service-delivery mechanisms also will continue through the dawn of the 21st century;

- metropolitan general purpose government is not inevitable in this or the next century; and
- an increasingly integrated network of regional problem-solving and service-delivery mechanisms will address regional challenges in the 21st century.

Finally, the SIGNET model assumes that intercommunity, and especially regional, problem-solving and service-delivery mechanisms are fully interactive. The intercommunity problem-solving mechanisms must be capable of developing visions and strategies for addressing crosscutting challenges and influencing their adoption and implementation by the intercommunity service-delivery mechanisms. In turn, the intercommunity service-delivery mechanisms must be capable of implementing the strategies as well as monitoring and evaluating their effectiveness while influencing the development of new visions and strategies. (Dodge, 1992)

New and more refined regional governance models are needed to offer tangible choices for community leaders and citizens.

Without question, more work needs to be done on regional governance models. In the short term, the best ideas will probably come from the experiences of community leaders and citizens designing visions and action plans for the future of regional governance (see Strategic #2). In the long term, academic and other observers might begin to devote more attention to developing models for consideration by community leaders and citizens. Maybe the National Civic League, which already prepares model city and county government charters, might be willing to host a competition, with the assistance of national foundations, to develop and test new models for regional governance.

Strategic #2
Design a Strategy for Achieving Regional Governance Excellence (SARGE) (new)

Make no small plans; they have no magic to stir the soul and probably themselves will not be realized.

— Daniel Burnham

To understand and strengthen regional governance, community leaders and citizens should conduct a broad examination that results in designing a consensus future vision for regional governance excellence and a coordinated action plan for achieving it.

Although more targeted examinations focus on specific crosscutting governance challenges, such as the future of a regional planning council or single-service authority, a broad examination is critical to developing an overall understanding of regional governance and guiding future experimentation in regional decision making. Without such a systemic examination, problem-solving and service-delivery mechanisms that appear successful individually might actually be undermining the efforts of other, even more important, decision-making processes.

This is not to suggest that such an examination needs to consume enormous resources over extended periods of time. Many examinations will require participating community leaders and citizens to meet regularly over a year or longer, enjoy the support of teams of hired staff and consultants, and produce a range of reports for various audiences. In fact, examinations in more complex regions might demand this rigor.

Productive examinations could be conducted in a series of day-long or weekend workshops in many regions, however, supported by loaned staff and the participants themselves. Task groups of participating community leaders and citizens could prepare materials in advance of each workshop. Workshop participants could discuss the materials and provide guidance for the next workshop. After a few workshops (between three and five, perhaps) a working group of participants could produce a report for regional discussion. Finally, workshop participants could create an ongoing group to monitor implementation of priority initiatives to strengthen regional governance.

The impetus for conducting a broad examination of regional governance could emerge from pursuing initiatives to make regional governance prominent, such as conducting an initial regional governance exploration, holding a regional governance symposium, or even launching a regional prominence campaign (see Prominent #1, 2 and 5, Chapter 3). Conducting such an examination could result in:

- further showcasing the importance and raising the stature of regional governance,

- designing a consensus vision of the future of regional governance for community leaders and citizens to achieve,

- developing a coordinated set of improvements or action plan for strengthening the network of regional problem-solving and service-delivery mechanisms, and

- making regional decision making more empowering, equitable, and effective.

While the specific components of the process for conducting a regional governance examination must be determined by the participants, it will probably include some of the following general tasks, which are presented graphically on the following page. More information on the design and implementation of regional governance examinations, can be found in *Shaping a Region's Future, A Guide to Strategic Decision Making for Regions,* a forthcoming publication of the National League of Cities.

Task 1: Organize a representative cross-section of community interests and the general public and design the examination process.

A regional governance examination can be initiated by individual community leaders or citizens and their organizations or, to share the responsibility, by an organizing committee of interested community leaders and citizens.

To be effective, however, the examination process itself needs to involve stakeholders across communities on a balanced basis, including representatives of existing regional problem-solving and service-delivery mechanisms and the general public. Since such an examination will be looking ahead for a few years to a few decades, it is important to include

Regional Governance Examination Process

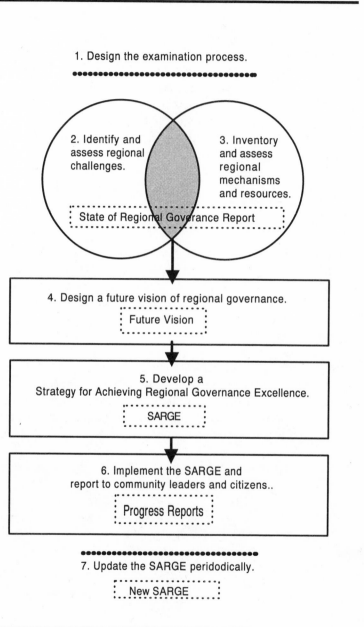

1. Design the examination process.

2. Identify and assess regional challenges.

3. Inventory and assess regional mechanisms and resources.

State of Regional Governance Report

4. Design a future vision of regional governance.

Future Vision

5. Develop a Strategy for Achieving Regional Governance Excellence.

SARGE

6. Implement the SARGE and report to community leaders and citizens..

Progress Reports

7. Update the SARGE peridodically.

New SARGE

future stakeholders, such as youth as well as community leaders and citizens from the outlying areas that will be part of the region of tomorrow.

Participants can be selected in a variety of ways, from designated representatives of various decision-making mechanisms and interests to those chosen at citizen forums. As potential participants are identified, they can be interviewed on their expectations for the outcomes of, other participants in, and perspectives on the design of the examination process. Since it is almost impossible to identify all important participants during the design of the process, it is usually advisable to provide the flexibility to add additional participants while conducting the examination. Moreover, since some important community interests will refuse to participate at the beginning of the examination, it is important to develop tactics for keeping them informed and, it is hoped, convince them to participate later in the examination.

Participants can be organized into a steering committee and task groups or periodically convened in stakeholder workshops. A regional planning council or other organization could serve as the secretariat for the examination or it could be a collective effort of two or more organizations, such as a regional chamber of commerce and college/university research institute.

Especially careful thought needs to be given to the design of the process for conducting the examination. While earlier efforts to develop regional plans or community goals might offer useful guidance, the process for developing a regional governance vision and action plan may need to be somewhat different.

For example, regional planning processes usually focus on developing initiatives for dealing with specific regional challenges, such as economic development or transportation, rather than improving problem solving and service delivery. Similarly, community goal-setting exercises often focus more on developing a vision and goals for the future of the region than on developing practical strategies for beginning to achieve them.

The following sections present the likely tasks in a regional governance examination, including:

assess.

- identify and assess past, present, and potential future regional challenges,
- inventory regional problem-solving and service-delivery mechanisms and resources and assess their strengths and shortcomings in addressing regional challenges,
- design a unifying/dynamic future vision of regional governance,
- develop a balanced Strategy for Achieving Regional Governance Excellence, a SARGE, to take advantage of priority opportunities for strengthening the regional governance network, and
- implement the SARGE, report regularly to community leaders and citizens, and update the SARGE periodically.

Regional governance examinations, no matter how well designed, never go according to the design. As a result, it is critical to develop contingencies for modifying them as inevitable obstacles are encountered. Participants need to monitor the process, to see if it is on time and within budget, and modify it in keeping with the desired outcomes of the participants. To facilitate modifying the process, part of the budget can be set aside as a contingency for allocation during the examination process.

Once the components of the examination process are determined, appropriate public involvement activities need to be developed for each of them. A variety of activities needs to be considered to attract the participation of as broad a range of citizens as possible and develop their "ownership" of the process. Since public involvement techniques have a mixed record of success, it's also important to assess their applicability and be prepared to shift to contingency activities as necessary.

Initial surveys, media announcements, descriptive brochures and community meetings can be considered at the launching of the examination. Public meetings, focus groups, study circles, surveys, periodic newsletters, newspaper inserts, and electronic regional meetings can be considered at key decision points in the examination process to provide reactions to pending decisions as well as guidance for the next tasks in the process. Hot lines, speakers' bureaus, and facilitation services could be provided throughout the examination process to respond to inquiries and suggestions and organize discussions on the examination process.

For example, William Hudnut, the former mayor of the consolidated government of Indianapolis, called Unigov, suggests providing "store front" offices — in city halls, public libraries or even shopping malls — to display information on the examination process and solicit comments on computer terminals. Lyle Wray, Director of the Citizens League of Minneapolis/St. Paul, suggests holding "speakouts" in which small groups of community leaders and citizens from throughout the region have an opportunity to dialogue on regional governance, maybe on a regional excellence day (see Prominent #5, Chapter IV).

Regional governance examinations can be conducted over a wide range of time. Given the complexity of the topic, however, it can easily take up to three months to design the examination process, mostly to assure representative participation, and from six months to a year to design a future vision and action plan and implement initial initiatives for improving regional governance.

On the other hand, some splendid "quick and dirty" examinations on similar topics have been undertaken in a series of weekend meetings, with considerable participant and staff work in between. For example, the Washington Regional Network for Livable Communities developed an alternative transportation plan for the National Capital Region in two weekend charettes.

Regional governance examinations can also be conducted with a wide range of resources. At least $25,000 to $50,000 in out-of-pocket and in-kind contributions is probably required to mount a thorough examination in the least complex regions; however, $100,000 to $250,000 or more could be usefully spent in educating and involving the public in the examination process. The more community leaders and citizens are involved throughout the process, the more likely they are to support the vision and implementation of the action plan.

Sufficient funding needs to be sought to design a vision and action plan as well as get the priority regional governance improvements over the hump into implementation. Funding can be sought from participants on a shared basis or community foundations can be approached for matching funds. Finally, participants can consider creating a regional governance fund or foundation to support conducting the examination as well as provide seed capital for launching the priority improvements in the resulting action plan. (see Strategic #5)

To convince reluctant community interests and citizens on the merits of conducting a regional governance examination, an examination prospectus can be prepared on the need for, and, it is hoped, compelling timeliness of conducting the examination. It could present potential benefits of such an examination, based on conversations with a cross-section of community leaders and citizens, along with some examples of regional governance improvements and their potential impact on regional decision making and the quality of citizens lives. The prospectus could suggest options for the involvement of community leaders and citizens in the examination process.

The prospectus could be prepared by the organizing committee or individuals familiar with regional governance in the region or nationally. If a prospectus helps foster the involvement of key community interests — the individuals and organizations that will be needed to implement key improvements in the action plan — it will be a worthwhile investment.

Finally, remember that the purpose of the regional governance examination is to improve regional decision making. Design and conduct the process so as to create momentum for implementation of improvements that strengthen the network for regional decision making. Encourage participants to stay involved through the implementation of the initial regional governance initiatives, but also respect their time and resource limitations and make the process as much fun as possible.

The product of this task will be a work program for the regional governance examination process that will probably describe:
- the desired outcomes of the examination,
- the components or tasks to be undertaken in the examination process,
- the individuals and groups to be involved in the examination process and the activities to involve the general public,

- cost estimates for conducting the examination and launching the action plan and prospective sources of technical and financial support,
- an approach for monitoring progress and associated costs and making modifications in the examination process, and
- the anticipated reports and other products of the examination and their potential users.

Task 2: Identify and assess past, present and potential future regional challenges

Past and present regional challenges are usually all too obvious. Emerging and especially potential future challenges are often more difficult to discover, but they need to be identified, given the future orientation of the examination. Often they can be identified by interviewing participants, regional scholars, futurists and other experts; reviewing newsletters and magazines for the new trends, events and developments that might become the regional "change-drivers" for the future; attending conferences on regional challenges; or conducting focus groups with community leaders and citizens.

For recent challenges, participants will probably want to examine how those challenges were addressed. Who addressed them? How much community leader and citizen involvement was there? Over what period of time? At how much cost? With what kinds of results? What impact did the decision-making processes have on addressing the next round of regional challenges? For some, if not most, unresolved and current challenges, participants will probably want to examine how these challenges are being addressed and with what results. For emerging and potential future challenges, participants will probably want to examine information that would help describe them and assess their probability and potential impact on the region.

Potential regional challenges of greatest interest will be those that are timely (they are likely to have an impact over the next five to ten years), critical (the consequences of not addressing them is worse than addressing them), and mysterious (they prompt the conclusion, "I do not understand this challenge; moreover, I don't know what to do about the potential opportunities or threats that it offers").

The product of this task could be a listing and brief analysis of past, present and potential future regional challenges. It might be useful to present these challenges, graphically, in chronological order of occurrence so as to facilitate tracking the changes in the numbers and nature of challenges over time, especially the current and potential future challenges. Or it might be possible to develop overlays of the geographic scope of these challenges, or even color-code them to display their relative intensity, so as to facilitate identifying the range, overlap and concentration of future regional decision making.

For example, the Greenbelt Alliance in the San Francisco (California) region color codes regional maps to display the risk to open space in the region, from dark green to identify low-risk publicly protected areas to angry red for high risk areas adjacent to already urbanized areas and along highway corridors. "It's a map that seems to be violently in motion, and when you look at it intently you can almost begin to see the pink areas (modest risk where land use controls are sketchy or partly effective) intensifying into red lands fading to gray (already urbanized areas)." (Hiss, 215)

Such color coding, possibly done electronically so as to be able to modify the combination and colors of overlays, could provide a powerful visual image of the changing regional reality.

Task 3: Inventory regional problem-solving and service-delivery mechanisms and resources and assess their strengths and shortcomings in addressing regional challenges.

Like regional challenges, active mechanisms for regional problem solving and service delivery will be the easiest to identify, such as regional planning councils and single-service authorities. Ad hoc and inactive mechanisms, such as regional alliances, or sub-regional and county-wide mechanisms, such as intergovernmental arrangements, will be the most difficult to identify. In general, the sources for identifying regional challenges will be useful in identifying regional decision-making mechanisms.

In addition, participants will probably want to identify resources currently available or potentially available, for at least the next few years, for strengthening regional governance. They include the individual regional "pioneers" — the regional entrepreneurs, wizards and champions — critical to conducting the examination and implementing its priority initiatives.

Finally, participants might want to survey community leader and citizen attitudes on regional governance. What is their awareness of regional problem-solving and service-delivery mechanisms? What is their sense of being regional as opposed to local leaders and citizens? What are their perspectives on intercommunity economic, racial and fiscal disparities? What are their attitudes towards improving regional governance?

In assessing the roles, responsibilities, and relationships of regional governance mechanisms, participants will probably want to explore recent experiences of problem-solving and service-delivery mechanisms in addressing regional challenges. Since these assessments overlap with those of Task 2, they could conduct the two tasks in tandem. In addition, they will probably want to track changes in the supply of regional "pioneers" and citizen attitudes and why they are changing.

In assessing the strengths and shortcomings of regional decision making, participants might want to utilize an assessment tool, such as the Civic Index developed by the National Civic League. John Parr, its recent president, coined the term "civic infrastructure" to describe "the complex interaction of people and groups through which decisions are made and problems resolved," or, in other words, the regional decision-making network. The Civic Index has ten components that describe the types of skills and processes that must be present in the civic infrastructure of a community, including a regional community, to deal effectively with its unique concerns. They are, with National Civic League comments:

- Citizen participation (making it a contact sport),
- Community leadership (it has to come from everywhere),
- Government performance (professional, entrepreneurial and open),
- Volunteerism and philanthropy (increasing the leverage of your local "points of light"),

- Intergroup relations (strength through diversity),
- Civic education (the community as classroom),
- Community information sharing (it takes more than watching the evening news),
- Capacity for cooperation and consensus building (turning potential conflict into positive action),
- Community vision and pride (you can't build the future without a common vision), and
- Intercommunity/regional cooperation (with whom are we really competing?).

The Civic Index has been used to initiate visioning processes in various regions and could provide a guide or checklist for inventorying and assessing individual regional decision-making mechanisms and their interactions. (National Civic League, *The Civic Index*, 1993)

Participants might also want to compare their regional decision making to other comparable regions, in what are often called *benchmarking* exercises. Although it is difficult to make rigorous comparisons for a topic as subjective as regional governance, the exercise might identify particular examples of problem-solving and service-delivery mechanisms that merit consideration or some aspects of the interconnections among mechanisms in other regional governance networks that might even merit emulation. For example, the Jacksonville, Florida, Community Council, Inc. has been measuring various quality of life indicators annually for the past decade. (Jacksonville Community Council, Inc., 1991)

Even better, participants might want to begin monitoring indicators of their own region governance over time, so as to have comparative data for periodic state of regional governance reports (see Strategic #4). Although the author is not familiar with any regular monitoring of regional governance indicators, the Citizens League of Greater Cleveland conducts semi-annual polls on various governance related questions, such as the quality of life and best things happening in Cleveland as well as its major concerns and image. (Citizens League of Greater Cleveland, "What We Think," 1992)

The product of this task could be the listing and analysis of the strengths, shortcomings and interconnections of mechanisms, and resources, that have been, are, or could potentially become available for regional decision making. As with the results of the previous step, it might be useful to diagram, possibly in a three-dimensional model, the present regional problem-solving and service-delivery mechanisms and their interrelationships to facilitate the analysis of the overall regional governance network. The connections could be color coded or thickened to indicate the range of interactions, from informal cooperation to formal agreements to state and federal government regulations, or their intensity (cooperative/difficult, frequent/infrequent, critical/trivial).

Together, the products of the first two tasks can be combined into a "state of regional governance report" for circulation to community leaders and citizens. Feedback in the form of oral and written comments or through focus groups, study circles and regional meetings can be used to guide the development of a future vision and action plan for strengthening regional governance.

Task 4: Design a unifying/dynamic future vision of regional governance.

With the common understanding provided by the state of regional governance report, participants can shift attention to designing a vision for the future of regional governance. Like playing winning chess, participants begin at the end and work backward; first, they design a vision, and then they develop an action plan for getting there.

A vision provides an image, or mental picture, of regional governance beyond the foreseeable future. It attempts to answer the general question: What does regional governance have the potential to be ten to twenty years in the future and beyond? What values will be honored, what impact will be made, what standards will be met in regional decision making? What image will regional governance project to community leaders and citizens? How will regional governance make the region preeminent, nationally and internationally? (Eadie, 100)

Regional governance visions need to be inspirational; they need to capture the hearts and minds of community leaders and citizens, to excite them about their common future potential, and to convince them to invest, collectively, in achieving it. As such, they tend to be rather emotional, visual and incomplete statements. They also need to be communicated to community leaders and citizens — to be "tangibilitated" according to William Hudnut — until they are understood, owned, and acted upon. (Governors State University)

Regional governance visions also tend to build upon what is good about the current reality of regional governance and improve the image of what is undesirable. They set standards for regional decision making that reflect the unique needs, circumstances, values, and overall culture of the region.

Regional governance visions might even define competitive niches or particular aspects of a vision that offer opportunities for the region to be preeminent, to be one of a handful of regions nationally or internationally renowned for a particular aspect of its regional governance. Just as the Indianapolis region defined itself as the "amateur sports capital" and the Baltimore region defined itself as the "global life sciences community," other regions could define themselves as the preeminent "public participation" or "celebrating diversity" regions. Or, as the Metropolitan Affairs Nonprofit Corporations, a group of privately sponsored urban affairs groups, once suggested, particular regions could be preeminent for their "regional productivity," their "overall effectiveness in combining human and natural resources and capital to achieve desired levels of service and environmental quality with minimum social and economic cost." (Metropolitan Affairs Nonprofit Corporations)

Regional governance visions are still relatively rare and imperfect, but recent efforts in the Pittsburgh and Denver regions illustrate their potential.

The Citizens League of Southwestern Pennsylvania developed a vision of governance by looking back from the future and indicating the improvements that would be made in regional governance by 2001. Collectively, these improvements begin to provide a mental picture of what governance could be, including:
- Regional governance gives balanced consideration to effectiveness, empowerment and equity.

Strategic #2

- Integrated state, regional, county and municipal planning efforts coordinate land use, infrastructure and economic development activities regionwide.

- Elected county councils and citizen advisory boards jointly develop county visions and strategic plans; professional county executives meet regularly with city managers and directors of councils of governments to implement county visions and strategic plans.

- Strengths of municipal level of governance are preserved, but its powers are balanced with neighborhood, intermunicipal, county and regional governance levels.

- Excellence in governance is recognized in annual regional governance awards.

- Community officials regularly participate in workshops on emerging regional challenges.

- Basic, adequate public services are provided efficiently to all of the region's citizens through coordinated public/private actions.

- Revenue sharing supports regional assets and fosters economic development in distressed communities.

- Governance excellence is a positive factor in attracting new and retaining existing businesses in Southwestern Pennsylvania. (Citizens League of Southwestern Pennsylvania, 1993)

The Denver Metro Forum developed a vision for a regional governance mechanism that states:

> The Metro Forum believes that the creation of an umbrella regional planning and service agency will provide the necessary institutional mechanism to expand local government capacity, to address development and service delivery issues, and integrate local governments and the existing regional agencies into a more effective governance and service delivery system.
>
> Once the umbrella agency is created, a regional vision should be crafted to help the new regional planning system guide the future development of the region and reach its full potential to solve regional issues.
>
> The new regional agency will enhance public accountability through citizen control of and participation in regional issues and

decisions. Local control and home rule authority will be preserved. (Metro Forum)

Various generally enjoyable approaches can be used to develop a regional governance vision with community leaders and citizens. All of them work best if participants are encouraged to let their minds wander, to advance any ideas, no matter how ridiculous, since visioning tends to work best when right brain intuition is overriding left brain control. Special encouragement should be given to the participation of youth, since they represent the future of the region. The approaches include:

- drawing graphic future visions, such as of the regional governance network,
- conducting imaginary trips through future region decision-making processes,
- pretending regional governance examination committee of 10 to 20 years in the future and writing a report on the accomplishments of the intervening years,
- exploring regional governance visions developed for other regions, and
- even assuming that no local or regional governance mechanisms exist in the region and developing an "ideal" vision for regional governance.

Finally, the regional governance vision options developed through these approaches can be considered by participants in brainstorming sessions. In these sessions, they can assess the options, such as by developing scenarios for the visions (what would a best-case, worst-case or trended-case version of the vision look like) or preparing hypothetical "snapshots" from the future. Often the preferred vision to emerge from these discussions is a hybrid based on desired components from a number of the vision options.

The product of this task is a vision for the future of regional governance. It can range in length from a few sentences to a few pages of text and is often combined with visual materials.

Task 5: Design a balanced Strategy for Achieving Regional Governance Excellence to take advantage of priority opportunities for strengthening the regional governance network.

Armed with the state of regional governance report and the vision statement, participants can begin to assess the alternative options — the regional governance initiatives — for strengthening regional governance. These initiatives can involve redirecting existing activities or launching new improvements to begin to achieve the future vision for regional governance. Collectively, the initiatives begin to move regional governance from where it is to where participants want it to be.

First, participants can identify options for regional governance initiatives.

Many of the options for strengthening regional governance that have been tried or considered are presented in the chapters on making regional governance prominent, equitable, empowering and institutionalized. As already advanced in the first hypothesis of this book, participants are encouraged to consider regional governance initiatives that address all of these five components of regional governance excellence. Moreover, they are encouraged to address the options for the first four components and then consider the fifth, the mix of region problem-solving and service-delivery mechanisms required to carry out the action plan.

Ideas for regional governance initiatives will also emerge from the examination itself, from the state of regional governance report (to address emerging regional challenges or overcome regional decision-making shortcomings) and from brainstorming potential accomplishments in improving regional governance (while designing the future vision for regional governance).

Regional governance initiative options can be considered for modifying the regional problem-solving and service-delivery mechanisms as well as for the policies, laws, rules, practices, and programs at all levels — local, regional, state and national — that govern their interrelationships. Special consideration should be given to the not-yet-tested options, since the already tested ones alone are generally failing to meet current challenges, much less achieve desired future visions for regional governance.

As many viable regional governance initiative options should be considered as possible. To assure that everyone has a role in strengthening regional governance, Rich Bradley, Director of the International Downtown Association, recommends using an *options matrix* to help identify possible initiatives. For example, the matrix developed by the National Civic League has the range of governance levels along one axis (neighborhood, city, county, region, state, and national) and range of governance sectors along the other axis (individual, civic, private, nonprofit, academic and public). Participants can be encouraged to fill in as many of the boxes as possible to make sure that all levels of governance and governance sectors are considered, such as what the private sector can do at the state level to strengthen regional governance.

Second, participants can select priority regional governance initiatives.

Selecting priority regional governance initiatives requires assessing options against criteria critical to participants. Such criteria often include:

- potential impact of the initiative on strengthening regional decision making and achieving the vision of future regional governance,
- feasibility of successfully implementing the initiative, such as availability of resources, acceptability to participants, legality, administratibility, consistency with regional values and timeliness,
- sustainability of initiative, such as resources to make it self-supporting once "seed funding" is exhausted; for example, developing a shared-ride taxicab business to institutionalize intercity-suburban mobility projects (see Equitable #3, Chapter 5) or holding an annual banquet to support a regional governance recognition awards program (see Prominent #4, Chapter 3), and
- compatibility with other regional governance initiatives as well as the existing regional governance network.

Participants could review regional governance initiative options in a two-step process. First, they could be subjected to a *threshold analysis* to determine whether the options meet some minimum expectations, such as having a tangible positive impact on improving regional decision making or being able to be administered in a cost-effective manner, or would be delayed by some fatal flaw, such as legality. Second, the options that survive the threshold analysis could be subjected to a *feasibility analysis* that would more rigorously assess their relative attractiveness.

Third, participants can determine which combination of regional governance initiatives best achieves the future vision for regional governance.

Rarely does a single regional governance initiative satisfy the desires of all participants, and especially communities. Only a balanced combination of initiatives — tied together in an overall action plan or "comprehensive deal" as it is called in one region — has the chance of satisfying the varying desires of participants while fairly distributing the costs of their implementation. Some of the important factors in testing for balance in the initiatives include:

- Balance in the benefits and costs for public and other community organizations responsible for implementing the action plan. Participants — central city and suburban and their various sectors — need to be able to extract tangible returns from their investments in the action plan.
- Balance in the equity, empowerment, efficiency and economic impact of improvements. Participants need to contribute to the action plan based on their fiscal abilities and be equally empowered to participate in its implementation. Moreover, resources need to be used efficiently and effectively and the overall action plan must foster economic competitiveness.
- Balance in interdependence versus self-determination. Participants need to be encouraged to cooperate with their neighbors, but assume primary responsibility for their own futures.
- Balance in comprehensive strategy versus incremental implementation. The action plan needs to set directions for achieving a broadly based vision, but strategically take advantage of opportunities for implementing timely initiatives.
- Balance in the long-term impact and short-term fiscal and political acceptability of the action plan. Participants need to be able to

experience short-term benefits even as they undertake long-term improvements in regional governance.

For example, a series of meetings among community leaders in the Dayton, Ohio, area identified a combination of four types of mechanisms to guide regional decision making:

- a regional challenge scanning "body, group, or process," to identify emerging regional challenges and recommend the appropriate existing or new mechanism for addressing them, potentially drawing upon the resources of a regional planning council (see Problem-Solving #1, Chapter 7),
- leadership networks or alliances, to design and guide the implementation of strategies for addressing recurring types of challenge topics, such as racial diversity, economic competitiveness, and regional governance (see Problem-Solving #5, Chapter 7),
- a service-delivery coordinating group, to facilitate the negotiation and implementation of strategies to address regional challenges, including the reallocation of responsibilities across local governments and other service deliverers (see Service-Delivery #5, Chapter 7), and
- an accountability "body, group or process," to independently monitor, evaluate, and report on and generally hold accountable, the mechanisms above (see Strategic #4), potentially drawing upon the resources of a college or university public service institute (see Problem-Solving #3, Chapter 7) or a regional civic organization (see Problem-Solving #4, Chapter 7). (Dodge, "Memorandum to Community Cooperation Task Force," 1992)

Looking at combinations of regional governance initiatives can also lead to development of overarching improvements that support the entire action plan. Participants could consider:

- drafting a "regional renaissance pledge" and securing the commitment of participants and other community leaders (see Strategic #3),
- developing the capacity to prepare a periodic report on the state of regional governance (see Strategic #4),
- creating a regional fund to provide seed or risk capital for launching regional governance initiatives (see Strategic #5),

- developing a regional clearinghouse to provide an ongoing source of information on regional challenges and the problem-solving and service-delivery mechanisms to address them (see Empowering #2, Chapter 6), and

- investing in developing the regional "pioneers" needed to make the regional problem-solving and service-delivery mechanisms effective, such as creating training programs or even a regional service corps (see Empowering #1, Chapter 6).

Fourth, participants can select an even smaller set of regional governance initiatives for initial implementation, due to their timeliness in addressing emerging regional challenges, their appeal to community leaders and citizens, and, especially, their impact on regional decision making.

George Latimer, a former mayor of St. Paul, Minnesota, and a former consultant to the U.S. Department of Housing and Urban Development, refers to using "urban, or regional, acupuncture" in selecting priority initiatives. He describes it as finding the key initiatives that will capture the essence of the vision and be a catalyst for community leader and citizen action, such as redeveloping a strategic corner parcel in a commercial redevelopment project. Peter Senge refers to finding the "trim tabs" on the "rudders" that move system "ships," to pursue the small targeted initiatives that will result in leveraging and shaping large regional challenges. (Senge, 64–65) To give these initiatives special attention, the priority regional governance initiatives could be called the "5" or "10" initiatives for regional governance excellence or even the "dream team" regional governance initiatives.

Fifth, participants can prepare an implementation work program for launching the priority regional governance initiatives.

An implementation work program indicates who will do what in which sequence with how much of whose resources to implement the priority initiatives. In addition, the implementation work program needs to specify the activities to be conducted from the completion of the action plan through at least the launching of priority regional governance initiatives. The time and costs of getting "over the hump" and implementing the initial initiatives can be equal to or even exceed the time and cost of getting the examination to this task.

Sixth, participants can design activities to monitor progress in implementing regional governance initiatives and evaluate progress towards achieving the future vision for regional governance.

Monitoring activities answer the questions:

- What will be monitored? (initiatives implemented, resources expended, time expired, outputs accomplished; also, possibly process followed and impact of initiatives)
- Who will be responsible for monitoring?
- How frequently will monitoring reports be produced (probably quarterly or semiannually)?
- How is monitoring to be used?

Evaluation activities answer similar questions:

- What will be evaluated? (impact of initiatives; also possibly impact on achieving the future vision, on stakeholders and on the region)
- Who will be responsible for evaluation?
- How frequently will evaluation reports be produced? (probably annually)
- How is evaluation to be used?

The product of this task is the Strategy for Achieving Regional Governance Excellence or SARGE, consisting of (1) the future vision for regional governance, (2) the priority regional governance initiatives for beginning to achieve it, (3) an implementation work program for launching the priority regional governance initiatives, and (4) monitoring and evaluation activities.

Task 6: Implement the action plan, report regularly to community leaders and citizens, and update the SARGE periodically.

The Strategy for Achieving Regional Governance Excellence should be circulated to community leaders and citizens for comment and commitments of support. Based on their comments, the action plan can be implemented, including tasks such as:

- Create an implementation group. The SARGE will need to be monitored during its implementation, possibly by institutionalizing the steering committee for the examination, turning responsibility over to a regional planning council or other organization or creating a new regional alliance to monitor and even evaluate strategy implementation. The organization responsible for monitoring will need to involve all participants in an equitable manner, be adequately staffed and funded to provide oversight, and perhaps have some authority or clout to influence the implementation process and update the SARGE.

- Negotiate the implementation of priority regional governance initiatives. Whereas participants can usually reach agreement in general about priority initiatives, they also usually "flee or fight" over responsibilities for their implementation. One regional alliance — Chattanooga Venture — schedules a priority strategic initiative for public consideration each month and uses this exposure to bring reluctant stakeholders to the table and encourage their commitments of support for its implementation. One regional planning council — the Southern California Association of Governments (Los Angeles) — offers a mediation/conflict resolution service with the range of professional skills needed to facilitate difficult negotiations.

- Establish monitoring and evaluation processes. Monitoring reports are often prepared by the organizations responsible for the implementation of priority initiatives; evaluations are usually conducted by independent individuals and organizations.

- Launch priority regional governance initiatives.

- Monitor implementation progress and making adjustments in the SARGE, as necessary.

- Report regularly to community leaders and citizens, through state of regional governance reports and conferences. These reports and conferences could share progress in implementing the SARGE and suggest modifications in regional governance initiatives as well as identify new emerging regional challenges and suggest how to address them (see Strategic #4).

- Evaluate implementation impact and update the SARGE, periodically. The SARGE should be updated periodically so that it provides a "moving picture" and not just a "single shot" of regional governance.

Two last considerations:

First, implementing regional governance initiatives depends on the convergence of preparation and opportunity. The best improvement sometimes has to await the removal of personal or legal obstacles; the unexpected opportunity sometimes makes it possible to implement a lower priority initiative. One of the main tasks of the implementation group is matching initiatives up against opportunities, or if they are especially entrepreneurial, creating opportunities for initiatives.

Second, even the most actively supported regional governance initiatives will probably not be fully implemented in a single step. More often, they are implemented incrementally, such as first as a demonstration, next for limited application possibly at a sub-regional level, and finally with broader powers regionwide. Allan Wallis recommends a two-phased model for building regional governance legitimacy and capacity: "...to start with strategic interests over which coalitions have already formed, and move iteratively and progressively toward developing the legitimacy and capacity of these collaborations so that they can form the basis for an institutionalized form of governance." (Wallis, 1994, 34)

Whereas there are real advantages to single step implementation, each incremental action should be celebrated as a partial success, not a partial failure. In the vicissitudes of regional governance, one has to always believe that the "glass is half-full."

The product of this task is the implementation of a Strategy for Achieving Regional Governance Excellence, including updating it, periodically, and reporting on the state of regional governance to community leaders and citizens, regularly.

Conducting Successful Examinations

Community leaders and citizens in a number of regions have conducted targeted examinations of regional governance that address many of the tasks described above. Few, however, have attempted to address the full scope of regional governance.

If a number of regions were to conduct regional governance examinations, participants in each of them would have an opportunity to make comparisons of similarities and differences in networks and improvement strategies. Initially, the networks and strategies might exhibit unique attributes, but common features will emerge over time, suggesting more general models for regional governance.

Various national organizations could aid and abet these examinations. The national organizations representing cities, counties, regional councils, public managers, chamber of commerce executives, citizens leagues, and others could support sharing information on regional governance examinations, including establishing a clearinghouse on regional governance. Moreover, academic and other research organizations could study regional decision making and develop regional governance models and initiatives for community leader and citizen consideration. For example, Wright State University has already sponsored a symposium of regional cooperation and is considering conducting regular dialogues on regional governance models. As already mentioned, the National Civic League and national foundations could sponsor a competition to spur the development of new regional governance models. All these national initiatives are presented in Chapter 8.

Without question, conducting such examinations will be demanding and initial iterations of the process imperfect at best. However, even these initial processes could begin to define visions and identify timely opportunities for strengthening regional governance, thus giving community leaders and citizens greater confidence that their efforts are contributing to a more effective network of regional problem-solving and service-delivery mechanisms.

Strategic #3
Adopt a Pledge to Strengthen Regional Decision Making (new)

Community leaders and citizens could encourage the adoption of a regional renaissance pledge to secure moral commitments to improving regional governance.

Such a pledge could be quite brief. It could commit community leaders and citizens to supporting and participating in processes for dealing with regional challenges, discussing and negotiating proposed developments with other communities they will affect, sharing community resources with less prosperous communities, supporting initiatives for improving regional decision making, and working for the general good of the region. A sample regional renaissance pledge can be found on the next page.

Although there do not appear to be any existing regional renaissance pledges, similar types of pledges have been made for other purposes:

- More than 600 corporations and more than 1,400 law firms, nationally, have adopted a pledge to use dispute resolution as an alternative to litigation. (Smith, Robert)
- The recent economic development strategy prepared by the Allegheny Conference on Community Development (Pittsburgh, Pennsylvania) called for a "Pittsburgh Pledge," an agreement to be "signed by business and labor leaders, committing them to use all means possible to resolve disputes without a strike." (Allegheny Conference on Community Development, 18)
- Similarly, local governments are beginning to enter into agreements for involving each other in their planning and regulatory changes, such as seven Maryland cities and counties in the Washington, D.C., area (see Equitable #3, Chapter 5), or for establishing principles of intergovernmental cooperation, such as between Champaign and Urbana, Illinois (Carter).

Regional renaissance pledges could be developed by those conducting regional governance examinations (see Strategic #2) and tailored to the priority initiatives in the action plan. They could also be developed by any regional problem-solving or service-delivery mechanism, or consortium of mechanisms, independent of such examinations. Community leaders and citizens, and their organizations, along with radio, television and the print media, could be involved in a campaign to secure commitments to the pledge. Costs should be minimal, except for conducting the campaign, publishing the names of signatories to the pledge, and issuing certificates to be hung in one's office or home, or even a bumper sticker to put on one's car.

Accomplishments

To be determined, but it is anticipated that the regional renaissance pledge would raise community leader and citizen awareness of regional governance. Moreover, it could encourage consideration of one's personal and community behavior in regional decision making and spur support and participation in regional decision-making processes.

Regional Renaissance Pledge

As a citizen of the _____ region, I recognize that my future is interwoven with that of my neighbors and that we must work together to address crosscutting challenges.

I, therefore, pledge to:

- support and participate in open processes for addressing regional challenges,

- discuss and negotiate proposed developments and other activities in my community, that have intercommunity and regional impact, with neighboring communities,

- share community resources with distressed communities to assure the provision of basic public services to my fellow citizens regionwide,

- support and participate in implementing critical initiatives for strengthening regional decision making (such as those developed in a Strategy for Achieving Regional Governance Excellence) and,

- generally work for the overall good of the region.

Together, I believe that we can successfully address cross-cutting challenges, be economically competitive in the global economy, and provide a high quality of life to all of our citizens.

Strengths and Shortcomings

The major strength of regional renaissance pledges is their potential to create widespread interest in, and support for, effective regional decision making, at minimal expense. The major shortcoming of regional renaissance pledges is their vagueness, making it difficult to hold signatories to more than a moral intent to behave positively in the interest of the region and regional decision making.

Potential

To be determined.

Contacts

- Pittsburgh Pledge: Allegheny Conference on Community Development, 412-281-1890
- Memorandum of Agreement (Maryland cities and counties): Maryland-National Capital Park and Planning Commission, 301-454-1740

Strategic #4
Report on the State of Regional Governance (new)

Community leaders and citizens could prepare periodic reports and hold conferences on progress made and initiatives still to be undertaken to improve regional governance.

Such reports and conferences could provide timely information on regional governance, share analyses of regional decision-making processes, recognize successful implementation of regional governance initiatives and their sponsors, identify emerging threats and opportunities for regional decision making, and suggest guidelines for the next round of regional governance improvements.

State of regional governance reports could be published, discussed with participants in follow-up conferences, and circulated to community leaders and citizens. State of regional governance conferences could allow participants to forge a consensus on the next round of regional governance improvements as well as provide recognition awards to successful regional governance initiatives and outstanding regional "pioneers."

Although regional governance does not appear to be the primary focus of any existing reports or conferences, the topic receives consideration in more general reports and conferences:

- Many regional decision-making mechanisms produce regular reports on their organizations and the regional challenges that they are addressing, such as the annual State of the Region Reports of the Economic Development Council of Northeastern Pennsylvania in the Scranton region (see Problem-Solving #1, Chapter 7) or the annual meetings of the Allegheny Conference on Community Development in the Pittsburgh region (see Problem-Solving #2, Chapter 7). The Ohio-Kentucky-Indiana Regional Council of Governments even convened a Commission on the State of the Region, composed of community leaders and citizens, to produce a State of the Region Report in 1993.
- Some of the comparative analyses of regions, often called "benchmarking" exercises, provide information on regional challenges,

such as the Rating the Region report of the Delaware Valley Regional Planning Commission in the Philadelphia region.

*   Various regional organizations, especially academic research centers, are already hosting annual conferences on regional topics, such as the Institute for Portland Metropolitan Studies (Portland State University) for community leaders, the Center for Greater Philadelphia (University of Pennsylvania) for state legislators, and the Urban Center (Cleveland State University) on economic competitiveness for community leaders. State of regional governance conferences could build upon the experience of these annual conferences.

State of regional governance reports and conferences could be instituted as annual followups on regional governance examinations, to report on progress and lay out the strategy for the coming year or years (see Strategic #2). They could also be launched by any regional problem-solving or service-delivery mechanism, or consortium of mechanisms, independent of such examinations. They could even cover additional regional topics and be called state-of-the-region reports or conferences.

Reports on the state of regional governance could be prepared by individual sponsors, by those responsible for implementing regional governance improvements, a college or university research institute or consultant, or some combination of the above. Models for these reports might be found in the less political state-of-the-state, -county, or -city reports, which are usually prepared by governors, mayors and county executives, or county and city managers, often as part of an annual budgeting process. Some costs would be involved in preparing and publishing the reports, as well as conducting the conferences, which could be covered by the sponsors, participants, community foundations, or even a regional governance fund (see Strategic #5).

Accomplishments

To be determined, but it is anticipated that state of regional governance reports or conferences would increase community leader and citizen awareness of regional governance, report on the regional governance initiatives accomplished and still to be accomplished, and help assess progress towards and support for achieving regional governance excellence.

Strengths and Shortcomings

The major strength of state of regional governance reports or conferences is keeping community leaders and citizens informed and involved in strengthening regional governance. The major shortcoming is that progress might be minimal in some years, providing little to report on since the last year, or relationships frayed at the time of the report, due to an especially conflicted regional challenge.

Potential

To be determined.

Contacts

- Economic Development Council of Northeastern Pennsylvania, Pittston, Pennsylvania, 717-655-5581
- Delaware Valley Regional Planning Commission, Philadelphia, Pennsylvania, 215-592-1800
- Ohio-Kentucky-Indiana Council of Governments, Cincinnati, Ohio, 513-621-7060

Strategic #5
Create a Regional Governance Fund/Foundation (new)

Community leaders and citizens could create a regional governance fund or foundation to provide a predictable source of financing for launching initiatives to strengthen regional governance.

It is always difficult to get good ideas over the hump into implementation. In spite of the fact that community leaders and citizens wholeheartedly endorse a particular regional governance initiative, they still might have lingering concerns or unanswered questions about its implementation. What's more, implementation of a particular initiative might require developing a more detailed work program, covering some "front-end" personnel and equipment costs, or even testing the initiative with a prototype demonstration. For any and all of these potential costs, a regional governance fund or foundation could be a resource.

A regional governance fund could be established in a number of ways. Community foundations, and even national foundations, could provide initial funding, possibly on a matching basis with public, private and other contributions. Or, a regional revenue could be earmarked to finance the fund, similar to the 1/10 percent sales tax being considered in the Philadelphia region for regional arts and culture initiatives (see Prominent #5, Chapter 3). Or, the fund could be supplemented with annual fund-raising campaigns or regional events, such as recognition awards for regional pioneers. Finally, the regional governance fund might get lucky and find a rich individual or family, or even business, that would want instant immortality for supporting regional governance excellence. The regional governance funds could be set up as nonprofit corporations, or even foundations, to facilitate receiving and distributing funds.

There are a couple of funds that might be models for a regional governance fund:

- The Southern Tier West Regional Planning and Development Board in the Jamestown, New York, region has created the Southern Tier West Development Foundation to support intermunicipal and regional planning. Seed money for the fund has been provided through the repayment of an economic development loan ($1 million over 20 years) and is being used to leverage other public, private and foundation funding.

- The Foundation for the National Capital Region, a regional community foundation, supports quality of life initiatives in the Washington, D.C., region, including the development of the Washington Regional Alliance (see Problem-Solving #4, Chapter 7).

- The Public Education Fund combined national and community foundation funding to establish local education funds in various central cities and urban counties over the past decade. These funds are used to finance education initiatives, such as by providing small grants to teachers or supporting examinations of public education challenges.

In addition, regional economic development funds have been established by regional chambers of commerce and other business organizations (see Problem-Solving #2, Chapter 7) to promote and finance critical development initiatives. For example, the Greater Denver Corporation was created by the Denver Metro Chamber of Commerce to conduct analyses and build support for a regional convention center and airport.

Finally, the Greater Minneapolis Chamber of Commerce encourages private corporations to join the Keystone Club and donate 5 percent of pre-tax profits to community charities, some of which serve the entire region. Similar efforts exist in other regions, such as 2 percent clubs, to raise the level of corporate giving above the national 1 percent average.

Accomplishments

To be determined, but the most important impact of regional governance funds might be on the mindset of community leaders and citizens. If they know that an ongoing source of funding already exists for improving regional governance, they might be inclined to take regional governance examinations more seriously and make sure that the resulting regional governance initiatives are "implementable."

Strengths and Shortcomings

The major strength of regional governance funds is providing some predicable funding for initiatives to improve regional governance. The major shortcoming is generating sufficient funding to support the ongoing experimentation needed to achieve regional governance excellence.

Potential

To be determined.

Contacts

- Southern Tier West Development Foundation: Southern Tier West Regional Planning and Development Board, Salamanca, New York, 716-945-5301
- Foundation for the National Capital Region, Washington, D.C., 202-338-8993
- Public Education Fund Network, Washington, D.C., 202-628-7460
- Greater Minneapolis Chamber of Commerce, Minneapolis, Minnesota, 612-370-9132

Chapter 5

Making Regional Governance Equitable: Economically, Racially, and Fiscally

Wholeness incorporating diversity is the transcendent goal of our time,
the task for our generation — close to home and worldwide.
— John Gardner

Economic disparities have created regions of have and have-not communities. Continued racial segregation has further differentiated many of these communities by race. The combination of economic and racial segregation has resulted in regions of widening extremes; rich and white communities continue to get richer and whiter with the fiscal capacity to do almost anything, poor and minority communities continue to get poorer and more African-American, Hispanic, and Asian with the fiscal capacity to do very little.

This widening gap in the capacity of communities to address challenges has become the Achilles heel of regional decision making. Cooperative decision making is best conducted among relatively equal partners, each of which has something to contribute to addressing common challenges. It is extremely difficult to make collaborative decisions, much less implement them, when disparities are already wide and widening.

As indicated in Chapter 1, poverty has become increasingly concentrated in the nation's central cities, resulting in central city per capita income falling to only 84 percent of suburban per capita income by 1989

---

and as low as 50 percent in some regions. This phenomenon appears to be moving outward with population; inner-ring suburbs are now becoming poorer as newer suburbs develop further out, and central counties are becoming poorer as the next ring of counties undergo development.

Communities seem to have become disposable.

As indicated in Chapter 1, racial segregation, as measured by racial dissimilarity indexes, appears to have persisted at all income levels over the past few decades of allegedly greater tolerance reinforced with civil rights legislation. White flight appears to be the continuing dominant practice in regions, though some central cities and inner-ring suburbs are witnessing some African-American and Hispanic flight as well, leaving the communities they are fleeing even more distressed. Many regions, however, and even the entire country, are rapidly becoming a mixture of white and other minorities. Henry Richmond makes a devastating historic comparison; "...there were 4 million Blacks in slavery in 1860, just before the Civil War, and ... today there are nearly 9 million black American citizens living in ghettos ... where poverty rates exceed 40 percent" (Richmond, 1995)

The impact of widening fiscal inequities between rich and poor communities is overwhelming. Poor communities tax their residents at higher rates, generate lower revenues, and have higher costs and fewer services than rich communities. Poor communities cannot keep the police on — or the snow off — their streets, making it virtually impossible to attract, much less keep, legal businesses. Moreover, the difficulty in keeping their schools competitive, or even open, along with the growing concentration of drug rings and youth gangs, makes it virtually impossible to attract, much less keep, residents. When rich communities face budget cutbacks, they have to trim services to growing populations; when poor communities fact budget cutbacks, they have to eliminate them for declining populations.

Rich communities seem to catch colds; poor communities, terminal illnesses.

And, as the studies in the Pittsburgh region indicated in Chapter 1, these disparities occur throughout the region, not just between central cities and their immediate suburbs, and they are getting worse over time.

As a result, most of the major regional challenges that have been "successfully" addressed — that is, action plans are developed and implemented — usually have some combination of the following characteristics:

- They offer a common challenge to rich and poor communities, such as the imposing of a new national or state government mandate or the departure of a major economic job provider.
- They can be substantially resolved without having to address economic, racial and fiscal disparity issues, directly, such as by financing strategies for addressing them with national or state government funding or a new regional source of funding that does not involve changing the status quo of the rich getting richer and the poor poorer.

In all too many cases, the challenges that have been most "successfully addressed" have either avoided economic, racial and fiscal disparities or pretended that they were unimportant.

Regrettably, economic, racial and fiscal disparities have been dealt with community-by-community with perverse consequences. Decades of exclusionary zoning strategies by suburban communities have wrought all the sins of sprawl. Attempts to establish new formulas for distributing state and national government assistance, such as for school aid, continue to underfund poor communities and "hold harmless" politically powerful rich ones.

Sometimes central cities appear to be fighting back with equally exclusionary funding strategies. A city budget that reduces the city government's match for state and national Medicaid and welfare funding, for example, can be interpreted as an attempt to reduce the number of poor residents by forcing them to choose between inadequate funding and moving elsewhere where public support might more closely approach the cost of subsistence living. And whether or not that is the strategy behind the budget, it is a possible outcome, as past experiences confirm that the poor do respond to changes in public support, and that they will move in response to them. (Gladwell)

Have our communities sunk to the behavior of feudal satrapies? How long can they go on pursuing "beggar-thy-neighbor" strategies that buy short-term advantage at others' expense? How much longer can we go on moving assets around the region, in the name of development, and abandon communities? What are the long-term consequences of widening fiscal inequities between rich and poor communities? When do regions have to face the music? Are regions already facing the music?

Thankfully, we are now realizing that we can no longer avoid economic, racial and fiscal disparities, even if we are not particularly excited about addressing them.

First, we are realizing that overcoming disparities and celebrating diversity are critical to the future economic competitiveness and quality of life of the region. We realize that communities across the region are interdependent; that the wider the disparities become, the more the region's economy suffers, as illustrated in Chapter 1. It is common to use the metaphor of boats in a harbor to illustrate this interdependency, suggesting that all rise and fall with an economic tide. However, one wag destroyed this metaphor for me by suggesting that one's economic health depended on the size of one's boat or its "location" in the harbor or, even worse, whether one is allowed to enter the harbor.

I prefer other metaphors to illustrate the interdependency of communities across a region. Jack Dustin, a professor at Wright State University, suggests a train track: "Perhaps the best way to visualize interdependency (of a region) is ... rails upon which people, goods and services move. Communities (of a region) ... are the rails guiding and supporting an economic locomotive. Letting any part of the track degenerate will ultimately cause serious problems." (Dustin, 1994, 20). Bruce Adams, urban consultant and former Montgomery County, Maryland, elected official, suggests thinking of the region as a quilt, which needs to "stitch" together its communities, if it is to provide "comfort" to its citizens. (Adams, 10-11)

Second, and related to the first, we are realizing that we are losing scarce human resources in poor communities; we are losing the future entrepreneurs and work force that are critical to the region's competitiveness. According to Ted Hershberg: "The future standard of the haves will be determined to a significant amount by the productivity of the children of the have-nots." (Hershberg, 1994)

Third, and related to the second, we are beginning to be concerned about the moral health of a society that continues to apply "band-aids" to the "open sores" of poor communities, but refuses to address the "diseases" causing their continued reinfection. We are becoming more concerned about finding the "soul" of the region, about what brings its residents "joy" and not just "nourishment." (Moore, Thomas) We increasingly want to live in a region that has "grace," one that is equitable — it offers equal opportunity to each citizen to live the good life — and, previewing the next chapter, empowering — it engages each citizen in an energizing regional community.

It is difficult to get rich communities to talk about disparities — "like going up a down elevator" according to some of the participants in a recent discussion on the topic. (National Academy of Public Administration, 1993) Maybe what's needed is a bit of Japanese Niaken therapy for the residents of rich communities. Niaken therapy uses people's guilt to encourage their gratitude, as well as self-sacrifice and service, towards those who have nurtured them, some of whom must live in poor communities. (Toms) Or maybe what's needed is a bit of old-fashioned grief and forgiveness, to allow the residents in rich communities, who still harbor the grief of being "pushed out" of central cities, or the residents in poor communities, who continue to harbor the grief of being "left behind," to forgive themselves and each other. Without letting go of the bitterness of the past, the "cold energy" of bad memories makes it almost impossible to accept one another; or replace the vision of "flight" with one of "interdependence"; or celebrate the richness of diversity; or deal openly with common challenges. (Erickson)

Fourth, we are realizing that regions will not prosper and thrive if they are segregated by race and class. We don't want to pursue regional strategies that "polish the apple of apartheid." (Kozul) And all too many have, both the big bucks strategies of the liberals and the bootstrap strategies of the conservatives. (Rusk, 1993, 121) Supporting regionwide efforts for celebrating diversity and overcoming disparities, such as sharing regional revenues, balancing economic development, or providing affordable housing regionwide is certainly preferred to the alternative of gated compounds or even gilded ghettos. As Henry Cisneros, Secretary of the U.S. Department of Housing and Urban Development, indicates; it costs only $80,000 to build an apartment and $5,000 a year to operate it in Rochester, New York, as opposed to $125,000 to build a jail cell and $30,000 per year per prisoner to operate it. (Cisneros)

Fifth, and most directly related to regional decision making, we are realizing that as disparities worsen, and become more central to addressing regional challenges, the more difficult it will be to bring rich and poor communities together, and negotiate cooperative arrangements among increasingly unequal partners.

Last, and maybe most important, we are beginning to believe that regions might offer the most appropriate arena for joint national, state and local experiments to address disparities; to "enfranchise minorities" (Toffler, 1995), "build a sense of common good out of diversity" (Peirce, 10), and create "pluralism with unity." (Etzioni)

Initiatives for Making Regional Governance Equitable

How can we overcome economic disparities and racial segregation and the resulting widening gap between rich and poor communities and develop an "equal opportunity playing field" for all citizens and communities regionwide?

Community leaders and citizens are only beginning to experiment with regional initiatives to address the economic, racial and fiscal disparities that undermine regional governance excellence. The preliminary conclusions of that experimentation appear to include:

- All three aspects of the disparity between communities — economic distress, racial segregation, and fiscal inequity — need to be addressed, preferably in coordinated initiatives.
- Direct, personal interaction needs to take place between rich and poor, white and minority communities, both in educating their residents and developing and implementing intercommunity and

regional strategies, preferably in neutral forums or through spending time on each other's "turf."

- Real people and dollar resources need to be devoted to breathing life into converting a region of "flight" into a region of "interdependence."
- Time is not on our side: disparities are worsening, and the price paid escalates daily.
- There are successful demonstrations of sharing regional revenues, balancing economic development and even integrating communities, as presented in the Equitable initiatives; however, few of them have been institutionalized on a local or especially a regional basis.
- Being willing to address the challenge of disparities directly, publicly, *and* regionally might be the most critical action to take for their resolution.

The initiatives for Making Regional Governance Equitable are:
- Equitable #1: Heighten regional interdependence awareness (new)
- Equitable #2: Share regional revenues (to address service inequity)
- Equitable #3: Target regional development (to address economic distress)
- Equitable #4: Integrate communities regionwide (to address racial segregation)

Community leaders and citizens could initiate the process of making regional governance equitable by conducting educational activities to heighten regional interdependence awareness (Equitable #1). Then they could launch the last three initiatives — sharing regional revenues (Equitable #2), balancing regional development (Equitable #3), and integrating communities regionwide (Equitable #4) — together to make regional governance equitable.

The performance of the Equitable initiatives in pursuing regional governance excellence can be measured by answering several questions. Does implementing the Equitable initiatives result in:

- pursuing coordinated initiatives to address intercommunity fiscal, economic *and* racial disparity?
- reversing the widening and beginning to close fiscal, economic *and* racial gaps among communities, regionwide?
- creating an "equal opportunity playing field" (basic quality services, equal economic opportunity, and racial integration) for all communities and populations in the region?

Equitable #1
Heighten Regional Interdependence Awareness
(new)

Community leaders and citizens could consider developing regional interdependence awareness programs to sensitize their communities to the threats of economic, racial and fiscal disparities and motivate them to take advantage of the opportunities offered by diversity and interdependence.

In most regions, a growing awareness of the challenges of diversity is being spurred informally and usually at a distance. Newspapers and community magazines and radio and television news programs and talk shows present intermittent "snapshot" stories that illustrate the challenges of disparities, such as one community's inability to provide 24-hour police protection, or the need for interdependence, such as the region's loss of a business opportunity due to intercommunity squabbles. A few emerging community leaders even receive some orientation to disparities in community leadership programs (see Empowering #1, Chapter 6).

Some informal interaction also takes place between residents of rich and poor communities and across racial lines. Local governments usually participate in associations that bring elected officials and professional managers together, likewise school board members and principals. Central city and suburban chambers of commerce sometimes come together to discuss common issues. But these encounters rarely take place in the poor communities and equally rarely focus their attention on economic, racial and fiscal disparities.

Some nonprofit organizations provide more structured interaction around the needs of poor and minority populations and their communities. United Ways and social service planning agencies bring providers and clients together to discuss these challenges and develop strategies for addressing them. Sometimes these discussions are primed with studies conducted by college or university research institutes and public service programs, or even national organizations, such as the Share the Wealth Project. Some religious groups also attract members from rich communities to provide assistance to residents of poor communities, such as through food banks and homeless shelters.

Then, too, ethnic festivals bring different groups together to share their foods, entertainment and cultures. Sometimes there are a series of such festivals, often held in the neighborhoods of the ethnic and racial groups.

For the most part, however, this interaction is often so informal that it misrepresents or oversimplifies the challenge of disparities and the potential of interdependence or it resembles "preaching to the choir" by involving only the already concerned community leaders and citizens. What is more, it does not provide the personal contacts or guidance to prepare community leaders and citizens to develop and support strategies for overcoming the disparities and fostering regional interdependence.

A few efforts strive to achieve the old English concept of "fellowfeel," which is "to feel in earnest how another person feels, to crawl practically under their skin to share their feelings and thereby make them feel better." One of the major reasons that medieval citizens engaged in fellowfeeling was to recognize "the mutual aim of ensuring themselves a comfortable 'chair day,' the evening of life when one is advanced in age and usually infirm. They thus prepared themselves and one another to be able to pass this time of life in peaceful ease and indulgence." (Sperling, 8-9)

For example, the Atlanta and Austin projects (see Empowering #4, Chapter 6) aggressively recruit residents of rich, especially suburban, communities to participate in poor inner suburbs and city neighborhood initiatives, such as mass inoculations of children. Communities sometimes sponsor special efforts to build intercommunity or interracial relations, such as the Day of Dialogue that sponsored simultaneous small group discussions across the Los Angeles region.

A few programs are specifically directed at building relationships across racial lines, such as the Program to Unlearn Racism in the Portland, Oregon, region, the Greater Philadelphia Urban Affairs Coalition, ERACE in the New Orleans Region, and the Cleveland Roundtable. They sponsor seminars and conferences, conduct studies and develop educational programs and collaborative public initiatives, such as in public education or fair housing, to address racial issues in their regions. (Stouffer, 13) ERACE , for example, gives bumper stickers reading "ERACISM" to participants in their weekly discussions on race. The Cleveland Roundtable is helping a group of suburban school districts recruit minority teachers and administrators, facilitating discussions of real estate agents and bankers regionwide to make housing mortgages more readily available to minority buyers, providing two-day Executive Forums on Diversity for groups of community leaders, and convening meetings of corporate human services coordinators to discuss diversity issues.

Most recently, diversity programs are beginning to be offered by larger businesses and local governments as they recognize that their work forces have become a more complex mix of race and gender. These programs bring employees together, across races, to discuss their racial prejudices, build personal and working relationships, and foster everyone's potential to contribute to their organizations. Similarly, many colleges and universities are now covering racial diversity in orientation courses for new students, such as by presenting "life sketch" skits at the University of Pennsylvania or reading *The Diary of Ann Frank* at the University of Maryland. (Sanchez)

Efforts to educate citizens on economic and fiscal disparities appear to be even rarer. At best, these are periodic topics on the agendas of college and university research institutes or public service programs, regional civic organizations, such as citizens leagues, or chambers of commerce and other business organizations (see Problem-Solving #3, 4, and 2, respectively, Chapter 7).

Accomplishments

Some outstanding single-shot efforts have been undertaken to educate community leaders and citizens on economic, racial and fiscal disparities. A few ongoing efforts have been undertaken to educate them on overcoming racial disparities and fostering racial diversity in communities and organizations.

Strengths and Shortcomings

Efforts to develop community leader and citizen understanding of economic, racial and fiscal disparities appear to be well-intended, but, with rare exceptions, they have failed to involve large numbers of individuals across regions in any sustained interaction on the topic. Unless residents of rich and poor communities are so engaged, it is difficult to engender their understanding of, and support for, initiatives to make regional governance more equitable.

Potential

The potential of regional interdependence awareness programs is unlimited, especially for ongoing efforts that develop community leader and citizen awareness and encourage them to pursue collaborative initiatives.

Sponsor ongoing education programs to build regional interdependence. Regional interdependence awareness programs could be sponsored by individuals or groups of organizations that have connections across the region — such as regional planning councils, chambers of commerce, colleges and universities, local governments, and religious and community groups. These programs could offer series of discussions or seminars for small groups of community leaders and citizens regionwide. The programs could be hosted on a rotating basis, in the communities or even homes of the participants.

Participants could be provided with relevant information on economic, racial and fiscal disparities to prime discussions on the implications of these disparities for their communities and themselves. They could discuss how these disparities impact on current and emerging regional challenges and develop collaborative initiatives, such as the ones discussed in this chapter, for addressing the disparities. It might be especially rewarding for participants from pairs of different communities (rich and poor, central city and suburban) to work as teams in developing these initiatives. Participants could even become involved in implementing short-term projects in each others' communities.

The seminars could be embellished with various written and visual materials, such as a series of brochures that could be used as newspaper inserts or a video that could be used in meetings with community groups or televised videoconferences. In general, these materials could be used to educate a larger audience and recruit participants in future seminar series.

Sufficient seminars and other activities should be undertaken to provide a basic understanding of disparities and develop personal relationships among participants. In addition, participants should have an opportunity to discuss and even design collaborative initiatives for fostering regional interdependence.

A model for these programs might be emerging in the Columbus, Ohio, and Washington, D.C., regions. In the Columbus region, the Young Women's Christian Association is inviting community leaders and citizens to participate in a three-month race relations program. Similarly, the National Conference on Christians and Jews is sponsoring a program in the Washington, D.C., region. Both begin with special events — a kickoff conference and electronic town meeting, respectively — and follow the study circle small group discussion model. (See Empowering #4, Chapter 6)

A variation on these programs could be developed for elementary and high school students and offered as part of their civics or social studies education. Or it could be offered to college and university students, possibly as part of a core curriculum for all undergraduates. A model for student programs might be the Greater Philadelphia High School Convocation Project. The Center for Greater Philadelphia convened high school students from across the region in a networking session to help city and suburban students discuss ideas and form teams to carry out projects. The results of those projects will be presented in the Greater Philadelphia High School Convocation. (Center for Greater Philadelphia, 1996)

Graduates of these programs could be encouraged to be mentors for the next round of seminars and recruited to pursue initiatives for addressing disparities, either by working with regional problem-solving and service-delivery mechanisms or with teams of other graduates. Students could also be offered opportunities to participate in efforts to address regional disparities; high school students could even use these activities to meet graduation requirements for community service.

Graduates of regional interdependence awareness programs and others could be offered additional training in developing initiatives for addressing regional disparities as well as technical assistance and even seed funding for pursuing them. They could become the regional governance "pioneers" needed to conduct a regional governance examination and implement strategic initiatives to achieve a future vision for regional governance (see Strategic #2, Chapter 4). They could even become the "interdependence police" and be charged to bring up economic, racial, and fiscal disparities as strategies are being developed for addressing regional challenges.

Launch a "Sister Communities" program to institutionalize intercommunity relationships. These regional interdependence awareness activities could be institutionalized in regional "Sister Communities" programs. Similar to the Sister Cities International program, which fosters the exchange of people, ideas, and cultures between communities and even regions in different nations, a Sister Communities program would develop special ties between communities in the same region, especially between affluent suburban and distressed central city and inner ring suburban communities. Beyond participating in education programs to build regional interdependence awareness, the pairs of communities could arrange joint meetings of similar types of business, government, academic and civic groups as well as schedule performances of each other's cultural groups. Most important, they could develop an ongoing dialogue between citizens of each other's communities on the common regional challenges facing them.

More than 2,000 communities in regions across this country have had success in developing close ties with Sister Cities in regions in more than 120 countries around the world. Maybe it would be equally rewarding, and timely, to develop similar relationships with communities in our own regions.

Contacts

- United Ways: United Way of America, Alexandria, Virginia, 202-836-7100
- Social service planning agencies: National Association of Regional Planning Councils, Dallas, Texas, 214-342-2638
- Share the Wealth Project, Boston, Massachusetts, 617-473-2148

- Greater Philadelphia Urban Affairs Coalition, Philadelphia, Pennsylvania, 215-851-0110
- Day of Dialogue, Los Angeles, California: Study Circles Resource Center, Pomfret, Connecticut, 860-928-2616
- ERACE, New Orleans, Louisiana, 504-866-1163
- Cleveland Roundtable, Cleveland, Ohio, 216-579-9980
- Race Relations Program, Columbus, Ohio: Young Women's Christian Association, Columbus, Ohio, 614-224-9121
- Race Relations Program, Washington, D.C.: The National Conference on Christians and Jews, Washington, D.C., 202-678-9400
- Sister Cities International, Washington, D.C., 202-466-8000

Equitable #2
Share Regional Revenues

Sharing regional tax and other revenues can help assure the availability of basic adequate municipal, public education, and other services for the residents of distressed communities and can even begin to provide some fiscal equity among communities.

Community leaders and citizens have considered and implemented various approaches for sharing regional revenues, in somewhat the following order:

1. Targeting service support to distressed communities

The most common approach for supporting the provision of services in poor communities has been targeted support by county, state, and national governments and nongovernmental providers. The Community Development Block Grant program at the national level, targeted aid for poor school districts at the state level, and county police patrolling and detective services at the local level are examples of such targeting. Communities and school districts that lack the economic base to balance their budgets are sometimes the beneficiaries of additional assistance as distressed communities, such as through special loans and grants in Pennsylvania. Unfortunately, this last assistance is usually tied to at least temporary ceding of community and school district budget authority to externally controlled oversight boards. Moreover, most of this targeted assistance is "soft" temporary money, tied to particular projects or programs, and does not provide "hard" ongoing support for basic public services.

2. Transferring service functions to higher levels of government

An alternate approach that has had some popularity, historically, is transferring functions to higher levels of government. Transit, many social and health services, some detective and special police services, and even some housing and redevelopment services have been transferred from municipal to county governments. Similarly, some public education services, such as special and vocational education, have been transferred from local school districts to intermediate, often county-wide, units. Although these transfers do not directly deal with inter-community disparities, they usually result in "leveling up" services, thereby raising the level of services in distressed communities to those in affluent communities. (National Academy of Public Administration, 1980, 38–41)

In some cases, these transfers have been specifically undertaken to address fiscal disparities. The Baltimore city government has transferred a number of its functions, such as the municipal jail, to the Maryland state government to help balance its budget.

Disincorporation has been suggested as maybe the most draconian form of transferring functions to higher levels of government. Frank Lucchino, the County Controller in Allegheny (Pittsburgh, Pennsylvania) County has proposed allowing distressed municipalities to disincorporate and become the responsibility of county government, thereby sharing the cost of their public services across the more affluent communities of the county. This should probably only be considered as a last resort, since it disenfranchises residents of their municipal citizenship. (Lucchino)

3. Reforming local tax systems

Changing the mix of local taxes, or giving distressed communities additional taxing authority, is another option that is often considered for dealing with intercommunity disparities. In addition, some reforms are directed at increasing the fairness of taxes, such as providing property tax exemptions and income or wage tax credits for the poor and food and clothing exemptions for sales taxes. Some reforms involve shifting from an undue dependence on usually regressive property taxes to sales or income taxes. Some reforms involve allowing distressed communities to use special tax "tools," such as tax abatements, to foster economic development.

Providing greater flexibility in the mix of taxing sources can increase the fairness, or unfairness, of taxing, depending upon how individual communities decide to use it. Flexibility, and especially "look-alike" taxes, can also facilitate intercommunity, county, and regional tax sharing.

Unfortunately, most of the tax reforms provide little assistance to poor communities in relation to their rich neighbors. Communities that have low assessed property tax valuations usually also have equally low income and retail sales levels. Providing additional tax options only further demonstrates the futility of trying to get blood from a turnip.

4. Sharing the revenues from regional developments

Sharing the benefits and costs of particular crosscutting economic development projects can begin to establish stable support for providing services in distressed communities. Unfortunately, the occurrences of such development projects are governed by economic opportunity, not community distress, and they may or may not provide greater intercommunity equity.

The Intermunicipal Tax Sharing Account, for example, shares the property taxes generated by the development of the Hackensack Meadowlands in New Jersey. Each of the fourteen participating towns is allowed to retain a portion of the revenues for public education and municipal services and contributes the balance to a fund that is redistributed based on relative acreage. The tax-sharing arrangement especially compensates towns where park and preservation zoning have precluded significant development. The Intermunicipal Tax Sharing Account is administered by the Hackensack Meadowlands Development Commission, which periodically explores problem areas with the mayors of the participating towns. (Smith, 19–21; Dodge, Greater Baltimore Committee, 1991, 4–5)

In a similar arrangement, the Chagrin Highlands Development shares the income tax proceeds from development of property owned by the city of Cleveland with the five communities in which the property is located. It also shares property tax revenues with the impacted school district. The communities have annexed the property and agreed to cover the costs of capital improvements required for its development. (Dustin, 1993)

5. Establishing new revenue sources for regional infrastructure and assets

Establishing new revenues, and often special districts, for regional transportation and other infrastructure projects and asset districts can relieve poor communities of the need to further divide up their meager resources to pay their share of the costs. However, these new revenues usually provide similar relief for rich communities and do not necessarily redress intercommunity disparities.

Regional taxes and special districts have been used frequently to finance regional infrastructure improvements, especially in transportation. In California, for example, counties are empowered to collect sales taxes for specified highways, bridges and transit projects or to be generally available for unspecified future improvements. They can be collected in perpetuity, periodically reenacted or enacted for the period of time required to pay for specific projects. Some counties have used the authority to finance a single project, such as widening Highway 101 in Santa Clara County; others have used it for comprehensive programs of regional and local transportation facilities and services, such as San Diego County. Sometimes, some of the resources are allocated by regional transportation commissions, such as the Metropolitan Transportation Commission in the San Francisco region. Similarly, local shares of capital and operating subsidies for regional transit authorities, and even airports and sports stadia, are financed with dedicated local sales and property taxes in many regions, nationally. (Dodge, Interstate Study Commission, 1994, 34–35)

Recently, this approach has been used to finance regional improvements in arts, culture, recreation, library and other "assets" of regional importance. Special arrangements have existed to finance specific facilities — such as the Metropolitan Service District (Portland, Oregon) for a zoo, convention center, coliseum, civic stadium and center for the performing arts (see Problem-Solving/Service-Delivery #3, Chapter 7) and the Zoo-Museum District in the St. Louis (Missouri) region for a zoo, art museum, science center, botanical garden and history museum (see Service-Delivery #4, Chapter 7).

In the Denver and Pittsburgh regions, however, piggyback sales taxes have been enacted to flexibly finance regional assets. The tax is collected by state government — 1/10 percent regionwide in the six counties in the Denver region (approximately $20 million annually) and 1/2 percent in Allegheny County, the central county in the Pittsburgh region (approximately $50 million annually) — and rebated to special districts — the Scientific and Cultural Facilities District in Denver and the Allegheny Regional Assets District in Pittsburgh — that allocate the revenues to priority regional assets. The regional assets district does not deliver regional services, it only contracts to support the operations of the regional assets. One of the major arguments for creating regional assets districts is to spread the fiscal responsibility, now often borne by central city and distressed communities, equitably across the region. (Parker, 3–5; Cisneros, 1995, 23–25; Dodge, Interstate Study Commission, 1994, 35)

In a variation on this approach, in the San Diego, Miami, and Columbus, Ohio, regions, the San Diego Commission for the Arts, Dade County Cultural Affairs Council, and Greater Columbus Arts Council, respectively, are being supported with dedicated percentages of hotel and motel taxes. (Neiman)

In another variation on this approach, the Baltimore Metropolitan Council called on county governments to contribute three-tenths of one percent of their general fund budgets to create a Regional Partnership for Cultural Development to support cultural institutions in the Baltimore region. (Baltimore Regional Council of Governments, 1990)

6. Sharing general tax revenues to redress intercommunity service inequities and achieve other purposes

Sharing general tax revenues or tax base to redress intercommunity fiscal inequities has been considered in various forms, but rarely implemented, and then only when combined with other, often more prominent purposes, such as to foster economic development or orderly growth. Even then, most of the successful experiences have been among a few communities; only one is fully countywide in its scope — the ED/GE program in Montgomery County, Ohio — and one regional in its scope — the Fiscal Disparities Program in the Minneapolis-St. Paul region. The forms include:

Sharing the public costs of "commuters" between central cities and suburbs: Local payroll taxes or income taxes are shared in a number of regions, including the Cleveland (Ohio) and Philadelphia (Pennsylvania) regions, for individuals who work in the central city and live in the suburbs. These commuter taxes have been established to recognize the respective public costs of supporting individuals where they work and live as well as to address fiscal disparities.

There is, however, a potential economic development down side of commuter taxes. They tend to further encourage businesses to locate in suburban settings where they do not have to pay the commuter tax and face lower local tax rates. There is also a potential political down side. For example, the threat of commuter taxes has helped poison the relations between the District of Columbia and its Maryland and Virginia neighbors, preventing constructive regional dialogue on the fiscal plight of the District of Columbia or sharing the costs of financing regional facilities and services.

Redistributing sales tax proceeds countywide to redress inter-community disparities: Sales taxes proceeds are redistributed in a few states based on the relative capacity of jurisdictions as opposed to being solely returned to the municipality or county of origin. In addition, counties in ten states have the option to establish their own formulas for the distribution of local and state sales tax proceeds, some of which consider intercommunity disparities. (Dodge, Greater Baltimore Committee, 1991, 7)

Reducing intercommunity disparities countywide and fostering cooperative economic development: The Economic Development/Government Equity (ED/GE)program fosters cooperative economic development among the jurisdictions of Montgomery County, Ohio, and shares some of the resulting growth in tax revenues with the most distressed communities, through two interrelated funds.

The Economic Development (ED) fund provides $5 million in county sales tax revenues annually for economic development projects. A selection committee, composed of officials from the participating jurisdictions and private leaders, reviews municipal applications, visits proposed project sites and meets with their sponsors, and jointly selects those that have the greatest areawide economic impact. Cooperative interjurisdictional projects are favored; interjurisdictional business prospect raiding is prohibited.

The Government Equity (GE) fund collects a portion of the increased property and income tax revenues resulting from economic growth and distributes it to nongrowing jurisdictions, based primarily on population and assessed property valuation. Contributions are calculated in early fall in advance of budget preparations and distributions are made in late spring after tax revenues are received. To provide year-to-year predictability, contributions are based on the past three years fiscal history and jurisdictions were required to enter into nine-year agreements to participate in ED/GE.

Twenty-nine of the thirty local governments in Montgomery County have voluntarily agreed to participate in the program. ED/GE is guided by an advisory committee of business, municipal and county government representatives and is administered by Montgomery County government. For smaller jurisdictions, ED/GE has invested in preparing collaborative economic development strategies, developing industrial parks, and providing key infrastructure projects, such as a water tank. For larger jurisdictions, ED/GE has invested in developing new businesses in the distressed western side of Dayton and saving a major shopping center in an inner suburb. In part due to ED/GE, the Dayton city government has been able to balance its municipal budget for the first time in the 1990s.

ED/GE also has fostered interjurisdictional cooperation. Most of the ED/GE jurisdictions just created a Regional Fire Alliance to foster cooperative fire services, an effort modeled on ED/GE and receiving ED/GE support. Two municipal consolidations have been approved since the launching of ED/GE. (Dodge, Greater Baltimore Committee, 1991; Austin, 1993; Schenking)

Reducing intercommunity disparities regionwide and fostering cooperative economic development: The only regional tax base sharing program in operation in the United States is the Minnesota Fiscal Disparities program. It serves the seven counties, approximately 190 municipalities, and half as many single purpose districts, and more than 2.5 million people in the Minneapolis/St. Paul region. It exists, in part, because it was seen as the best of a number of options to address intercommunity disparities; it did not set up a new taxing authority or threaten municipal government powers.

Enacted by Minnesota state government in 1971 and implemented in 1975, the Fiscal Disparities program distributes 40 percent of the increase in commercial and property tax base (not tax revenues) since the benchmark year of 1971, an amount that now equals approximately 30 percent of the commercial and industrial tax base. In 1994, part of the residential tax base was added to the shared pool, on houses with assessments of over $200,000, to prevent undue distributions to affluent suburban communities. To distribute the tax base, an index is calculated for each local government jurisdiction, based primarily on population and assessed property valuation. Administration of the Fiscal Disparities program is rotated among the participating county governments. (Smith, 1994, 18–19; Dodge, Greater Baltimore Committee, 1991, 2–4)

Equalizing fiscal disparities in other countries: Other countries, especially those with strong central or state governments, have tended to establish sophisticated programs for distributing central or state government funds to local governments to equalize their relative fiscal disparities and meet their varying service needs. Distribution formulas in these countries, such as Australia (States Personal Income Tax Sharing Act) and Japan (Local Allocation Tax Law), take into consideration not only relative fiscal capacities but also relative service levels in calculating formula distributions. Although these programs are more like national and state revenue sharing programs in this country, their formula distributions and administrative arrangements, and political acceptance, offer insights for designing income tax sharing arrangements for this country.

Accomplishments

When fully implemented, either on a county or regional basis, revenue sharing has a significant impact, even at the level of less than a million dollars annually in the ED/GEprogram in Montgomery County (Dayton, Ohio). Born in the throes of parochial criticism, including fighting a law suit initiated by four of the municipalities, ED/GE has been an unexpected catalyst for interjurisdictional cooperation, substantially curtailing beggar-thy-neighbor behavior and encouraging intermunicipal development.

At the more significant level of redistributing more than $2 billion in tax base in the Minneapolis/St. Paul region, the Fiscal Disparities program appears to have reduced fiscal inequities considerably: from 12 to 1 to 4 to 1. Without the Fiscal Disparities program, disparities would have grown to 22 to 1. (Smith, 18) Most researchers suggest that the Fiscal Disparities program has also had a favorable impact on discouraging destructive economic competition among communities.

Strengths and Shortcomings

The major strength of sharing regional revenues is their direct impact on reducing intercommunity inequities in basic public and other services and their indirect impact on facilitating regional decision making and cooperation. The major shortcoming is the difficulty of convincing community leaders and citizens to create them and withstanding the initial law suits and continuing pressure of contributing communities to weaken or terminate them. In no small part, both the ED/GE and Fiscal Disparities programs have survived because the receiving communities have always outnumbered the contributing communities, at least politically.

Potential

Although the potential of sharing regional revenues is considerable and critical, the pursuit of such initiatives is difficult. Key to the success of any initiative could be a few rounds of regional interdependence awareness education (see Equitable #1) to convince community leaders and citizens that an investment in distressed communities pays economic and quality of life returns for rich and poor communities.

Approaches to sharing regional revenues that merit consideration include:

Providing targeted general assistance to distressed communities: Suggestions continue to be made for providing national and state financial adjustments for communities with declining populations and fiscal capacity, such as targeted general revenue sharing for central cities, but the odds against their passage, especially in times of growing national government deficits, appear to be overwhelming. (Downs, 100)

Financing more public services regionally: Many public works, such as transportation facilities and services and recreational and cultural assets, are financed regionally, as are national and international marketing and other economic development activities, in part as a result of national and state government funding incentives.

Community leaders and citizens, especially in response to national and state government incentives, could consider regional financing of other public services. The State of Connecticut, for example, provides support for regional magnet schools, such as the New London Regional Magnet. The Magnet is an initiative of the Southeastern Connecticut Task Force on Racial/Ethnic Equity, which is composed of superintendents and board of education members from ten school districts. (Connecticut Public Television, 38) The state has also considered passing out school aid on a regional basis to encourage local school districts, collectively, to devise strategies for providing quality, integrated public education to residents of rich and poor communities. (*New York Times*, 1993)

Similarly, dedicated regional financing could also overcome some of the resistance to commuter taxes. In the District of Columbia, for example, a regional tax that covered the cost of regional transportation improvements and picked up the community shares of transit system subsidies could relieve some of the burdens of the District of Columbia for maintaining existing facilities as well as assist Maryland and Virginia communities to invest in new facilities.

Establishing enhanced boundary review or service equalization commissions: Boundary review commissions (see Problem-Solving/Service-Delivery #2, Chapter 7) in California are increasingly becoming involved in negotiating tax sharing arrangements associated with boundary changes, according to the Advisory Commission on Intergovernmental Relations. Especially when incorporated jurisdictions attempt to annex unincorporated county land, county governments are requiring the sharing of sales tax revenues to compensate for the loss of property tax revenues. To date, the boundary review commissions in California and in other states with similar organizations (Iowa, Minnesota, Michigan, New Mexico, Oregon, Utah, Virginia and Washington) have primarily considered the fiscal capacity of annexing jurisdictions, but a few are beginning to note the relative fiscal disparities of the jurisdictions losing land as well. (Advisory Commission on Intergovernmental Relations, 1992; Dodge, Greater Baltimore Committee, 1991, 10)

Regions, with the help of state enabling legislation, could establish commissions to deal with the relative disparities of communities in annexation and boundary change cases. Moreover, the commissions could be empowered to more broadly explore tax equity. They could, for example, conduct studies and recommend appropriate approaches for financing regional services, for consideration of community officials and citizens. In addition, they could conduct studies of state funding and recommend appropriate approaches for "regionalizing" its distribution, such as for state aid to public education. Most important, they could conduct studies and recommend appropriate approaches for overcoming intercommunity disparities and guaranteeing basic public and other services in all communities throughout the region. Boundary review or service equalization commissions could also assist in administering these arrangements, such as those for collecting and distributing regional revenues, as necessary.

To assure local support for their recommendations, the governing bodies of boundary or service equalization commissions could be composed of local elected officials and other community leaders and citizens, appointed by both state and local governments. To assure close ties to regional transportation, environmental and land use planning, regional planning councils (see Problem-Solving #1, Chapter 7) could even be designated as staff to or administrators of boundary review or service equalization commissions.

Establishing combination tax sharing programs: Given the virtual impossibility of passing state mandated tax sharing programs and the equally difficult task of selling voluntary approaches by themselves, combination programs that include "carrots" or even occasional "sticks" might offer the best approach to launching successful tax sharing programs.

Like the ED/GE program in the Dayton region, economic development funding could be offered as an incentive to participate in a tax sharing program. National, state or even regional economic development funding could be made available, on a competitive basis, to any community, or group of communities, that enters into a tax sharing agreement. Long term agreements — ten years or longer — are probably necessary to provide an opportunity for participants to experience the long-term impact of tax sharing, such as being net contributors as well as recipients of the tax sharing program.

New funding, such as a regional sales tax, would potentially provide the most desirable incentive, but embellished existing funding could offer a similar incentive. For example, counties and especially state governments could offer to increase various pots of funding for communities if they would agree to distribute the funding cooperatively and enter into tax sharing arrangements.

Similarly, conditions that overcome intercommunity fiscal inequities could be added to annexations and other actions desired by communities. For example, annexations could be tied to long-term agreements for sharing revenues between annexing and annexed communities, as in the county-city agreements in Virginia, especially when they involve poor and rich communities (see Service-Delivery #1, Chapter 7).

Contacts

- Municipal/School District Distress Programs: Department of Community Affairs, State of Pennsylvania, Pittsburgh Region, 412-565-5002; Department of Education, State of Pennsylvania, Harrisburg, Pennsylvania, 717-783-6788
- Intermunicipal Tax Sharing Account: Hackensack Meadowlands Development Commission, Lyndhurst, New Jersey, 201-460-1700
- Economic Development/Government Equity Program: County Administrator, Montgomery County government, Dayton, Ohio, 513-225-4693
- The Scientific and Cultural Facilities District, Denver, Colorado, 303-860-0588
- Allegheny Regional Assets District, Pittsburgh, Pennsylvania, 412-227-1900
- Minnesota Fiscal Disparities Program: Metropolitan Council, Minneapolis/St. Paul, Minnesota, 612-291-6359

- New London Regional Magnet: Connecticut Public Television, Hartford, Connecticut, 203-278-5310

Equitable #3
Target Regional Development

Targeting regional development can help build the economic base that distressed communities need to provide public and other services, as well as begin to provide balanced economic equal opportunity for communities regionwide.

Community leaders and citizens have considered and implemented various approaches for sharing regional development, in somewhat the following order:

1. Targeting economic development support to distressed individuals and communities

The most common approach for fostering economic development in poor communities is targeting support by county, state and national governments and nongovernmental organizations. The Enterprise Community/Empowerment Zone (EC/EZ) initiative of the U.S. Departments of Agriculture and Housing and Urban Development is an example of such targeting that has included the involvement of all levels of government. The Atlanta and Austin projects (see Empowering #4, Chapter 6) are examples of initiatives that have especially mobilized nongovernmental resources to address the needs of poor inner-city and suburban communities.

Similarly, community development corporations (CDCs) have been established in many poor communities, with outside support from national organizations, such as the Local Initiatives Support Corporation and The Enterprise Corporation or regional entities, such as the Pittsburgh Partnership for Neighborhood Development in Pittsburgh and Neighborhood Progress, Inc. in Cleveland. The number of CDCs has increased ten-fold over the last decade and their impact has been significant. One study by Rene Berger of 2,000 CDCs indicated that they had built or refurbished 320,000 homes, developed 17.4 million square feet of commercial and industrial space and created 90,000 jobs. (Putnam, 1995; Peirce, 1993, 25)

Finally, many state and national income assistance programs provide support to individuals and families in distressed communities. Some local governments and school districts, such as those in Baltimore and Milwaukee, are now adopting living wage policies to assure that their employees, as well as those of their contractors and grant recipients, receive adequate wages to support a family of three, generally $6 to $8 per hour.

2. Linking job and development activities of rich and poor communities

A number of actions have been taken in recent years to link the development of rich and poor communities.

Some actions have been directed at linking residents in distressed city neighborhoods to suburban job opportunities, and are often referred to as "reverse commuting" or "mobility" projects. Suburban Joblink, Inc. in the Chicago region operates a fleet of buses, organizes carpools and vanpools, and subsidizes the cost to commuters through contributions from employers. The Southeastern Pennsylvania Transit Authority provides more than fifteen bus routes to move central city residents from commuter rail system stops to suburban employers, again supported with subsidies from employers. Project BREAC (Break Barriers Employment Assistance Collaborative) in the Hartford region helped city residents get driver's licenses, lease cars, or form carpools to get to suburban jobs. (Rainbow Research, Inc., 48–49) Some have even recommended developing shared ride taxicab businesses as a way to institutionalize this capacity in distressed city neighborhoods.

The U.S. Department of Housing and Urban Development has launched a national demonstration project, called Bridges-to-Work, in six cities (Baltimore, Chicago, Denver, Milwaukee, Philadelphia, and St. Louis). Administered by Public-Private Ventures, each of the regional partners has developed a combination of transportation, placement, and counseling services to help approximately 500 persons move to suburban jobs over a four-year period.

A recent Urban Institute study concluded that there has been too little experience to fully assess the impact of reverse commuting projects, but that the efforts to date do open up new jobs and bring income into poor city neighborhoods. The study recommended that reverse commuting experiments merit at least modest investments, especially given the massive investments that have been made in transportation systems to move suburbanites in the opposite direction. (Barringer)

Some initiatives have been directed at linking the development of desirable and undesirable parcels, at least between rich and poor neighborhoods of central cities. The City of Boston has packaged the sale of such parcels to attract developers' interest in using the profits from the former to subsidize development of the latter.

3. Developing arrangements for mediating and resolving intercommunity conflicts over development projects

A number of actions have been taken in recent years to involve neighboring communities in reviewing each other's development decisions. Some are more generally directed at sharing proposed planning and regulatory changes, others at resolving conflicts over proposed developments with intercommunity implications. Whereas none of these is currently focused on narrowing the economic gap between rich and poor communities, they offer approaches that could be so targeted.

Seven Maryland cities and counties in the Washington, D.C., region have entered into a memorandum of understanding to notify each other of proposed planning and regulatory changes before public announcement; establish repositories within each jurisdiction to facilitate citizen and official review; develop common approaches to data collection, analysis and mapping; and convene quarterly meetings of planning department representatives to discuss issues of common concern (see Problem-Solving #1, Chapter 7). (Dodge, Interstate Study Commission, 11) The San Diego Association of Governments (SANDAG) has established a self-certification process that allows local jurisdictions and regional agencies to certify the consistency of their plans, policies, and ordinances with the SANDAG regional plan. (Sulzer) New York and New Jersey are using "cross-acceptance" agreements to achieve consistency and compatibility among local land use plans in the state. (Wallis, 1993, 133)

Some states and regions are also providing mediation and dispute resolution services to resolve planning, zoning, and development conflicts between communities:

- The State of Washington created boards to resolve disputes concerning the establishment of urban growth boundaries. (Wallis, 1993, 133)
- The San Diego Association of Governments established a conflict resolution procedure for resolving interjurisdictional conflicts concerning the SANDAG regional plan. (Sulzer)
- The Southern California Association of Governments offers conflict resolution and negotiation services to its member governments to resolve intercommunity land use, environment and development challenges that are especially contentious. (Dodge, Interstate Study Commission, 1995, 27)

The Kettering Foundation has experimented with negotiated investment strategies to foster intergovernmental agreements for particular development projects or programs. (King; Moore, Carl) Finally, the National Institute for Dispute Resolution maintains information on mediation centers that have been established in communities in various regions, nationally.

4. Managing growth to balance development region-wide.

Some states and regions are developing special review processes for developments of regional impact (Wallis, 1994, 18) and establishing urban growth boundaries to refocus growth on already developed, and often, poor communities, and protect open space and agricultural land. Such boundaries limit the provision of water, sewage and some transportation services to areas within the boundaries. In the Portland, Oregon, region, the urban growth boundary has been in existence for approximately two decades, long enough to influence development. It has helped to increase the proportion of multi-family housing (to approximately 50 percent of new housing), reduce the size of single family lots (from approximately 13,000 to 9,000 square feet), and foster infill development in already developed communities. (Downs, 126, 153-5) Both of these tools — regional impact review and urban growth boundaries — offer new opportunities for poor and rich communities to address the economic disparities between them.

Growth management programs have been mandated by a number of states to guide the use of these tools for shaping balanced, sustainable growth across regions. Among the states that have created these programs are Florida, Georgia, Hawaii, New Jersey, Vermont, Maine, Oregon, and Washington. Regional growth management boards, often administered by regional planning councils (see Problem-Solving #1, Chapter 7), review the consistency of local jurisdiction development projects with regional or state growth management plans. They are authorized to take various actions, including mediating differences and referring unresolved disputes to state courts or administrative judges. In addition, more than two dozen states can override local zoning, if there is a compelling state environmental, historic, or other interest.

Oregon, for example, established the Land Conservation and Development Commission in the 1970s to set statewide planning goals and oversee the preparation of city and county plans that meet those goals. To conserve outlying farm land and stabilize inner-city downtowns and neighborhoods, an urban growth boundary was established to accommodate anticipated growth for the next two decades but limit it primarily to already developed areas in the Portland region. Metro, the regional mechanism that combines regional planning council and service-delivery responsibilities in the Portland region (see Problem-Solving/Service-Delivery #3, Chapter 7), is now developing a new regional plan that is attempting to improve development patterns within the existing urban growth boundary as opposed to expanding the boundary into undeveloped areas. (Berke)

In other countries, national, and sometimes, state governments have even greater influence on regional development. At times, they have expanded the boundaries of central city governments and created greenbelts and growth corridors to preserve the economic competitiveness of central cities as well as shape sustainable, balanced growth regionwide.

Accomplishments

Targeting economic development activities on distressed communities appears to have had the most visible impact on disparities, but far from enough to deter the widening gap between rich and poor communities. Linkage projects have potential but thus far have only been applied on an experimental basis, such as "reverse commuting." Most linkage of development parcels has occurred within the confines of a single community, such as a central city; it has had little application across community boundaries. Similarly, most of the regional growth management programs are still too new, or are being implemented so slowly that they have had little impact to date. Where they have been in place for some time, such as in the Portland, Oregon, area, they appear to be having a positive impact on development in city and, possibly, distressed communities.

Strengths and Shortcomings

Approaches for overcoming economic distress would almost automatically resolve fiscal inequities and probably improve racial relations. Unfortunately, not enough experimentation has been pursued to assess the impact of linkage projects between rich and poor communities and regional growth management programs.

Potential

Although the balancing of regional development has considerable and critical potential, the pursuit of such initiatives is almost as difficult as sharing regional revenues.

Community leaders and citizens in rich communities are increasingly aware, however, that poor communities need to contribute to the regional economy if they, in turn, are to prosper. But they are generally unwilling to make investments if they believe that they will be at the expense of their own future development. Again, key to success of any initiative could be a few rounds of regional interdependence awareness education (see Equitable #1) to help convince community leaders and citizens that an investment in distressed communities pays economic and quality of life returns for poor, and rich, communities.

The greatest benefit for economically distressed communities might come from combining incentives for shared economic development between rich and poor communities with regional growth management programs. Such a combination also offers the potential to take advantage of opportunities that go beyond the capacity of individual communities and foster balanced development regionwide.

The components of this combination could include the following:

Fostering the development of rich-poor community linkage projects: As the supply of developable land shrinks in many rich communities, it continues to grow in many poor ones. As regions seriously consider establishing urban growth boundaries to channel development and keep transportation and other infrastructure costs from escalating further, it might make this supply of land even more valuable. Agreements could be negotiated that allowed rich communities to develop parcels in poor communities and share the resulting tax benefits. Even though these arrangements might work best between adjoining communities, they could also work between nonadjoining communities that have similar economic interests.

Providing the benefits of projects of regional significance to distressed communities : Projects of regional significance — such as major employment centers, shopping malls, or major sports and other installations — could be developed cooperatively among the impacted communities. The costs and benefits of these projects for poor and rich communities could be assessed to determine equitable distribution of tax revenues. Most of the tax revenues from these projects could be used to support public and other services in impacted communities, but some could be invested in other regional economic development projects that would benefit poor communities.

Shaping future growth to balance development of all communities regionwide: A regional growth management program could shape future development by negotiating regional agreements on transportation, environment, housing and land use; preparing regional growth strategies; and setting and enforcing urban growth boundaries. Such a regional growth management program could include strategies for shaping growth that use market incentives, such as Montgomery County, Maryland, which uses market incentives to discourage the development of agricultural land. The county government allows developers to buy development rights in one area, such as from farmers in an agricultural area, and use them to increase the density of development in another area, thereby protecting the agricultural area from further development. (Wallis, 1994, 40)

Existing regional economic development organizations could take the lead for individual linkage or regional significance projects. Or an existing or new organization could be designated to foster development of either or both types of projects, possibly modeled after the Southern California Regional Partnership, a public-private partnership created by the Southern California Association of Governments to develop new transportation technologies (see Service-Delivery #2, Chapter 7). In either case, the organization, or organizations, could conduct studies of the regional impact of particular developments and negotiate development linkage strategies among the appropriate rich and poor communities. It could begin with an infusion of seed funding and use part of the tax revenues resulting from successful developments to support future rounds of projects.

Finally, a regional growth management board could operate the regional growth management program, such as a regional planning council (see Problem-Solving #1, Chapter 7). It would need to be empowered by state government and administered by community leaders and citizens regionwide.

Contacts

- Local Initiatives Support Corporation, New York, New York, 212-455-9800
- The Enterprise Corporation, Columbia, Maryland, 410-964-1230
- Pittsburgh Partnership for Neighborhood Development, Pittsburgh, Pennsylvania, 412-471-3727
- Neighborhood Progress, Inc., Cleveland, Ohio, 216-268-6240
- Suburban Job-Link, Inc., Chicago, Illinois, 312-522-8700, 312-521-8226
- Southeastern Pennsylvania Transit Authority, Philadelphia, Pennsylvania, 215-580-7800

- Bridges-to-Work: Public-Private Ventures, Philadelphia, Pennsylvania, 215-557-4400
- San Diego Association of Governments, San Diego, California, 619-599-5305
- Southern California Regional Partnership: Southern California Association of Governments, Los Angeles, California, 213-236-1800

Equitable #4
Integrate Communities Regionwide

Just as sharing regional revenues and balancing regional development is critical to reversing the widening gap between rich and poor communities, integrating communities racially is critical to building effective working relationships to address the crosscutting challenges to regional economic competitiveness and quality of life.

Community leaders and citizens have considered and implemented various approaches.

Sharing leadership in regional decision-making mechanisms: Many regional problem-solving and service-delivery mechanisms have multiracial participation, but few have multiracial leadership that reflects the racial composition of the region. For example, the Richmond Renaissance has biracial leadership to help build bridges between the African-American and white populations in the community. Biracial leadership helps assure that both populations are involved and facilitates their participation in decision making.

Providing regional fair share housing: Although state court decisions and national legislation have established the principle of providing a "fair share" of affordable housing in every community, programs to facilitate equal access to housing regionwide are still mostly experimental.

The Hartford, Connecticut Department of Housing has placed more than 400 households, mostly African-American and Hispanic, in suburban housing projects. The suburban communities to which they relocated are more than 80 percent white and have an average poverty level of 7 percent compared to the city neighborhoods they left, which are 75 percent minority and have a poverty rate four times as high as that of the suburban communities. (Cisneros, 1995, 10-12) Similarly, Hillcrest Housing Services had provided low interest loans (up to $5,000 at 5 percent for 5 years) to help more than 100 minority families buy houses in six predominantly white suburban communities in the Cleveland, Ohio, region. Initial funding was provided by community foundations and private corporations; continuing funding is provided through the recycling of loan repayments. In addition to mortgage assistance, Hillcrest Housing Services helps homebuyers develop networks of support services in the communities.

On a larger scale, the Gautreaux program, sponsored by the Leadership Council for Metropolitan Open Communities, a court-appointed nonprofit corporation in the Chicago region, has offered vouchers to more than 5,600 inner city, mostly African-American, households to relocate over the past two decades. Approximately two-thirds have relocated into more than 115 suburban communities. The Council also offers moving assistance and counseling to relocating households. Follow-up studies indicate that "members of most households improved their living standards, level of employment, and school performance, and were satisfied with the move." (Downs, 108; Gurwitt, 1995, 21) Of the families moving to suburban locations, 64 percent of the mothers, many of whom were former welfare recipients, were working; 95 percent of the children were graduating from high school and 44 percent were moving on to higher education; and 75 percent of the youth were working. (Rusk, 1993, 114-5)

Some experimentation has also taken place in creating metropolitan housing commissions, authorities and coalitions. The Dayton/Montgomery County, Ohio, Housing Authority, funded with proceeds from a local option sales tax, finances affordable housing projects in suburban locations. Some of the public housing authorities have an almost metropolitan scope: the Albuquerque, New Mexico, Housing Authority facilitates pursuing a policy of small projects, no more than sixty units, that are economically mixed on scattered sites throughout the city. (Rusk, 116) In the Minneapolis/St. Paul area, more than 350 suburban churches have become part of a coalition to bring "fair share" housing to the suburbs. (Cisneros, 1995, 16)

State legislation requiring local governments to accept a "fair share" of affordable housing has been enacted in Connecticut and Massachusetts. Recent legislation in Minnesota, the "Metropolitan Livable Communities Act," offers financial incentives, such as cleaning up waste sites and subsidizing transit-oriented development, to communities that pursue affordable housing strategies. (*The Public Innovator*, 1996) Similar ordinances have been adopted by various communities, such as Tallahassee and Tampa. Montgomery County, Maryland, requires all new developments with 50 or more residential units to set aside at least 15 percent of the units for low and moderate income renters or buyers. In return, developers receive a bonus of 22 percent more housing units than is usually allowed by zoning. Up to 40 percent of the set-aside units may be purchased by the county's Housing Opportunities Commission and nonprofit organizations. Buyers of subsidized units are required to share any appreciation in value with the Housing Opportunities Commission if they sell their houses in the first ten years, to avoid any undue appreciation. More than 9,000 low and moderate income units have been provided by this policy, resulting in a county population that is more racially diverse, going from 92 percent white in 1970 to over 27 percent minority in 1990. (Cisneros, 1995, 17–19)

A recent study by the Urban Institute, *Housing Mobility: Promise or Illusion?*, reports on a range of housing mobility programs in various regions of the nation. (The Urban Institute)

Maintaining community integration: There has been some experimentation to maintain racial balance in communities, usually in more affluent suburban communities. The cities of Cleveland Heights and Shaker Heights offer low-interest mortgage assistance to both white and African-American families to maintain racial balance in these and other eastern suburban communities of the Cleveland area. Initial financing was provided by community foundations and private corporations; continued funding is provided through the recycling of loan repayments.

Accomplishments

Experimental programs to integrate communities appear to work.
- Poor, and mostly African-American, households participating in the Gautreaux program in the Chicago region found employment and pursued schooling at rates that mimic their suburban counterparts. A substantial proportion of the families qualified to move have not found housing, however, suggesting that the difficulty of locating suitable housing in unfamiliar communities might be a major impediment to mobility programs.

- Racial maintenance projects in the eastern suburbs of Cleveland, Ohio, appear to be succeeding at modest investments.
- Affordable housing units in Montgomery County, Maryland, have integrated the county and held their value. In fact, affordable housing units appreciated at a faster rate than market rate units in a study conducted by one of the developers.
- In a study in Albuquerque, New Mexico, students moving from public housing projects in poor neighborhoods to scattered-site housing units in middle class neighborhoods improved their third and fifth grade testing scores by 13 percentile points, in the same city and school district. (Rusk, Atlanta Regional Commission, 1995)

Strengths and Shortcomings

The major strength is that experiments in racial integration appear to succeed. The major shortcoming is that there is rarely the will of community leaders and citizens to pursue and sustain them. For example, the U.S. Department of Housing and Urban Development has launched a Moving to Opportunity for Fair Housing Demonstration Program that replicates many of the features of the Gautreaux program in Boston, Baltimore, Chicago, New York, and Los Angeles, but had its second year of funding canceled, in part due to opposition to the program in relocation neighborhoods. Even so, 1,300 vouchers will be made available, and control groups established, to test the impact of mobility programs on families and neighborhoods.

Potential

Although integrating communities regionwide has considerable potential, the will of community leaders and citizens to achieve it is uncertain. Again, the key to success for any initiative could be a few rounds of regional interdependence awareness education (see Equitable #1) to help convince community leaders and citizens that an investment in racial integration pays economic and quality of life returns for rich and poor communities.

And a reasonable investment could have a substantial impact. If only 5 percent of the new suburban housing units built in the 1980s had been set aside in the suburbs of the forty-four largest cities, 12.7 percent of poor city households could have moved to the suburbs; in thirteen of these regions, more than 30 percent could have moved to the suburbs. "Suburbs would not have to be overwhelmed by out-migrants from central cities to achieve significant reductions in the poor (and minority) populations of many central cities." (Downs, 110) This, of course, begs the question of what happens to distressed city neighborhoods, which need to continue to be the focus of targeted economic development efforts, but the resulting redistribution of population could facilitate their redevelopment and regional decision making.

Therefore, a major approach to integrating communities regionwide could be to take the narrow experiments and institutionalize them, regionally, including considering:

- establishing region-wide housing commissions, authorities and coalitions,
- requiring and providing affordable housing in all communities, mostly as part of new construction,
- offering open school enrollments across school district lines,
- monitoring racial change and providing low-interest mortgages and other strategies to maintain racial balance, and
- providing regional interdependence awareness programs for community leaders and citizens.

Contacts

- Richmond Renaissance, Richmond, Virginia, 804-644-0404
- Department of Housing, City of Hartford, Connecticut, 203-543-8640
- Gautreaux program: Leadership Council for Metropolitan Open Communities, Chicago, Illinois, 312-341-5678
- Dayton/Montgomery County Housing Authority, Dayton, Ohio, 513-224-0060
- Hillcrest Housing Services, Lyndhurst, Ohio, 216-691-9696
- Heights Fund, Cleveland Heights, Ohio, 216-291-5959

Chapter 6
Making Regional Governance Empowering: Regional Citizenship and Community

What both Democrats and Republicans fail to see is that the government and the market are not enough to make a civilization. There must àlso be a healthy, robust civic sector — a space in which the bonds of community can flourish. Government and the market are similar to two legs of a three-legged stool. Without the third leg of civil society, the stool is not stable and cannot provide support for a vital America.

— Senator Bill Bradley

Suburban sprawl has created regions of local communities that mimic the neighborhood rivalries created by the earlier expansion of central cities. Traditionally, these communities and neighborhoods have been fiercely independent and competitive, cooperating with their neighbors primarily when facing an overwhelming outside threat. Now even this sense of local community is being shattered by a combination of events.

To begin with, our sense of local community has been weakened by sprawl itself, making it very difficult to find community in the hodge-podge of employment centers, shopping malls, and multi-lane high-ways, or within the confines of arbitrary jurisdictional boundaries that place more importance on geography than people. Even worse, it has contributed to the decimation of central city neighborhoods, making it difficult to hold on to community amidst boarded-up and burned-out buildings.

The threats of economic upheaval and crime and violence have further discouraged building a sense of community, in central city as well as suburban communities, driving citizens into the private worlds of their own homes where they continue to be barraged by "drive-by debates" on radio and television talk shows. What's more, residents have lost faith in being able to overcome the "sour power" of special interests that seems to prevail in major decisions, regardless of the wishes of the general, and usually more passive, public. (Chesnut)

As a result, residents have all too often ceased to participate in community affairs or commit other acts of citizenship. Even worse, they may choose to participate in urban riots, which Mark Pisano, Director of the Southern California Association of Governments, calls the "voice of the unheard." (National Academy of Public Administration, 1993)

Another factor weakening our sense of local community has been the explosion of crosscutting challenges, ones that cannot be addressed, at least not successfully, by individual communities.

Many of these crosscutting challenges cannot even be addressed with neighbors but require the difficult process of involving and developing a new sense of community with unknown people from equally unknown parts of the region. (Gerston, 65) At times, these challenges are beginning to foster some regional thinking, such as the recent rise and fall of the Disney America theme park in the National Capital Region, and even some support for regional cooperation. Before the Disney America debate, most National Capital Region citizens primarily thought about the consequences of the location of the theme park; they tended to behave like NIMBYs (Not-In-My-Back-Yard). After the defeat of Disney America, they began to think about the regional implications of development; they began to behave like budding "regionalists." (Kristin Pauly, Governors State University RAP2000+ Idea Fair)

But we are still relatively ignorant about these regional challenges, much less about what to do about them, or we are reluctant to behave like regional citizens and leaders, in the unknown regional community. We know something about how to influence decisions at the most local level, such as whether to build a housing subdivision or block a highway. We know little about how to influence decisions at the regional level — how to scatter affordable housing, for instance, tie highways to transit systems, or shape regional growth.

This disenchantment with community does not appear to be diminishing our interest in becoming involved. More people claim to be volunteering than ever; a recent survey indicated that about half of the adult population, more than 89 million, volunteers an average of over four hours a week. Even so, the best hard evidence of regular volunteering shows a decline of 15 to 20 percent over the past three decades. Little of this volunteering might be in making decisions on the future of our communities, much less our regions. Our desire to volunteer, however, might offer a way to reconnect us with the political process. (Patterson/Kim, 228; Putnam, 1995)

Community and citizenship, therefore, need to be built anew at the regional level, as well as rebuilt at the local level, if regions are to be competitive and offer citizens a high quality of life. Citizenship and a sense of community are critical to creating "a parade for politicians to lead," according to Kristin Pauly of the Chesapeake Bay Foundation. Unless regional initiatives are rooted in the collaborative consensus of citizens, they are liable to be supported by little more that hot air.

Citizens and community leaders need to think of themselves as citizens of the region, as well as their neighborhoods and local communities, and invest in achieving governance excellence or what John Parr, former President of the National Civic League, calls creating a healthy civic infrastructure: "the formal and informal processes and networks through which communities make decisions and solve problems." (Parr, 93; Putnam, 1995)

Robert Putnam, whose report on the experiences of creating regional governments in Italy was presented in Strategic #1, Chapter 3, uses the term social capital to make the same point.

Regions that invest in the social capital required to achieve coordinated actions, he writes, reap returns in more productive economies and a higher quality of life.

...social capital, as embodied in horizontal networks of civic engagement, bolsters the performance of the polity and the economy, rather than the reverse: Strong society, strong economy; strong society, strong state." Participating in parent teacher organizations is as critical to making schools work as raising teacher salaries; knowing one's neighbors is as critical to crime control as hiring additional police officers; even trusting one's co-workers is critical to building competitive businesses in the global economy. (Putnam, *Making Democracy Work*, 176; Putnam, 1995)

The stock of a region's social capital is determined by the capacity of the region's norms of reciprocity and networks of civic engagement to develop, together, the social trust required by citizens to undertake "coordinated actions." Social capital is like the "Powdermilk Biscuits" of regional decision making, to borrow an image from Garrison Keillor; it gives citizens "the strength to do the [regional] things that they know they need to do." (Keillor)

Norms of reciprocity and networks of civic engagement are forged by the interactions of citizens over time. In ancient Rome, Cicero stressed the importance of the norm of generalized reciprocity, "There is no duty more indispensable than that of returning a kindness. All men distrust one forgetful of a benefit." For example, cutting one's grass or voting can be an important norm of community; if one does either, regularly, one can be accepted; if one neglects either, one can become an outcast. Regrettably, the grass cutting norm is often more important than the voting norm. The more established and practiced the norms, especially surrounding the values that guide decision making, the more social capital a community has to invest.

Similarly, networks of civic engagement, especially those that are primarily horizontal — such as the social clubs, sports teams, singing groups, community associations, cooperatives, intercommunity associations, and citizen-based parties of Italy — contribute to the stock of social capital by:
- fostering robust norms of reciprocity,
- punishing violators of norms of reciprocity,
- facilitating communication and improving the flow of community information, such as to perceive threats and recognize common opportunities, and

- embodying past success at collaboratively mobilizing resources and providing the template for future cooperation. (Putnam, *Making Democracy Work*, 171–174)

In contrast, vertical networks of civic engagement, such as patron-client organizations or rigid business or government hierarchies, cannot develop social trust and cooperation primarily because information flows are less reliable than those of horizontal networks and the sanctions for violators of norms are less likely to flow up. Putnam also argues that strong interpersonal ties (kinship, intimate friendship, even family) are less important than weak ties (acquaintanceship and shared membership in associations), since the latter reach across social cleavages and help participants solve dilemmas of collective action, and build social capital. (Putnam, *Making Democracy Work*, 174–175)

Putnam's comments are especially applicable to the regional community. Regional norms of reciprocity are established across a wide range of intercommunity and regionwide interactions, from the mutual aid agreements covering police, fire and emergency medical services to regional marketing networks. They are also established by the way communities involve each other in their deliberations on policies, practices, programs and actions that have an impact on their neighbors, such as zoning, transportation and economic development decisions. Horizontal networks of civic engagement include many of the same types of organizations active in the Italian regions, as well as our own variations, such as sports leagues, singing groups, intercommunity symphonies, parent-teacher organizations and regional civic organizations (see Problem-Solving #4, Chapter 7).

Unfortunately, too few regional norms of reciprocity and networks of civic engagement — and therefore stock of social capital — are formed among and "connect" people from widely different, rich and poor, communities, or regionwide, often because of geographic dispersion or the lack of regional citizen-based organizations. As a result, we fail to develop a civic culture of connectedness and trust and learn Jane Jacobs' "first fundamental of successful city life":

> People must take a modicum of public responsibility for each other even if they have no ties to each other. This is a lesson that nobody learns by being told. It is learned from the experience of having

other people without ties of kinship or close friendship or formal responsibility take a modicum of public responsibility for you. (Jacobs, 82)

Putnam sums up the need for this bridging social capital:

> In some respects, the most important single problem facing our country today is the absence of bridging social capital — that is, the absence of connections, friendships or bowling league partnerships or whatever, that cross racial and social class lines." (Putnam, 1995)
> Building social capital will not be easy, but it is the key to making democracy work. (Putnam, 1993, 177-185)

Regrettably, the polarized politics of the past few decades have diminished our social capital just as our civic infrastructure is facing heavier "decision loads."

E. J. Dionne argues that the Sixties Left and Eighties Right created a "false polarization" that has poorly prepared community leaders and citizens for finding the political center critical to solving problems:

> The Sixties Left and Eighties Right had far more in common than either realized. If they shared a virtue, it was their mutual, if differently expressed, hope that politics could find ways of liberating the potential of individuals and fostering benevolent communities.... Americans yearn simultaneously for untrammeled personal liberty and a strong sense of community that allows burdens and benefits to be shared fairly and willingly, apportioned through democratic decisions. (Dionne, 329)

Dionne argues that the elevated aspirations of both groups left the American middle class feeling cheated. It diverted community leaders and citizens from addressing the practical concerns of the electorate as well as the serious challenges facing them, such as economic competition. He believes that community leaders and citizens lost all sense of the public good and concluded that politics is no longer a deliberative process through which people resolve disputes, find remedies and move forward. He harkens back to President Franklin Delano Roosevelt's New Deal which was able to motivate citizens by enlightened self-interest, not altruism, and by capturing the American imagination for supporting a "great act of civic inclusion." (Dionne, 338, 355)

Alvin and Heidi Toffler argue that the future will present community leaders and citizens with increasingly heavier "decision loads," making wider community leader and citizen participation in new forms of decision making a necessity, not a nicety:

> The creation of new political structures will not come in a single climatic upheaval but as a consequence of a thousand innovations and collisions at many levels in many places over a period of decades... Elites, no matter how enlightened, cannot by themselves make a new civilization. The energies of whole peoples will be required... (Toffler, 1995, 105-8)

In sum, developing regional citizenship and sense of community builds the social capital critical to addressing crosscutting challenges.

General guidelines for developing regional citizenship and sense of community, for making regional governance empowering, could include:

Define the attributes or ingredients of regional citizenship and sense of community. We could possibly draw upon those ingredients suggested for building community by John Gardner:
- wholeness incorporating diversity
- a reasonable base of shared values
- caring, trust and teamwork
- effective internal communications
- affirmation, confidence in itself
- links beyond the community, especially across rich and poor communities: "The sound community has seemingly contradictory responsibilities: it must defend itself from the forces in the outside environment that undermine its integrity, yet it must maintain open, constructive, and extensive relations with the world beyond its boundaries." (Gardner, 1991, 24)
- development of young people, especially the citizenship of children, the inheritors and, according to Lewis Thomas, the potential

shapers of the region: "The long period of childhood is not just a time of fragile immaturity and vulnerability, not just a phase of development to be got through before the real show of humanity emerges onstage. It is the time when the human brain can set to work on language, on taste, on poetry and music, with centers at its disposal that may not be available later in life. If we did not have childhood, and were able to leap catlike from infancy to adulthood, I doubt very much that we would turn out human." For example, Thomas speculates that children invented language, based on looking at earliest languages and comparing them to children's language as well as nursery rhymes which have a remarkable similarity across languages. (Thomas, Lewis, 174)

- a forward view
- institutional arrangements for community maintenance (Gardner, 1991, 24)

Some organizations are beginning to develop tools for assessing regional citizenship and community. One such tool is the Civic Index (Strategic #2) developed by the National Civic League. Another, a "social capital index" to measure the state of "connectedness" in regional communities, is being developed by the Institute of Portland Metropolitan Studies.

Focus on people, not geography (a collection of boundaries on a map) or things (the roads and bridges, airports, sewer and water lines). (Foster-Bey, National Academy of Public Administration conference) (Cisneros, 1995, 8-9)

Develop the capacity of citizens to act out of enlightened self-interest in pursuit of regional betterment. Anthony Downs, in referring to the tensions created by the economic impetus towards interdependence and the social and political impetus towards smaller groups, suggests:

> The ultimate solution to this dilemma involves convincing the members of each metropolitan locality, especially nonpoor suburban members, that the interests they share with all parts of their metropolitan area are more important to their long-rum welfare

than the conflicting interests they more easily perceive. (Downs, 204)

Encourage a "community-out" *and* a "bottom-up" approach to developing regional community and citizenship. Reinforcing this guideline are John Parr, John Gardner, and President Bill Clinton.

The key component of creating a healthy civic infrastructure or investing in social capital has to be an employment strategy that starts from the bottom up and not the top down. (Parr, 100)

The diverse, sometimes, extremely hostile, elements must learn the arts of communicating across boundaries and building consensus. The basic rules are that each group must be respected, and each group must reach back toward the whole community. (Gardner, 1994, 377)

There must be more responsibility for all of our citizens...A lot of our people don't have the time or the emotional stress, they think, to do the work of citizenship....For years we've mostly treated citizens like they were consumers or spectators, sort of political couch potatoes who were supposed to watch the TV ads, either promise them something for nothing or play on their fears and frustrations....But the truth is, we have got to stop seeing each other as enemies just because we have different views...We simply cannot wait for a tornado, a fire, or a flood to behave in dealing with one another. (Clinton)

Provide citizens with the tools to be effective regional citizens. Sherry Arnstein differentiates various forms of citizen involvement in a "ladder of citizen participation." Her ladder has two levels of nonparticipation — manipulation and therapy; three levels of tokenism — informing, consultation and placation; and three levels of citizen power — partnership, delegated power and citizen control.

Ethan Seltzer, Director of the Institute of Portland Metropolitan Studies, has modified Arnsteins's ladder to suggest a "ladder of metropolitan interaction."

At the bottom is isolation, where organizations proceed with little attention to neighbors or potential partners, and the firm belief that all forces can be held accountable at the local or organizational level.

Next comes communication, marked by a willingness to let others know what they plan to do, and an awareness that others are taking action or addressing an issue of common interest.

The third rung is coordination, where organizations begin to move beyond largely ceremonial communication to more functional interactions that synchronize actions in time or results in space.

A more fundamental merger of interests occurs at the fourth level of collaboration, where individuals recognize the taking action together, making several actions into one, can make it possible to achieve individual objectives more efficiently, leveraging more out of the same net level of effort expended through coordination.

Finally, partnership, is the fifth rung, marked by the development of common objectives and a true merger of interests. Here responsibility for the outcome, good or bad, is assigned to the partnership rather than to the individual collaborators.

Regional citizens need to be primarily provided the tools to be involved in the citizen power, and especially partnership, mechanisms of regional decision making. (Arnstein, 216-24; Conner, Desmond; Henderson; Seltzer, 11)

Present regional challenges in language understood by community leaders and citizens. Regional challenges need to be explained to community leaders and citizens in "concrete, household-scale ways," according to Henry Richmond, founder of the National Growth Management Leadership Project. He illustrates with the example of sprawl and the need to explain:

Why sprawl is not economic development, but, instead, often simply a process of moving assets around in a region, exchanging economic abandonment in one part of the region for advantage in another — why sprawl is not the unalterable result of market forces, but, instead, caused largely by a highly fragmented local government structure supercharged by the local implementation of a mass of uncoordinated state and federal programs — everything from building highways to insuring mortgages for single-family homes. Together, these policies foster, if not compel, the development patterns we have. (Richmond, 2)

Develop regional leadership and followership. In an editorial in *Time* magazine, Lance Morrow speaks to the types of leaders needed today:

> The sort of leader needed today is the kind who can assume a reasonable well-educated and informed electorate but help it sort through the inundations of information and opinion (much of it corrupt, self-serving, pseudo-moral) towards solutions. Americans need leaders who will not so much enforce a vision (though visions remain indispensable) as lead people to understanding the problems they face together and the costs and effort necessary to solve them — the changes in behavior and attitude, sometimes the sacrifices, and above all the need to think and adapt. The key to leadership now is to get Americans to act in concert and take responsibility for the courses that they have set for themselves. (Morrow)

Robert Kelley, in *The Power of Followership,* calls for exemplary followers, the individuals who actually contribute more than 80 percent of the success of any initiative:

> On one hand, they (exemplary followers) exercise independent, critical thinking, separate from the leader or the group. Leaders and co-workers describe them as 'thinking for themselves'. They 'are their own persons,' they are 'innovative and creative,' 'give constructive criticism,' and 'are willing to stand up to leaders.'
> On the other hand, exemplary followers are actively engaged, applying their talents for the benefit of the organization [or region] even when confronted with bureaucratic inanities and nonproducing co-workers. It is said that they 'take initiative,' 'assume ownership,' 'support team and leader,' 'are extremely competent,' and 'go above and beyond the job.' (Kelley, 126–127)

Regional governance excellence demands community leaders and citizens that evidence exemplary leadership and followership traits.

In sum, we need to build regional citizenship to help citizens overcome their alienation and anger and become stewards of the regional community. To paraphrase two old sayings: whereas "all politics might still be local," it is going to "take an entire (regional) community to address a crosscutting (common) challenge."

Initiatives for Making Regional Governance Empowering

How can we develop our individual regional citizenship and create an overall sense of regional community that enables us to govern together regionwide?

The initiatives for Making Regional Governance Empowering are:
- Empowering #1: Develop regional citizenship skills
- Empowering #2: Disseminate regional governance information

    In addition, the Prominent initiatives in Chapter 3 complement Empowering #1 and #2.
- Empowering #3: Establish regional community identity
- Empowering #4: Forge a city/suburb regional constituency (new)
- Empowering #5: Empower citizen standing in regional decision making
- Empowering #6: Establish regional problem-solving centers (new)
- Empowering #7: Develop a regional citizens charter (new)

    In addition, Problem-Solving #4 in Chapter 7 (citizen regional problem-solving mechanisms) complements the Empowering initiatives.

Community leaders and citizens could initiate the process for making regional governance empowering by developing the regional citizenship skills of citizens (Empowering #1) and providing them with regional governance information (Empowering #2). Then they could launch one or more of the remaining five initiatives (Empowering #3 through #7) to make regional governance empowering.

The performance of the Empowering initiatives in pursuing regional governance excellence can be assessed by answering several questions. Does implementing the Empowering initiatives result in:

- enabling citizen interaction across communities and regionwide?
- empowering citizen involvement in regional decision making?
- building regional citizenship and a sense of regional community?

Empowering #1
Develop Regional Citizenship Skills

Developing the regional leadership, followership and overall citizenship skills of community leaders and citizens prepares them to become involved in regional decision making.

Most of the current regional efforts are directed at developing the leadership skills of emerging and already recognized community leaders (through leadership and visitation programs) although new experiments are being conducted in developing citizenship skills through national efforts such as the Kettering Foundation, the Civic Network Television, and the Center for Living Democracy.

Community leadership programs, especially those with a regional orientation, can help develop the skills of emerging community leaders and citizens and prepare them to become involved in regional decision-making mechanisms. Community leadership programs are offered in the central cities, as well as some of the suburbs, of many regions. Most are year-long, day-a-month programs, that often begin or end with an overnight retreat. Some also require teams of participants to analyze community issues during the program.

Some of these leadership programs have taken on a more regional flavor over the years, and in a few regions, separate regional leadership programs have been offered to focus on regional challenges and prepare leaders to serve on regional organizations. Participants in the regional leadership programs are recruited from all parts of the region and often include alumni of the community leadership programs. Graduates of the regional leadership programs are tapped to serve on regional organizations or otherwise participate in developing regional initiatives.

The Leadership Miami Valley program, offered in the Dayton, Ohio, region by the Dayton Area Chamber of Commerce, provides an example of this kind of leadership program. Following an overnight retreat, participants visit each of the counties in the region in successive months. Participants from the host county help plan the itinerary and topics to be discussed for the visits. The Triad Leadership Network program, offered in the Greensboro/Winston-Salem/High Point region of North Carolina by the Piedmont Triad Partnership, also begins with an overnight retreat and devotes a day-a-month to particular regional challenges.

In another approach, individuals tapped to serve on regional organizations, who have not been through a leadership program or are new to the region, are offered an intensive orientation to help them become effective regional leaders. For example, leaders in the Atlanta region participate in a week-long regional leadership program, called the Regional Leadership Institute, that is offered by the Atlanta Regional Commission, a regional planning council, and the Metro Business Forum, a consortium of the chambers of commerce throughout the region.

Graduates of many leadership programs also participate in alumni groups to maintain contact with each other and sponsor joint activities. Alumni of the Regional Leadership Institute in the Atlanta (Georgia) region, for example, have formed the Regional Leadership Foundation which sponsors a regional newspaper, *The Region Dialogue,* and forums on timely topics facing the region, such as the 1996 Olympics.

Leadership training for particular types of leaders and professional staff also touches on regional citizenship. In the Pittsburgh area, for example, the Local Government Academy offers an intensive orientation for newly elected officials as well as seminars on timely regional challenges for appointed and elected officials. The Allegheny County Community College offers periodic courses on participating in community organizations. Regional citizenship training is being considered in elementary and high schools in the Philadelphia region. (Hershberg, 1994 National Civic League Conference) Finally, some national training programs, such as for city managers and chamber of commerce executives, help develop the skills of professionals involved in regional decision-making mechanisms.

Regional visitation programs offer another approach to develop regional leadership skills. In these programs, delegations of a few dozen to scores of leaders from one region visit another for an intensive two to three day visit. The visits bring community leaders together for a couple of days, to share mutual concerns with community leaders in another region, and to "beg, borrow, or steal" good ideas that might have application at home. These visitations are annual events for a number of communities and are often organized by chambers of commerce or leadership program alumni. As a variation on regional visitation programs, delegations in a couple of regions are visiting themselves for a couple of days, following the same type of process, to better understand and solicit good ideas from community leaders and citizens.

Finally, a few citizenship skills development programs are being offered by national foundations and academic institutions. For example, the Kettering Foundation sponsors National Issues Forums, public dialogues that "bring back the tradition of the town meeting in which each member of the community has an opportunity to contribute to the discussion of important issues." Each year, it prepares discussion materials on three issues of citizen concern and works with various academic institutions to train citizens on conducting National Issues Forums. (Center for School Study Councils)

Videoconferencing is beginning to be used to develop the community building skills of community leaders across the country. The Civic Network Television(CNT), a satellite-delivered training and information network, is attempting to create an interconnected set of learning centers throughout the regions of the country. Its first two series of programs, on community building and regional collaboration, are being offered in approximately fifty regions to several thousand participants. Tuition is $285 per person up to the first 20 persons or approximately $5,700 per site. CNT anticipates offering new series on other related topics, as well as developing materials for unique audiences or organizing electronic town meetings on timely topics. According to Ralph Widner, its director, CNT wants to become a "talent fire house" that can be quickly accessed online to address particular community and regional challenges. (Widner, 1994 National Civic League conference)

Finally, various national organizations develop training materials for citizenship programs. The Public Broadcasting System series, *The American Promise,* provides excellent examples of citizens coming together to address crosscutting challenges. The Center for Living Democracy has developed an excellent guide, entitled *The Quickening of America,* on mastering the ten arts of democracy:

- active listening: encouraging the speaker and searching for meaning,
- creative conflict: confronting others in ways that produce growth,
- mediation: facilitating interaction to help people in conflict hear each other,
- negotiation: problem-solving that meets some key interests of all involved,
- political imagination: reimaging our futures according to our values,
- public dialogue: public talk on matters that concern us all,
- public judgment: public decision making that allows citizens to make choices they are willing to help implement,
- celebration and appreciation: expressing joy and appreciation for what we learn as well as what we achieve,
- evaluation and reflection: assessing and incorporating the lessons we learn through action, and
- mentoring: supportively guiding others to learn these arts of public life. (Lappé, 239)

Accomplishments

Regional, and some community, leadership programs help develop the regional citizenship skills of emerging community leaders, especially if they graduate into a leadership position in a regional organization. National organizations, such as the Kettering Foundation and the Center for Living Democracy, are beginning to offer materials that can be used in more broadly based regional citizenship programs. Video-conferencing is beginning to offer targeted community-building training to community leaders, interactively and nationally.

Strengths and Shortcomings

The major strength of regional leadership programs is their preparation of emerging leaders to assume leadership positions in regional organizations. The major shortcoming is their focus on a select few leaders and offering little followership or citizenship skills for citizens at large.

Potential

The future potential for developing regional citizenship skills is almost unlimited. It could include several approaches.

Expanding the curriculum of regional leadership programs to include followership and citizenship: Robert Kelley suggests a followership perspective in *The Power of Followership* that could be added to leadership programs. In addition, the materials developed for regional interdependence awareness education seminars (see Equitable #1, Chapter 5) could be incorporated into citizenship training to expose participants to the special challenges of fiscal, economic, and racial disparities. Most important, the curriculum could focus on the basic questions of regional citizenship:

- What is the regional community, in terms of people, geography and interests? How have the characteristics of the regional community changed over time? How might the characteristics change in the future?
- How well does the regional community cooperate and make decisions? What is the state of its regional civic infrastructure, its stock of social capital to strengthen regional decision making?
- What are the rights and responsibilities of regional citizenship and how is that similar to or different from local citizenship?
- How can one exercise his or her regional citizenship? What skills does one need to develop? How does one develop his or her regional citizenship skills?
- How can one help build regional community? What are the regional norms of reciprocity and the regional decision-making processes and mechanisms?

Offering regional citizenship skills programs to a broader audience: In addition to expanding the curriculum, these emerging regional citizenship programs could be offered to a wider cross-section of citizens. One-day, one-evening- or one-weekend-a-month, up to year-long programs, could be offered to selected citizens from throughout the region, possibly with an emphasis on ones who have been involved in citizen-based organizations. Other approaches could be used as well, such as by offering special courses at community colleges or videoconferences for community organizations. Maybe a special training academy could be established to focus on providing regional citizenship education.

Most important, regional citizenship programs could be offered to young people, the inheritors of the region. For example, the participants in the Vision 2020 strategic planning process in the Atlanta region have committed to implementing a "Passport to the Atlanta Region" program to teach youth about the Atlanta region, including News for Kids, a special news section in the *Atlanta Journal Constitution; Access Atlanta,* online local news and information; and VOX, a regional student newspaper as well as classroom instruction. Other programs have been initiated to develop the citizenship skills of youth, including Networking for Youth, a collaborative mentoring program in Eugene, Oregon; Build Peoria, which offers education, job-readiness skills, short-term jobs and job training for at-risk teenagers in Peoria, Illinois; and St. Louis KidsPlace, which brings groups of young people together with community leaders to discuss youth concerns. (Kemmis, 1995, 35–49)

Graduates could be recruited to participate in regional decision-making mechanisms, especially citizen-based ones, such as regional civic organizations (see Problem-Solving #4, Chapter 7), or to help design and implement public involvement activities for particular decision-making processes.

Providing follow-up training and support to develop the skills of regional governance "pioneers:" General regional citizenship programs could provide an initial orientation to regional citizenship, but follow-up efforts could help hone the skills of citizens to participate in particular regional governance mechanisms or decision-making processes. Graduates of the basic program could move on to advanced training in becoming regional governance "pioneers" — regional entrepreneurs who could instigate regional problem-solving processes, regional wizards who could facilitate or staff such processes, or regional champions who could build support for such processes.

Other approaches to providing follow-up training and support could include initiating:
* Regional mentoring programs to pair up individuals in regional citizenship programs with seasoned regional "pioneers" who could counsel them on practicing regional citizenship. Graduates of the

basic or advanced citizenship programs could become mentors for the next "class" of regional "pioneers."

- Regional user groups of similarly skilled individuals to share experiences and receive guidance from skilled "pioneers" on making regional decision-making processes work.

- Regional exchange or service corps similar to the National Service Corps, to develop the regional citizenship skills of individuals and provide support for regional organizations. A regional exchange program could focus on exchanging residents of rich and poor communities to assist in developing collaborative efforts; a regional service corps could operate similar to the National Service Corps and assign individuals to work in regional organizations for up to a year on a part- or full-time basis.

- Regional citizenship guides to help community leaders and citizens become involved in addressing regional challenges. A guide could be developed on things to do before complaining to a regional organization, such as gather facts, talk to neighbors, and identify solutions.

- A regional game to give community leaders and citizens an opportunity to participate in interactive simulations of regional challenges. A regional game could be modeled after the World Game, which uses a basketball-court-size map and props symbolizing resources to allow participants to trade resources, negotiate treaties and develop strategies to address global challenges.

Contacts

- Leadership Miami Valley: Dayton Area Chamber of Commerce, Dayton, Ohio, 513-226-8231
- Triad Leadership Network: Piedmont Triad Partnership, Greensboro, North Carolina, 910-668-4556, 800-669-4556
- Regional Leadership Institute: Atlanta Regional Commission, Atlanta, Georgia, 404-364-2610
- Local Government Academy, Pittsburgh, Pennsylvania, 412-322-2626
- Regional visitation programs: Community leaders in Denver, Nashville, Portland, and Seattle conduct regular visitations to other regions.

- Kettering Foundation, Dayton, Ohio, 513-434-7300
- Public Policy Institute, Center for School Study Councils, University of Pennsylvania, 215-898-7371
- Civic Network Television, Washington, D.C., 202-457-5353, 703-960-9626
- The American Promise: KQED, Los Angeles, California, 800-204-7722
- Passport to the Atlanta Region: Atlanta Regional Commission, Atlanta, Georgia, 404-363-2500
- World Game: World Game Institute, Philadelphia, Pennsylvania, 215-387-0220

Empowering #2
Disseminate Regional Governance Information

Regional governance information is critical to graduates of regional citizenship programs as well as other community leaders and citizens participating in activities to make regional decision making prominent, strategic, equitable, empowering and institutionalized.

The Institute of Portland Metropolitan Studies at Portland State University is developing a number of "tools" for providing regional governance information to "potential collaborators and partners," its term for community leaders and citizens. These tools include:

- A Metropolitan Clearinghouse to "alert a wide range of organizations to others sharing the same interest, and to provide a consistent point for information and referral." It collects reports, studies, policy documents and papers, indexes and abstracts them, publishes the results semiannually in *Metropolitan Clearinghouse Abstracts,* and distributes copies to jurisdictions, planners, faculty and elected officials. The Abstracts also include short features on timely regional issues.

- A Metropolitan Briefing Book to "better acquaint decisionmakers with the region, and to help them literally locate their interests relative to others." It includes a list of critical metropolitan issues, based on public opinion and community leader surveys; essays on demographic trends and the economy of the region; and maps showing concentrations of poverty, income, age distribution, racial and ethnic communities and trends for communities. It is mailed to elected officials and civic and business leaders and will be updated periodically.

- *Metroscape,* a newsletter intended to "be an accessible chronicle of metropolitan cultural, political, economic, and social interaction, past, present and future...to make the notion of 'metropolitan' strategically useful to residents and decisionmakers." The first issue has been developed and the feasibility of making it a business enterprise is being assessed.

- Metropolitan Newsnet to use "telecommunications technologies to promote interjurisdictional collaboration." The Institute has established a pilot on-line service but technological difficulties have brought the project to a halt. (Seltzer)

These four tools echo experimentation that is taking place nationally. The Center for Greater Philadelphia at the University of Pennsylvania, for example, prepared a Regional Network Directory, which provides background on the importance of regional cooperation, a listing of regional organizations and their purposes, and a listing of regional initiatives organized by topic. Most regional planning organizations maintain regional databases of census and other information and many highlight this information in reports or newsletters that are circulated to local governments and other organizations. Some regional decision-making mechanisms are tracking information in competitive or comparable regions and provide periodic "benchmarking" reports that include regional governance mechanisms being considered or implemented in the sample of regions.

A number of community and regional organizations are experimenting with electronic data bases, which have the potential to deliver instant regional governance information to citizens. A number of local governments provide electronic kiosks, sometimes called 24-hour city halls in government buildings and other prominent locations, such as libraries and shopping malls. Users can almost always obtain information on local government services and calendars of upcoming community events and guidance on applying for licenses and permits. Sometimes they can access information on the history of the community and timely community topics or opportunities for participating in community decision making or volunteering in community organizations. In some cases they might have the opportunity to ask questions for on-line or later responses by government employees or volunteers. Finally, users can often access other data bases through the Internet.

The Mercer Island, Washington, city government sponsors INFO/isle (Krupp-Wilmeth); Santa Monica, California, city government sponsors the Public Electronic Network (Lappé, 127–128); and Unigov (the Consolidated Government of Indianapolis and Marion County, Indiana) sponsors CivicLink (Government Technology, 18). A Colorado Springs, Colorado, resident has established sixty-five bulletin boards to connect people who have common interests. The bulletin boards also provide pending city government ordinances for callers to download, rewrite, and upload for others to review. (Lappé, 127–128) In Cupertino, California, residents can use their home computers to send electronic messages to the city council during a meeting. (International City/County Management Association *Newsletter,* July 10, 1995)

In another example, the California Secretary of State and the League of Women Voters' Education Fund have been experimenting with on-line information on candidates for elected office and ballot propositions. In the California demonstration, up to 15,000 requests were received daily before the November 1994 elections. (*The Public Innovator,* "The Dawn of CyberPolitics"). Various community-based electronic data bases also have the potential to provide information on regional governance, such as FreeNet in the Cleveland area.

Periodic regional governance symposia, similar to those described in Prominent #2, Chapter 3, offer another approach for regularly providing timely information on regional governance to citizens and community leaders.

Some of these symposia are specifically directed at the public, such as the recent Citizens Summit on Regional Transit sponsored by the Institute for Public Policy and Management at the University of Washington and the Municipal League of Seattle-King County. The Summit was preceded by a survey of the more than 500 participants, the responses to which were shared at the day-long summit. The results of the workshop and plenary sessions at the summit were summarized in a report that was provided to participants and a regional planning committee examining regional transit. The participant registration fee (including lunch) was only ten dollars, thanks to foundation support. (Dodge, Interstate Study Commission, 1994, 31)

Some of these symposia are specifically directed at volunteers, many of whom are citizens. For example, the Federation for Community Planning in the Cleveland region holds an annual health and human services institute that attracts hundreds of volunteers to address specific regional challenges. Based on the discussions in these workshops, task forces are established to design and oversee the implementation of various initiatives, such as the establishment of an affordable housing trust fund. (Wallis, 1994, 29)

Accomplishments

The experiments in providing citizens and community leaders with information on governance have been positive, as measured by the use of electronic data bases and the participation in citizens summits. Some reservations have been raised about whether electronic data bases might discourage personal interaction, that the Internet might be an information highway not unlike the ones for cars that separate us. Computer information networks might make it unnecessary to learn how to communicate; what's more, they can't "download" the capacity to connect and could create a "silicon curtain" between citizens with and without the resources to own computers. What is most regrettable, however, is that few experiments on disseminating regional governance information have been undertaken, and most of them have not been institutionalized long enough to assess their ongoing usefulness to citizens and community leaders.

Strengths and Shortcomings

The major strength of providing residents with regional governance information is that it responds to and supports their understanding of regional challenges and fosters their regional citizenship. The major shortcoming is the difficulty in institutionalizing the capacity to provide continuing information on a timely basis.

Potential

The potential of providing regional governance information to citizens and community leaders is unlimited, in any of the current forms — clearinghouses, newsletters, electronic databases, seminars, etc. — or potential new ones — such as accessing "mailing lists" and "home pages" on the Internet or using videoconferencing or interactive television to not only provide information but facilitate dialogue with citizens and even poll their attitudes on approaches to dealing with timely regional topics. Just as some communities are now referring to themselves as electronic villages capable of providing information electronically and interactively to all citizens, some regions will probably do likewise before the turn of the century.

The major challenge appears to be to create enough of a critical mass to launch and sustain these activities. A couple of approaches might help.

One would be to designate an existing regional organization to design and implement the tools for providing regional governance information to citizens and community leaders. An academic public research institute (see Problem-Solving #3, Chapter 7), regional planning council (see Problem-Solving #1, Chapter 7), or regional civic organization (see Problem-Solving #4, Chapter 7) could assume this responsibility. Ad hoc efforts to provide such information appear to have extremely short half-lives. Finding or creating a home for these tools might be the critical threshold step in providing such information.

Another approach would be to develop a business plan for sustaining the existence of tools for providing regional governance information. Equally critically, it appears that considerable thought needs to be given to sustaining these efforts before launching them. Whereas it might be possible to secure "seed" funding, initially, from foundations and others, a reliable group of paying clients is probably critical to the ongoing dissemination of regional governance information. A business plan could test the potential marketplace, from determining how much organizations or individual citizens would pay for what kinds of regional governance information in what types of formats.

A third approach would be to establish state or national regional governance clearinghouses to support regional efforts. The International City/County Management Association and the National Association of Regional Councils are considering establishing regional governance clearinghouses. These, or other state and national efforts, possibly with foundation support, could also disseminate technical and financial assistance in designing, financing, and operating regional governance clearinghouses and other tools to provide regional governance information to citizens and community leaders. State or national clearinghouses could provide assistance in networking regional databases so as to facilitate making regional comparisons or generating national information on the state of regional governance (see State-National #7, Chapter 8).

Contacts

- Institute of Portland Metropolitan Studies, Portland State University, Portland, Oregon, 503-725-5170
- Center for Greater Philadelphia, University of Pennsylvania, 215-898-8713
- INFO/isle: City of Mercer Island, Washington, 206-236-5300
- CivicLink: Unigov, Indianapolis, Indiana, 317-327-3141
- Municipal League of Seattle-King County, Seattle, Washington, 206-622-8333
- Federation for Community Planning, Cleveland, Ohio, 216-781-2944, 216-249-9644

Empowering #3
Establish Regional Community Identity

Regional identity programs are directed at making the region better known and appreciated by community leaders and citizens.

It is ironic that most of the existing regional identity programs are directed at making the region better known outside the region, both in this country and abroad. These are the marketing campaigns coordinated by chambers of commerce and public-private partnerships to promote the region's products or to attract new businesses to the region (see Problem-Solving #2, Chapter 7). They use a combination of strategies, including producing written materials and videotapes that tout the region's products and advantages, attending and sponsoring trade shows, sending individual "ambassadors" and trade delegations to other regions, developing regional networks of economic development organizations to respond to potential prospects, and establishing electronic databases on the Internet. Regrettably, very little of this material is used *within* the region to educate community leaders and citizens.

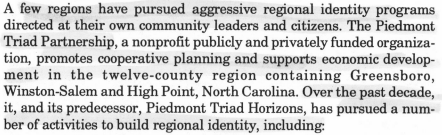

A few regions have pursued aggressive regional identity programs directed at their own community leaders and citizens. The Piedmont Triad Partnership, a nonprofit publicly and privately funded organization, promotes cooperative planning and supports economic development in the twelve-county region containing Greensboro, Winston-Salem and High Point, North Carolina. Over the past decade, it, and its predecessor, Piedmont Triad Horizons, has pursued a number of activities to build regional identity, including:

- a regional postmark, "North Carolina's Piedmont Triad. We deliver opportunities;"
- signs in communities, identifying them as Piedmont Triad communities;
- local toll-free dialing among telephone area codes in the region;
- a regional tourist service, including regional maps, promotional items and souvenirs;
- license plates with the Piedmont Triad logo;
- regional real estate listing guides and telephone yellow pages;

- a regional information system, including brochures and videos on various topics;
- leadership development programs for current and emerging community leaders;
- a periodic newsletter on regional activities; and
- an annual meeting to report, informally, on the state of the region.

Other regions have taken similar actions to establish regional identity, including distributing satellite photographs of the region or maps of the region in the form of a puzzle with the label, "It all fits together, so let's work together."

Accomplishments

The Piedmont Triad Partnership has helped establish a regional identity among community leaders and citizens in the Greensboro/Winston-Salem/High Point area. Its regional identity activities have facilitated developing cooperative strategies for pursuing economic development opportunities as well as building partnerships for addressing crosscutting threats, and they have helped generate participation in, and support for, developing a regional economic development plan.

Strengths and Shortcomings

The Piedmont Triad Partnership campaign has substantially increased community leader and resident awareness of the region, especially its geographic scope and some of its economic and other challenges. It has, however, provided less exposure for the regional problem-solving and service-delivery mechanisms and initiatives being undertaken or considered to strengthen regional decision making.

Potential

Regions that have not conducted regional identity programs could consider designing and conducting them, drawing upon the experience of the Piedmont Triad Partnership and others. Even regions that have conducted such programs realize that they have only tried a few of the potential strategies that could be pursued to establish regional identity. Future regional identity programs could focus specifically on regional governance, and educate community leaders and citizens on how regional challenges are addressed and what is being done to strengthen regional decision making.

Finally, future regional identity programs could help develop a regional story, a narrative that describes how the citizens and institutions of the region are linked, historically and culturally. Such stories need to be personal, so as to share the joys and sufferings of citizens and their communities, as well as interactive, so as to understand how the individual stories are woven into an overall regional story, according to Harold McDougall, Director of the Law and Public Policy Program at Catholic University. He suggests especially encouraging the inheritors of the region — that is, high school students — to develop the story, through sponsoring essay contests or organizing study circles (see Empowering #4). One such regional story — a comic book titled *The Legend of the Allegheny Traveler* — has been prepared by the Southwestern Pennsylvania Heritage Preservation Commission.

Contacts

- Piedmont Triad Partnership, Greensboro, North Carolina, 910-668-4556, 800-669-4556
- Regional Puzzle: Allegheny Conference on Community Development, Pittsburgh, Pennsylvania, 412-281-1890
- The Legend of the Allegheny Traveler: Southwestern Pennsylvania Heritage Preservation Commission, Holidaysburg, Pennsylvania, 814-696-9380

Empowering #4
Forge a City/Suburb Regional Constituency (new)

Forging a regional constituency among city and suburban citizens, especially one that cuts across the communities with the widest fiscal, economic, and racial disparities, is critical to developing a consensus among community leaders and citizens on strategies for addressing regional challenges.

The Regional Unity Program in the Dallas-Fort Worth region and The Atlanta Project in the Atlanta region show how a regional constituency can be forged among city and suburban residents.

The Regional Unity Program is an effort recommended by Vic Suhm to the North Texas Commission, a regional organization in the Dallas-Fort Worth region. Though directed primarily at community leaders, it could be easily expanded to include residents as well, as suggested in the brackets. It provides a useful framework and set of activities for forging a regional constituency, including:

– Activities to discourage adversarial behavior and encourage collaboration by bringing leaders [*and residents*] together to get acquainted, recognize commonalities, build relationships and establish trust:

organize small groups of leaders and their families [*and residents*] to attend regional events, such as cultural events and baseball games

organize regular dinners to bring regional leaders and their spouses [*and residents*] together, such as individuals active in local government, chambers of commerce, academic institutions or other areas of similar interest

organize small in-home dinners for regional leaders and their families [*and residents*]

– Activities to build a regional constituency, increasing understanding of the importance of regional unity, the adverse consequences of disunity, and the appropriateness and effectiveness of collaboration in lieu of competition in reconciling differences, resolving conflict, and developing integrative strategies and solutions within the region.

establish a speakers bureau to address meetings of civic clubs, service organizations, professional organizations and citizen groups on regional topics

challenge emerging leaders to become good regional citizens, by conducting a one-day program each year for current graduates of community leadership programs throughout the region; encourage them to hold joint meetings of alumni groups

survey regional leaders [*and residents*], conduct seminars and workshops, (such as an annual one-day forum on the state of the region as well as a longer retreat on specific regional challenges and visits to other regions; with the assistance of colleges and universities), initiate a visioning process and form alliances and workshops

Vic Suhm recommends creating a Regional Unity Task Force to oversee program activities, with subcommittees and activity leaders responsible for each program activity. In addition, he recommends assembling a directory of regional community organizations (see Empowering #2) that could be involved in, and serve as partners in, recruiting community leader and citizen participation in regional citizenship activities. (Suhm)

The Atlanta Project (TAP), launched by former President Jimmy Carter, focuses on the city and suburban areas with the highest teen-age pregnancy and single parent family rates. It is backed with tens of millions in corporate contributions, and supported by more than 100,000 volunteers. According to Dan Sweat, its director, "TAP provides shovels to communities to allow them to burrow up through the layers of policy and program, the 'turf' that buries them."

TAP's efforts are focused on twenty communities centered around a central city or suburban high school. Each of these communities (or clusters or villages, in TAP's terms) has a community council to involve residents in designing community development initiatives, and a coordinator and small staff to guide their activities. Most importantly, each cluster has a corporate and academic partner to assist in implementing priority initiatives. These partners, in turn, recruit suburban volunteers to work with cluster residents to carry out the initiatives, such as the more than 7,000 who participated in a project to vaccinate more than 17,000 cluster children. (The Atlanta Project)

Accomplishments

The Regional Unity Program offers an example of a set of activities that could be undertaken to forge a regional constituency between city and suburban citizens and community leaders which could contribute to building regional citizenship and a sense of regional community. The Atlanta Project demonstrates that city and suburban citizens can be brought together on the common regional challenge of intercommunity disparity.

Strengths and Shortcomings

The major strength of bringing city and suburban citizens together is its power to forge the personal relationships needed to build the regional constituency required to achieve regional governance excellence. The major shortcoming is that none of this will happen overnight: it will take years, if not generations, to develop personal relationships, change pre-existing biases and find the common ground necessary to build regional citizenship and sense of community. At best, it is a process of two steps forward and one step back; at worst, it can be two steps backward and one forward for the foreseeable future.

Potential

The potential of forging a regional constituency among city and suburban citizens is almost unlimited compared to the activity to date.

Beyond the ideas suggested by the Regional Unity Program and The Atlanta Project, it could be useful to develop direct contact between specific city neighborhoods and suburban communities. For example, a proposal to develop The Allegheny Project in the Pittsburgh region suggested that a suburban community partner be identified for each of the distressed central city neighborhoods or suburban mill towns. (Dodge, "Southern Plan," 1993) Or a regional problem-solving organization, such as a regional planning council (see Problem-Solving #1, Chapter 7) or a regional civic organization (see Problem-Solving #4, Chapter 7) could sponsor dinners or discussions that brought residents from city and suburban communities together to discuss regional challenges.

Study circles, too, could bring together residents from pairs of city and suburban communities. A study circle, according to the Study Circles Resource Center:

> is made up of five to twenty people who agree to meet together several times to learn about a social or political issue in a democratic and collaborative way. Complex issues are broken down into manageable subdivisions, and controversial topics are dealt with in depth. While single-session programs can result in meaningful and productive dialogue, multiple sessions generate continuity and camaraderie within the group. (Study Circles Resource Center, 3)

In a regional context, study circles composed of people from pairs of communities could address regional challenges. Background materials could be provided to participants; professional facilitators or trained participants could guide discussions. The study circle meetings could result in improved understanding of regional challenges and perspectives on what to do about them. They also could lead to developing collaborative strategies for city and suburban citizens and their communities.

Finally, *citizen juries* could bring citizens together regionwide to address crosscutting challenges. Citizen juries are "randomly selected representative panels of citizens that meet for several days at a time to examine major policy decisions and evaluate key issues in political campaigns." (Jefferson Center)

Prototypes for paired study circles have already been tested among the members of different church congregations on the topic of racism, such as by the Coalition Unity Task Force among twelve congregations in Lexington, Kentucky. (Study Circles Resource Center) A new program,

COMMONPLACE, in the Philadelphia region, plans to promote small group discussions on race, so as to develop a consensus on new strategies for thinking and talking about race and other important social issues.

Linkages also could be developed among similar groups across a range of communities, perhaps by community organizations or religious groups. Some religious coalitions, such as Shelby Interfaith in the Memphis region, and The Church in the City in the Cleveland region, have had great success in bringing citizens across congregations and communities together to address common concerns. (Lappé, 184–185) Linking up the residents of individual rich and poor communities could hasten the process of developing working relationships and foster intercommunity awareness, often an important step to regional citizenship.

Finally, a number of these activities could be initiated under the umbrella of a "Sister Communities" program. Such a program could be launched to develop an ongoing dialogue between community leaders and citizens in pairs of communities across the region, including arranging exchanges of cultural and other groups and pursuing joint activities in each other's communities (see Equitable #1, Chapter 5).

Contacts

- Regional Unity Program: North Texas Commission, Victor Suhm, Dallas, Texas, 214-328-5001
- The Atlanta Project, Atlanta, Georgia, 404-881-3400
- Study Circles Resource Center, Pomfret, Connecticut, 203-928-2616
- COMMONPLACE, Philadelphia, Pennsylvania, 215-898-7032
- The Church in the City: Catholic Diocese of Cleveland, Ohio, 216-696-6525

Empowering #5
Empower Citizen Standing in Regional Decision Making

Empowering citizen standing in regional decision-making mechanisms can have an instant impact on regional citizenship. Involving citizens intermittently, such as in community meetings or public hearings, elicits public input on crosscutting challenges, but generally it lacks the interaction with other communities and sustained involvement required to develop one's sense of regional community.

The most commonly used approaches have been to create citizen advisory committees or appoint citizen representatives to the governing bodies of regional problem-solving and service-delivery mechanisms. Elected citizen advisory boards have been established in a few central city governments, but they have not yet been tried at the regional level.

Create citizen advisory committees for regional decision-making mechanisms. Many citizen advisory committees are voluntarily created by regional decision-making organizations, to provide customer input to organizations such as sewer, water, or transit authorities. Some, however, are mandated by national and state governments. For example, the Intermodal Surface Transportation Efficiency Act, known as ISTEA, requires widespread citizen participation in the planning of regional transportation systems, usually resulting in the creation of citizen advisory committees. Similar requirements are usually established for national and state community and economic development programs. In either case, they usually have authority only to advise the governing body or staff of the organization. For some citizen advisory committees required by state or national government legislation, the right of appeal to state or national government agencies is available if the input of citizens is thwarted; citizen advisory boards for Florida's regional growth management boards, for example, may appeal to the state government. (Wallis, 1994, 41)

Citizen advisory groups are usually informal groups, but some are considering nonprofit incorporation. One of those is the Regional Advisory Council (RAC) of the Southern California Association of Governments, which serves the Los Angeles region. RAC is also creating a "regional citizenry," an informal group of 1,000 citizens who will be kept informed about regional challenges through newsletters, fax, Internet, and media channels and who will be able to participate in activities to address them through the same channels. (Around the Region)

Appoint citizen representatives to governing bodies of regional decision-making mechanisms. The governing bodies of regional decision-making mechanisms are usually primarily composed of specific types of representatives, such as elected officials or business leaders. Some even call for citizen members, often by exclusion, such as by requiring nonelected official members. Most of the citizen members, however, are usually selected by the other board members. As a result, few governing bodies of regional decision-making mechanisms have balanced representation from all community sectors and citizens, given the "birds of a feather" tendency of these appointments.

Elect citizen boards to participate in central city decision making. All of the examples of elected citizen boards are in central city governments, in part because few regional governance mechanisms themselves have directly elected governing bodies, such as the Metropolitan Service District in the Portland, Oregon, region. These boards are either required by local government charters or are established by local government ordinances and generally have mandatory review and comment powers, often some limited service-delivery responsibilities, but no taxing authority. (National Academy of Public Administration, 1980, 55)

For example, Dayton, Ohio, has had a system of statutory neighborhood councils, called priority boards, since 1975. These priority boards identify and present community priorities to city government, monitor and make recommendations on public services, review city government plans and budgets, and take other actions to improve the quality of neighborhood life. The priority boards are elected by neighborhood residents and are staffed by city government employees.

Over the past two decades, the Dayton priority boards have become quite influential. They have led campaigns to clean up neighborhoods, set up community development corporations, and developed annual agendas of capital projects and legislation for city government action.

The boards meet frequently with city officials, including monthly meetings with the city manager and department heads. Not surprisingly, they provide the most beaten path to higher elected office in city government and beyond. (Gurwitt, 1992; City of Dayton)

Citywide systems of neighborhood organizations also exist in Portland, Oregon, and St. Paul, Minnesota, with a similar emphasis on developing neighborhood priorities and reviewing city government plans and budgets. Similar empowered boards have been recommended for particular purposes, such as environmental advisory boards to influence environmental policies and services, by James Harless of the Institute of Public Service at the University of Tennessee. (Harless)

Many communities without statutory citizen advisory boards are attempting to solicit similar input from neighborhood organizations. In Jersey City, New Jersey, for example, the city government is offering choices of contractors to neighborhoods for cleaning graffiti, removing debris and pruning trees, all with city funds, and requiring police on night patrol to check in with designated neighborhood residents who brief the officers on problems that have arisen that day. (Vise, 15)

Elected and empowered citizen boards fit Mike Eichler's model of consensus organizing:

> ...Consensus organizers focus on the traditional processes of leadership development among neighborhood residents, in the hope of creating viable neighborhood institutions that can produce tangible improvements for their communities. But in sharp contrast to earlier community organizing approaches, consensus organizing incorporates a second fundamental element; collaboration with a city's powerful interests — businesses, governments, foundations and downtown civic leaders. The resulting alliances produce more than one time civic gestures. A set of enduring relationships begins to emerge. (Eichler, 1)

Accomplishments and Strengths and Shortcomings

Recently, Jeffrey Berry, Kent Portney, and Ken Thomson of Tufts University examined the experiences of statutory, elected citizen boards and similar citywide systems of neighborhood associations in

Dayton as well as Portland, Oregon, Birmingham, Alabama, and St. Paul, Minnesota, and concluded in general that, "In the four citywide systems, the neighborhood associations have substantial authority over decisions that affect the quality of life in their communities, and they facilitate participation of rank-and-file citizens in face-to-face settings." (Berry, 283)

They also raised some basic questions about citizen participation and provided answers, based on their examination of the four cities and interviews in eleven other comparison cities without similar citywide systems of neighborhood associations:

Is participation possible? They conclude that, on one hand, voting requires little effort or reflection, not enough for responsible citizenship; and, on the other hand, individual neighborhood associations are respected, but still do not bring people out of the woodwork, especially low-income citizens. "In the real world, even the most open and democratic political meetings can be perceived as intimidating...or uninteresting or less exciting than other pursuits." (Berry, 285) They found, however, than in the four cities with citywide systems of neighborhood organizations — "structures of strong democracy" — more political activity falls into the strong participation category (involved in neighborhood or issue groups, contacting such groups, and working with others to solve problems in the community) than in comparison cities, where more weak participation dominates (working in social or service groups or contacting government officials). Moreover, they found that citizen activism in the four cities is channeled towards neighborhood associations.

> In the final analysis, citywide systems of neighborhood associations do affect participation in the city. Even though they fall short in getting more people to become active in the political world and getting more low income people involved, neighborhood associations do nurture face-to-face participation. This participation, channeled into neighborhood-based activity, changes the balance of power in the city. (Berry, 286)

Does government respond? They conclude that city government support is critical to the survival of neighborhood associations. "The greatest difficulty neighborhoods in local politics face in influencing city hall is simply getting organized in the first place." (Berry, 287). They also concluded that citywide systems of elected citizen boards and neighborhood associations change the balance of power with businesses. For example, businesses have to negotiate in good faith with the neighborhoods, since citizens can rise up in opposition to any development proposal. Moreover, with citywide systems of neighborhood associations, there is an almost guaranteed certainty of response to development proposals.

On one hand, they conclude that neighborhood boards have less influence on citywide politics than individual community concerns. The neighborhood boards are also relatively weak initiators of citywide issues. None of the citywide systems of neighborhood associations are federated in an effective way and there is no correlation between levels of participation and concurrence on citywide issues.

On the other hand, they found high correlation on neighborhood issues. They also found that neighborhood opinions are heard at city hall by institutional arrangements, not osmosis. Neighborhood activists are part of citywide planning, zoning and budgeting and city officials are on call to neighborhood associations. Overall, they found "...there are rich, dense communications networks between the neighborhood associations and city officials." (Berry, 288)

They also found that city officials respond to neighborhood boards because they know they have the support of rank and file residents. City administrators have found that being in open conflict with neighborhood boards can be damaging to their careers. Overall, cities with neighborhood boards run against the grain of most studies that find few effective community or interest groups present in city politics. "Citywide systems of neighborhood associations do contribute to the responsiveness of city governments. In a variety of ways, city hall has been shown to be responsive to the needs of individual neighborhoods because of the advocacy of the neighborhood associations." (Berry, 289–290)

Does participation empower? Berry and his associates found that the most striking impact of neighborhood boards is on residents' sense of community. They found, for example, that participation in neighborhood board activities was strongly linked to a positive attitude on sense of community. Although cause and effect were difficult to relate, they also found that residents in cities with high participation rates have higher levels of trust in local government and more knowledge of the governmental systems and how to get things done. They found no evidence that participation brought out the wrong people and led to undermining society.

Their overall conclusion was that elected citizen boards and similar citywide systems of neighborhood associations empower citizens in a representative democracy. "Empowerment does come with participation. Face-to-face activity may not transform people to the degree that participation theorists have anticipated, but it does make a difference in the attitudes of people who become involved in such political activities." (Berry, 291)

Active citizen involvement takes time, an average of four years for major projects in Dayton. But, even in Jersey City, the mere requirement that police check in daily with neighborhood representatives has empowered citizens and made officers more accountable.

Moreover, Berry and his colleagues concluded that the potential payoff of citywide systems is high, but so is the risk. Involving people in systems that are ineffectual (long on rhetoric, short on support) is sure to alienate them and damage the reputation of the incumbent administration. (Berry, 294)

They recommend three critical steps to make elected citizen boards and other citywide systems of neighborhood associations work.
- Turn exclusive powers over to the citizen boards. They cannot just be planning boards and advisory committees, but need to have authority to allocate some significant goods and services in their communities. In the four cities examined, for example, a substantial part of zoning authority is transferred to the community. "What neighborhood groups do must be integrated into the existing administrative structure of the city...(and not be) dependent on the administrators' willingness to meet with them." (Berry, 295)
- Develop an administrative plan that specifies sanctions and rewards for city hall administrators who interact with citizen

boards. Such a plan needs to discourage rearguard actions, in part, by making the personal future of administrators tied to the success of the citizen boards.

- Make the citizen advisory boards citywide in their coverage. They recommend that there be a single, officially recognized group with defined boundaries for all neighborhoods, not just for minority or poor neighborhoods, to avoid an us-versus-them mentality, especially between neighborhood and racial groups.

In addition to the three critical recommendations above, they recommend additional factors of success, including:

- giving citizen boards control over significant discretionary financial resources,
- providing adequate resources to citizen boards to allow communication with every household at least annually,
- making citizen boards be feeders to other citizen participation structures, especially citywide ones,
- establishing an early warning system in city government to notify neighborhoods of pending city activities that will affect them,
- limiting terms of office for officers of citizen boards to avoid development of oligarchies, and
- prohibiting citizen boards from involvement in electoral activity. (Berry, 297)

Berry and his associates found no evidence that neighborhood parochial interests have damaged the broader well-being of cities. Nor did they find any evidence that citizen boards undermine economic development. Although citizen boards exercise considerable control over the nature of neighborhood businesses, they don't stop, but only negotiate arrangements with, major developments. (Berry, 298)

They concluded that more power could be turned over to communities:

The real risk to central cities is not giving up power to the neighborhoods but from failing to do enough to nurture the sense of community in their neighborhoods... Neighborhood associations are creative mechanisms for tying people into their communities....These modest, voluntary neighborhood organizations are places where the grass roots of democracy may be nourished. (Berry, 299)

Potential

The potential for empowering citizen standing in regional decision making is complicated by the problematic powers of most regional governance mechanisms.

Unlike local governments, which operate under state statutes or home rule charters, most regional problem-solving organizations have vague powers, and most regional service-delivery organizations are limited to the powers of special purpose authorities or districts. Moreover, most of the governing bodies are composed of appointed members, making it difficult to have popularly elected citizen boards reporting to them.

In sum, it is difficult to see how regional citizen standing can be empowered, when it is difficult to pin down the powers and authorities of regional governance mechanisms themselves.

The models that have worked at the local government level, however, merit consideration at the regional level, especially since they could have the same potential to build regional citizenship and sense of community as have the neighborhood-based citizen boards.

Approaches to empowering citizen standing in regional decision making organizations include:

Creating regional citizen advisory committees for individual regional decision-making mechanisms. Regional citizen advisory committees could be modeled after the committees created for the ISTEA process and follow the guidelines emerging from the examination of citizen boards by Berry and his colleagues.

Sub-regional committees could also be created, possibly for groups of contiguous communities, or for each county in larger regions. To discourage parochial discussions, representatives of rich and poor, city and suburban communities could be assigned to each sub-regional group. These sub-regional groups could address similar topics, in simultaneous meetings. The results of their deliberations could be reported directly to the regional decision-making organization. Alternatively, a committee of chairs or representatives of these sub-regional groups would prepare a consolidated report, to foster regional citizenship and community.

Appointing or electing citizen board members of regional decision-making mechanisms. Citizens could be appointed or elected to boards of regional decision-making mechanisms as at-large representatives or as representatives of particular geographic areas of the region. If appointed, nominations could be solicited from community and other citizen-based organizations.

Creating an elected regional citizens board to advise various regional decision-making mechanisms. As an alternative, an elected regional citizens board could be created to be generally available to advise regional governance mechanisms. Such a board could be drawn upon by the appointed boards and staffs of existing regional organizations to help develop citizen involvement in their activities. Members of the regional citizens board could be elected by sub-regional areas and could even organize sub-regional committees in their areas to participate in the activities of regional organizations.

The powers and authorities of an elected regional citizens board could be limited to advising regional decision-making organizations and helping them in generating citizen input into the regional challenges they are addressing. Alternatively, it could be authorized to serve as a watchdog for regional organizations with strong planning and implementation responsibilities, such as regional growth management or transit authorities, and be able to appeal to the voters (through referenda) or state and national governments (through administrative or legal reviews) if they believe citizen input is being thwarted or disregarded. Some dedicated funding, such as a minuscule part of a local sales tax, could be used to finance a small staff and the operations of the regional citizens board.

Creating regional coalitions of citizen-based organizations. As an alternative to an elected region citizens board, citizen-based organizations could create a regional coalition to provide input to regional decision making.

Coalitions of citizen-based organizations have been created in a number of regions, especially for neighborhood organizations across central cities, such as the Neighborhood Network in Chattanooga, Tennessee, and even central counties. (James Catanzaro, Governors State University RAP 2000+ Idea Fair) Regional civic organizations have also been created, but they have primarily drawn their membership from individuals, not citizen-based organizations. (See Problem-Solving #4, Chapter 7.)

A regional coalition of citizen-based organizations could be created by neighborhood and community associations but could also be open to other citizen-based organizations, such as those interested in environmental, transportation, or other particular regional topics. It could develop regional citizenship skills (see Empowering #1), provide citizens with regional governance information (see Empowering #2) and assist regional organizations in developing citizen input into the challenges they are addressing.

The regional coalition could have a small staff and be supported by dues of citizen-based organizations as well as contracts with regional organizations and fees from information forums, training programs, publications and other activities supportive of citizen-based organizations. An example or a coalition of citizen-based organizations could be the Regional Council of Neighborhoods and Community Groups being created in the Atlanta region to "facilitate communication of common challenges and solutions and develop consistent and equitable regional policies and practices." (Atlanta Regional Commission, 1993)

Fostering use of citizen initiative and referenda on regional topics. Initiative and referendum could offer citizens an opportunity to recommend regional challenges for agendas of regional-decision making mechanisms or to express their opinions about strategies under consideration by these mechanisms, respectively. Their use might be especially appropriate for sorting our citizen preferences for alternative options for dealing with conflicted regional challenges.

Some critics fear that citizen initiative and referendum can be easily abused, especially if the ballot questions are vague or misleading, citizens are uninformed or seriously misled on the regional challenge being addressed, or the signature requirements are outrageously high.

But citizen initiative and referendum can provide important guidance to regional decision-making organizations and others charged with dealing with crosscutting challenges.

Regrettably, it is virtually impossible to put a regional citizen initiative or referendum on the ballot in most states since it cuts across normal jurisdictional boundaries and would require either look-a-like wording in each county (and perhaps city) or state empowering legislation. Recognizing the difficulty in putting regional questions to the voters, Confluence St. Louis, a regional civic organization in the St. Louis area, recommended creating a directly elected Metropolitan Board (see Problem-Solving #1, Chapter 7) whose primary duty, and power, would be to put regional citizen initiatives and referenda on the ballot.

Emerging electronic technology allows a highly interactive form of initiative and referendum. Citizens could have the opportunity to express their concerns on regional challenges and options for addressing them, directly from their homes, to regional decision-making mechanisms. Demonstrations of this technology have already occurred, beginning with the Qube cable television system in the Columbus, Ohio, region, which enabled citizens to vote from their homes and participate in the discussion of actions being considered by a local planning commission. This "semi-direct democracy," a middle ground between representative and direct democracy, might offer an approach for facilitating reaching a consensus on conflicted regional challenges before the turn of the century. (Toffler, 1995, 98)

Contacts

- Southern California Association of Governments, Los Angeles, California, 213-236-1800
- City of Dayton, Division of Neighborhood Affairs, Dayton, Ohio, 513-443-3775
- Altanta Regional Commission, Atlanta, Georgia, 404-364-2500

Empowering #6:
Establish Regional Problem-Solving Centers (new)

Regional problem-solving centers could facilitate regional decision making by providing comfortable settings in which citizens and community leaders have access to facilitators and regional experts, decision-making electronic software, and best practices information from other regions.

For example, The Atlanta Project (Empowering #4) developed a Collaboration Center with two large meeting rooms, a training room, a strategic planning room and a presentation room, most of which can be readily rearranged for different types of groups. The facility has access to a databank and resource center for anti-poverty initiatives that provides written text, photographs and even videos on best practices in other regions. It also has satellite access to other regions, making it easy to set up videoconferences with groups in other regions.

The Collaboration Center is available for meetings of groups from one or more of the cluster neighborhoods, which often include residents from the cluster along with representatives of agencies participating in The Atlanta Project. In a typical meeting, participants can use keyboards to participate in simultaneous "brainstorming" sessions in which they can see their responses as well as those of other participants on their computer monitors or an overhead screen. Similarly, participants can simultaneously express their opinions on particular questions, review the responses of others, and develop collective positions. Everyone has a chance to be "seen" and "heard," precluding participants from being excluded from or dominating the meeting. At the conclusion of the meeting, any of the information reviewed, topics discussed, and results reached can be compiled into a report, copied and distributed to participants, instantaneously.

The approximately $5 million cost of the Collaboration Center was covered largely from contributions to The Atlanta Project, reducing the out-of-pocket cost to only $800,000. In addition, the staff will help community groups use the facilities of the Collaboration Center and facilitate meetings. (The Atlanta Project)

Collaboration centers can be provided at less expense and still provide problem-solving venues for citizens. Special rooms in community schools or public libraries have been provided for use of community groups, especially in poor neighborhoods and communities, and could be equipped as collaboration centers. Similarly, rooms used by governing bodies of public, private, academic, nonprofit and civic organizations are often equipped with audio-video capabilities. Classrooms in colleges and universities are being similarly equipped for audio-video and distance learning capabilities.

Informal collaboration centers are critical for facilitating conversations between friends and neighbors. Front porches often provide such informal collaboration centers in residential neighborhoods. Maybe a program to provide a "front porch" on every block could provide a critical complement to more high-tech collaboration centers.

Another form of high-tech collaboration center is the array of bulletin boards or home pages on the Internet. For free, or for a small fee, one can create and access a file on the Internet and share comments with others interested in the same topic. A community values bulletin board already exists that shares thoughts on the values of community. Such bulletin boards provide opportunities for "more dedicated" citizens to share their thoughts with other individuals in a free-flowing discussion. Given the rapid increase in the use of electronic information services, special bulletin boards could be established on regional topics for participants in a particular region or nationally.

Accomplishments

According to officials of The Atlanta Project, the Collaboration Center has "already altered the way meetings are conducted and, as people become adept in the technology, promises to speed them up. Even "traditional" meetings seem to go more smoothly, as participants trained in the new technology become more respective of each others' opinions and less combative." (The Atlanta Project, *32)*

Strengths and Shortcomings

The major strength of collaboration centers is their ability to facilitate citizen involvement in regional decision making. Their major shortcoming appears to be the cost of establishing and operating them.

Potential

The future potential of regional problem-solving centers is illustrated in a proposal of the National Civic League for establishing "community-building and collaboration centers."

The community-building and collaboration centers would be led by a "distinguished board and would consist of a core staff and network of affiliate organizations and individuals" who would provide collaborative planning, consensus building, facilitation, leadership consultation, training and community problem-solving services. The centers facilities might include:

- a meeting center, for groups ranging from 10 to 100 people;
- computer-assisted meeting management and decision-making support programs, sometimes called groupware;
- computer simulation services for design-development-planning issues, such as to assist in modifying site or building configurations for physical developments or costing out alternative approaches for addressing a regional challenge;
- a computer-assisted data-base management support system, to facilitate accessing information located elsewhere in the region or in other regions;
- a video library, such as of best practices in other regions; and
- teleconferencing capabilities to connect with local and national networks, such as community cable television channels or the Civic Network Television (see Empowering #1).

The National Civic League estimates that the cost of converting an existing space to a community building and collaboration center would be $25,000 to $300,000. Equipping a facility with computer-based keypad technologies and ten to twelve microcomputers would cost approximately $100,000.

Staffing of the center could be done on an incremental basis as its use, and supporters, increase. For example, the Team Technology Center of the Federal Aviation Administration has four staff, including two facilitators and two "technographers." The National Civic League estimates operating costs could range from $100,000 to $500,000 a year.

The cost of equipping and operating a center could be reduced if it were done on a collaborative basis with a college or university, government or other facility. (National Civic League, "Proposal to Establish a Community Building and Collaboration Center," 1993)

Contacts

- The Atlanta Project, Atlanta, Georgia, 404-881-3400
- National Civic League, Denver, Colorado, 303-571-4343
- Institute for Awakening Technology, Lake Oswego, Oregon, 503-635-2615

Empowering #7:
Develop a Regional Citizens Charter (new)

A regional citizens charter could present the rights and responsibilities of regional residents, the opportunities for citizen involvement in regional decision making, and the standards for services provided by regional governance mechanisms.

The Citizen's Charter developed by the administration of British Prime Minister John Major provides a model for a regional citizens charter.

The Citizen's Charter focuses on principles of public service and setting standards for achieving the principles. According to John Major:

> The Citizen's Charter is about giving more power to the citizen. But citizenship is about our responsibilities — as parents, for example, or as neighbours — as well as our entitlements. The Citizen's Charter is not a recipe for more state action: it is a testament to our belief in people's right to be informed and choose for themselves. (Great Britain, Government of)

The principles of public service laid out in the Citizen's Charter include:
- standards — explicit standards, published and prominently displayed at the point of delivery
- openness — there should be no secrecy about how public services are run, how much they cost, who is in charge, and whether or not they are meeting their standards.
- information — Full, accurate information should be readily available, in plain language, about what services are being provided.
- choice — The public sector should provide choice wherever possible.
- nondiscrimination — Services should be available regardless of race or sex.
- accessibility — Services should be run to suit the convenience of customers, not staff.
- And if things go wrong? — At the very least, the citizen is entitled to a good explanation, or an apology. There should be a well-publicized and readily available complaints procedure. If there is a

serious problem, it should be put right. And lessons must be learnt so that mistakes are not repeated.

- scope — The Citizen's Charter applies to all government services.
- cost — The Charter programme is about finding better ways of converting the money that can be afforded into even better services.

Standards are given for each government service — waiting time guarantees for medical services from the National Health Service, on-time guarantees for the trains of British Rail. Redress for failing to meet standards is also outlined for each government service — provision of health services from independent providers, or partial or full refunds of fares, even additional compensation for late or canceled trains. Only those government services meeting the Charter Standard are entitled to display the Chartermark of compliance with the Citizen's Charter. (Great Britain, Government of)

Accomplishments

The Citizens Charter has had an impact on the attitudes of government employees and citizens just by being produced, forcing both to consider appropriate standards of service and how to achieve them. The initial implementation of the Charter standards has also had an impact on the consumer relations and budgets of various government services; people were not only more likely to register complaints but to collect some financial compensation from government services. The long-term impact on the quality, choice, value and standards of government services is yet to be analyzed.

Strengths and Shortcomings

The major strength of the Citizen's Charter is specifying the rights and responsibilities of the recipients of public services. The major shortcoming is defining acceptable standards and fairly enforcing their implementation.

Potential

The potential of developing a regional Citizen's Charter could be enormous.

A regional citizens charter could build upon the Citizen's Charter example and include a number of components, such as:

- stating the rights and responsibilities of regional citizens — a first cut at defining regional citizenship,
- defining opportunities for citizen involvement in regional decision making, which could be adopted by regional governance mechanisms — covering topics such as the powers and responsibilities of governing bodies for citizen involvement, the selection of citizen members of governing bodies and advisory committees, and the opportunities for citizen involvement in planning processes and consumer participation in service delivery, and
- establishing principles and standards for the delivery of regional services, including guidelines for developing and posting standards and processes for compensating people for violations.

There are several ways to initiate the regional citizens charter. It could be done as part of a regional governance examination (see Strategic #2, Chapter 4), through the collaboration of citizen-based organizations across the region or by a regional civic organization (see Problem-Solving #4, Chapter 7), by a regional service-delivery coordinating group (see Service-Delivery #5, Chapter 7), or by other regional decision-making mechanisms.

It would need to be developed in cooperation with regional problem-solving and, especially, service-delivery mechanisms. The completed charter could be adopted by individual regional mechanisms. Monitoring and updating the regional citizens charter could be assigned to a regional civic organization or a special committee composed of citizens and representatives of regional decision-making mechanisms.

The cost of preparing and monitoring the implementation of a regional citizens charter is probably minimal; the improvement in citizen involvement in regional decision making could be considerable.

Empowering #7:

Chapter 7

Making Regional Governance Institutionalized: Regional Problem Solving and Service Delivery

The point is that we either can be scorpions in a bottle or follow the pattern of bees in a beehive capably working together.

— *Clarke Thomas*

Experimentation with regional problem-solving and service-delivery mechanisms has exploded in the 1990s. On bad days, it looks chaotic and seems to be getting worse with each new experiment; on good days, it provides early evidence of governance in the 21st century.

This new experimentation is significantly different than that of past decades.

First, a greater proportion of today's governance experimentation is focusing on intercommunity and regional challenges, especially economic competitiveness. Community leaders and citizens are increasingly addressing the need to provide effective governance where challenges are emerging, at the regional and neighborhood levels.

Second, regional governance experimentation is more inclusive, involving community leaders from all sectors, not just elected and other public officials. The intercommunity and regional challenges of the 1990s not only impact all sectors of the community, they almost always require their collective involvement to address them successfully.

Third, regional governance experimentation has moved away from looking for the single all-powerful governance mechanism — the "will-o'-the-wisp" metropolitan government — to creating a network of mechanisms.

In the 1960s, the prevailing vision of regional governance was a single metropolitan government consolidating and replacing all local governments, such as was proposed by the Committee for Economic Development (CED). (Committee for Economic Development) In practice, during this decade, national and some state governments, in conjunction with local governments, breathed life into regional planning councils that were established in most regions during the decade.

By the 1970s, the prevailing vision of regional governance was multi-tier, with a hierarchy of regional, county and municipal governments in multi-county regions — which were becoming more prevalent across the nation — such as was proposed by the CED and analyzed extensively by the Advisory Commission on Intergovernmental Relations (ACIR). (Advisory Commission on Intergovernmental Relations, 1974) In practice, some top down central city-county consolidation was pursued during the 1970s, generally unsuccessfully; but bottom-up voluntary cooperation efforts expanded enormously, and succeeded overwhelmingly, among groups of local governments.

By the 1980s, the prevailing vision of regional governance was a combination of neighborhood (such as empowered neighborhood councils) and regional mechanisms (such as single purpose districts and authorities, empowered/federated urban counties in single county regions and regional planning councils and service districts in multi-county regions), as was proposed in the National Academy of Public Administration guide on metropolitan governance. In practice, shrinking national and state government assistance during the 1980s fostered some fend-for-yourself behavior among local governments, but inter-community and regional partnerships, involving all sectors, began to be established to address crosscutting challenges in almost all regions. (Dodge, "Regional Problem Solving in the 1990s," 1990)

This experimentation needs to take yet a different approach to make regional governance preeminent in the 21st century, as described in Chapter 2. In the past, equity and empowerment concerns were only considered as criteria for assessing alternative regional service-delivery mechanisms. Little concern, and considerable reservation, was given to institutionalizing regional problem-solving mechanisms. Community leaders and citizens seemed to assiduously avoid making regional governance either prominent or strategic. Almost the entire focus of regional governance explorations was on selecting mechanisms for delivering regional services, usually through transferring functions to county governments or creating special single or multiple-service authorities.

Future regional governance experimentation will have to begin with making regional governance prominent and strategic; raising its stature and developing a future vision and action plan for its excellence — a Strategy for Achieving Regional Governance Excellence (SARGE). Developing the SARGE includes examining all aspects of regional governance and selecting initiatives for making it equitable and empowering as well as institutionalizing an integrated network of regional problem-solving and service-delivery mechanisms that has the geographic scope and functional latitude to achieve the vision.

The SARGE, and the regional governance mechanisms themselves, need to be flexible so that they can be modified over time to be responsive to emerging regional challenges. In general, the emphasis should be on institutionalizing flexible decision-making collaboration, not rigid decision-making mechanisms.

Over the past few decades, various typologies have been developed to organize the range of options for intercommunity decision-making mechanisms, including regional mechanisms. Many emerged from the experience of intergovernmental service delivery and range from informal ad hoc cooperation to formal ongoing structured service-delivery mechanisms.

Dave Walker, the provocative observer of intergovernmental cooperation, developed a list of seventeen options that, in his characterization, range from "pabulum" to "castor oil." Drawing on the work of Roscoe Martin (Martin), he presented them in an article titled "Snow White

(Metro America) and the 17 Dwarfs: From Metro Cooperation to Governance." David Parry added boundary commissions and nongovernmental alternatives to the list. (Parry) And Jay Goodman shortened it and called it a "continuum of radicalness of metropolitan governmental forms." Drawing on these various typologies, Pat Atkins, Consulting Director of The Institute for the Regional Community at the National Association of Regional Councils, has produced a master list of "different ways to organize services and governments for citizens," which ranges from lesser to greater change. (See next page.)

I concur with making these typologies more inclusive by adding non-public sectors, and more experimental by combining regulatory "sticks" and public and market "carrots" for addressing regional challenges.

I suggest one additional modification, however: Give equal billing to problem-solving and service-delivery mechanisms. Most of the historic emphasis has been on finding, and usually creating, the appropriate mechanism to deliver a new regional service or consolidate a fragmented service delivered by multiple local governments or private businesses.

Less emphasis has been placed on creating mechanisms to design strategies for addressing regional challenges, except for the continued reference to regional planning councils and councils of governments, which are usually dominated by public sector members. Now that all sectors have become involved in addressing regional challenges, this diversity needs to be better reflected in the typology. More importantly, as community leaders and citizens become increasingly aware that they lack the mechanisms to address emerging regional challenges, design strategies and negotiate implementation responsibilities, they are focusing more attention on creating effective problem-solving mechanisms, such as regional alliances and citizens leagues.

A suggested continuum of regional problem-solving and service-delivery mechanisms is presented in the remainder of this chapter.

The overall purpose of these mechanisms is to provide community leaders and citizens with workable approaches to manage cooperatively what they cannot respond to alone. Community leaders, such as elected officials and professional managers, are primarily trained to deal with

Pat Atkins' Typology of Options for Intercommunity Decision Making

Some of the options for delivering services require very little change for the typical local government. Others are more drastic. This list slides from lesser change to greater change.

Volunteerism: The provision of all or part of a public service through the use of trained and supervised volunteer personnel, employed without pay for a local government.

Informal Agreement: An agreement, not backed by law, between two or more units of local government that pledges them to common improvement in a targeted service.

Formal Agreement, Joint powers: A legal agreement permitting two or more jurisdictions mutually to plan, finance, and deliver a service for their constituencies.

Interlocal Service Contract: A local agreement permitting one government to supply a specified service for a fee to another government.

Privatization: The provision of public services for local governments and their constituency by the private sector.

Multicommunity Partnerships: An intergovernmental entity that ranges from loosely connected and informal to formal complex long-term networks, including joint public-private citizen associations, private business-industry alliances with government, and others.

Intersectoral Cooperation: Creation of mutually beneficial alliances between government, the nonprofit public sector, and the business sector to best finance and deliver services.

Negotiated Boundary: A contract between two jurisdictions that legally secures a mutual boundary for the specified time period of 10 to 20 years and may include services agreements as part of the contract.

Nonprofit Public Corporation: A legal entity used by local governments to own a company jointly and manage it through a board of directors representing the local governments.

Extraterritorial Power: A state statute-bestowed grant of power enabling a local government to exercise specific powers or services beyond its legal territorial borders.

Regional Council: A voluntary regional organization, regularly convening appointed and elected representatives of area local governments to discuss, study, and adopt multiple purpose cooperative plans and programs.

Federally Induced Regional Body: A single-purpose regional body established or mandated by the national government, as with a metropolitan transportation planning agency.

Local Special Purpose Services District: A single-purpose unit legally established to handle one service and not required to follow existing local boundaries.

Transfers of Functions: The legal transfer of one or more services from one government to a second, deemed more able in resources or area to provide the service.

Annexation: An attachment of a portion of unincorporated territory to the contiguous annexing local jurisdiction.

Incorporation: A legal process whereby a given community or part of a community is transformed into a legal municipal corporation endowed in law with specific duties, services, rights, and liabilities.

Unified Property Tax Base Sharing: A formula that allows a percent of any new industrial-commercial property development within a region, with that percent accruing to a general pool which is then shared regionally by a weighted formula.

Government Equity Fund: A voluntary redistribution by a region's local governments based on a complex formula that considers aggregate growth in property values, income and property tax revenues, so that communities not experiencing growth still receive a share of the fund.

Services Consolidation: A merging of two services into one delivery mechanism without changing the underlying local governmental structure.

Reformed Urban County Government: The rechartering of a county government to undertake municipal-type services delivery, usually in conjunction with the establishment of an elected country executive.

Regional Special Purpose Services District, Regional Joint District: As the local special district, but geographically larger, created to provide a single service to many local jurisdictions.

Regional Special Authority: As the regional special district, but with stronger and more extensive powers surrounding its specified service.

Regional Delimited Purpose Multiservices District, Metropolitan Services Authority: As the metropolitan or regional government, but with responsibilities restricted to a cluster of interrelated services.

Consolidated Government: Merger of two or more entire governments into one new unit that replaces them.

Metropolitan Government, Regional Government: Incorporation of a new general purpose government encompassing a complete metropolitan area or rural area, which may or may not replace all existing local governments.

Federated Metropolitan Government: Incorporation or merger of local governments into one large government containing two tiers, one to handle areawide services and the other, which consists of preexisting local jurisdictional boundaries, to handle local services.

what they can control, the challenges that are contained within the borders of their communities. Given the explosion of crosscutting challenges, they can no longer control the responses to the challenges; instead they must develop intercommunity and regional mechanisms to manage these challenges, cooperatively, with their neighbors or regionwide.

Finally, I would like to suggest a few general guidelines for considering the regional problem-solving and service-delivery mechanisms:

Experiment with mechanisms before institutionalizing them; then empower them with "laces." Test experimental regional governance mechanisms on smaller challenges or sub-regional challenges; if they work, assign them larger, regionwide challenges. If they work for a range of challenges, and there will be a continuing need for them in the future, consider their roles, responsibilities, and relationships to other governance mechanisms, and empower them: Provide them with the requisite authorities and resources — "laces" — to carry out their responsibilities.

Provide for reauthorizing mechanisms to protect against institutionalizing dinosaurs. Similarly, protect against institutionalizing regional governance, and especially service-delivery, mechanisms beyond the need for their existence. Regions and their governance are changing so rapidly that almost any mechanisms require evaluation and even reauthorization every five to ten years.

Continually monitor the overall effectiveness of the regional governance network; designate regional governance monitors. Designate one or more organizations to monitor the overall effectiveness of regional governance mechanisms and their relationships in a regional governance network, including their ties to neighborhood organizations and local governments. This organization (or organizations) could conduct annual audits of the progress and accomplishments of regional governance mechanisms and suggest corrective actions for addressing obstacles encountered and making them more effective components of the regional governance network. This organization{s} could even prepare periodic reports and hold conferences on the state of regional governance (see Strategic #4, Chapter 4).

Initiatives for Making Regional Governance Institutionalized

How can we foster experimentation that results in institutionalizing a regional decision-making capacity to address emerging challenges? How can we experiment with existing and probably many new regional problem-solving mechanisms, until known and unforeseen crosscutting challenges are addressed in a timely manner? How can we redistribute responsibilities among existing and probably few new regional service-delivery mechanisms, until strategies for addressing crosscutting issues are implemented flexibly?

The initiatives for responding to these questions include regional problem-solving mechanisms, regional service-delivery mechanisms, and combined regional problem-solving/service-delivery mechanisms.

Regional Problem-Solving Mechanisms

Public, private, academic, and civil sectors are initiating regional problem-solving mechanisms to address crosscutting challenges. In an increasing number of cases, these mechanisms include representatives from other sectors or even exchange members from other regional decision-making mechanisms. Many of the newer problem-solving mechanisms are being launched as joint efforts of various sectors within a region.

Initiatives for Making Regional Governance Institutionalized are:

- Problem-Solving #1: Public regional problem-solving mechanisms (ad hoc intercommunity problem-solving groups and regional planning councils)
- Problem-Solving #2: Private regional problem-solving mechanisms (regional chambers of commerce and growth associations and business leadership organizations)
- Problem-Solving #3: Academic regional problem-solving mechanisms (college and university research institutes and public service programs)
- Problem-Solving #4: Citizen regional problem-solving mechanisms (regional civic organizations)

- Problem-Solving #5: Multi-sector regional problem-solving mechanisms (regional alliances)

Regional Service-Delivery Mechanisms

Intergovernmental arrangements and regional single-service authorities are the most popular regional service-delivery mechanisms, but there is growing interest in other than public regional services, regional multiple-service authorities, and regional service-delivery coordinating groups.

Initiatives for Making Regional Governance Institutionalized are:
- Service-Delivery #1: Intergovernmental service-delivery arrangements
- Service-Delivery #2: Other than public regional services
- Service-Delivery #3: Regional single-service authorities
- Service-Delivery #4: Regional multiple-service authorities
- Service-Delivery #5: Regional service-delivery coordinating groups (new)

Regional Problem-Solving and Service-Delivery Mechanisms

A couple of regional governance mechanisms combine regional problem solving and service delivery. Empowered counties and central cities and central city-county government consolidations have the potential to provide both aspects of regional decision making in primarily one-county regions. Regional planning and service districts — such as the directly elected Metropolitan Service District (Portland, Oregon region), state-mandated Metropolitan Council (Minneapolis/St. Paul, Minnesota region), and provincial regional districts in British Columbia — have the potential to provide both aspects of regional decision making in multi-county regions.

Initiatives for Making Regional Governance Institutionalized are:
- Problem-Solving/Service-Delivery #1: Empowered counties and central cities

- Problem-Solving/Service-Delivery #2: Municipal/county government modifications, federations and consolidations (municipal modification, such as incorporation, combination, disincorporation; central city annexation; and central city-county government federations and consolidations)
- Problem-Solving/Service-Delivery #3: Regional planning and service districts

In addition, regional single- and multiple-service authorities (Service-Delivery #3 and #4) have the potential to provide both aspects of regional decision making for particular types of regional challenges; however, their service-delivery responsibilities often preclude them, administratively or politically, from taking the lead in addressing emerging regional challenges.

Community leaders and citizens could initiate the process for making regional governance institutionalized by exploring all of the existing regional decision-making mechanisms as part of a regional governance examination (see Strategic #2, Chapter 4). Then they could modify existing mechanisms or create new ones — such as multi-sector regional alliances (Problem-Solving #5), regional service-delivery coordinating groups (Service-Delivery #5) and regional planning and service districts (Problem-Solving/Service-Delivery #3) — to make regional governance both institutionalized and networked.

The performance of the Institutionalized initiatives can be measured by answering two questions. Does implementing the Institutionalized initiatives result in:

- experimenting with regional problem-solving and service-delivery mechanisms that efficiently guide community leaders and citizens through equitable and empowering processes for effectively addressing the most pressing challenges?
- building a "honeycomb network" of regional problem-solving and service-delivery mechanisms that interact seamlessly to provide regional governance excellence?

Problem-Solving #1
Public Regional Problem-Solving Mechanisms

The most common examples of regional problem-solving mechanisms over the past few decades have been the publicly initiated ad hoc intercommunity problem-solving groups and regional planning councils.

Ad Hoc Intercommunity Problem-Solving Groups

Many crosscutting challenges are addressed by ad hoc groups, established by local government officials, especially challenges that are sub-regional and primarily affect neighboring municipalities or counties.

Ad hoc intercommunity problem-solving groups or task forces have been used to address almost any crosscutting or common challenge. The four communities in the northern part of Allegheny County (Pittsburgh, Pennsylvania), for example, created a committee of municipal officials and citizens to explore the crosscutting need for information services. They developed a proposal for jointly providing a main library in the central community and satellite facilities in the school libraries in the other three communities. Their proposal is being implemented by the governing bodies in the communities with the assistance of committee members. (Dodge, *Final Report, Northern Tier Library Services Feasibility Study,* 1994)

Temporary local and state study commissions have also been established to explore various aspects of intercommunity governance.

Local study commissions generally are established to consider changes in individual local governments, such as to draft or revise a home rule charter. When these commissions look at county government, however, they often consider the relationships of county to municipal governments, including their respective responsibilities, and other intercommunity topics. For example, the ad hoc Des Moines Area Commission explored alternative forms of local government and their financing, including federating or consolidating the central city and county governments. (Hamilton, 504)

State study commissions often have a broader mandate. The State Commission on the Capital Region, established by the New York state government, is charged with studying ways to strengthen regional problem solving and service delivery in the six adjoining counties making up the Albany/Schenectady/Troy region. (State of New York)

Finally, informal groups of elected officials have convened themselves on a periodic basis to address crosscutting challenges. The mayors of jurisdictions in the Denver region, for example, meet for half a day each month to address air quality compliance and other regional challenges.

Various tools have been developed to help community officials and citizens participating in ad hoc intercommunity problem-solving groups. These include:

Guidelines for establishing ad hoc intercommunity problem-solving groups. Seven Maryland jurisdictions (the counties of Anne Arundel, Carroll, Frederick, Howard, Montgomery, Prince George's and the City of Laurel), for example, entered into a memorandum of understanding to notify neighbors of proposed planning and regulatory changes, before public announcements; establish repositories within each jurisdiction to facilitate citizen and official review; develop common approaches to data collection, analysis, and mapping; and convene quarterly meetings of planning department representatives to discuss issues of common concern. (Dodge, Interstate Study Commission, 1994, 11) Similarly, Champaign and Urbana, Illinois, along with two school districts and one park district, have adopted a joint resolution on principles of intergovernmental cooperation. (Carter)

Processes for conducting ad hoc intercommunity problem-solving groups. The Negotiated Investment Strategy, developed by the Kettering Foundation to negotiate strategies for the coordinated investment of national, state and local, including private, resources into developing distressed communities, is an example of such a process. In Gary, Indiana, teams of national, state and local government representatives, and an observer from the USX Corporation, used the process, with the guidance of a mediator, to negotiate a $250 million strategy for improving the City. (Moore, Carl, 298)

Sources of funding for ad hoc intercommunity problem-solving groups. The Western Pennsylvania Division of the Pennsylvania Economy League, for example, provides financial assistance to groups of communities interested in conducting cooperative strategic planning processes or consolidation studies. Funded by community foundations, it has resulted in the consolidation of two municipalities and development of intercounty service delivery. (Pennsylvania Economy League, Descriptions, 1992) (Thomas, Clarke, 1994)

Regional Planning Councils and Councils of Governments

Regional planning councils or councils of governments are associations of local governments, usually state and national government mandated and supported, that oversee regional transportation, air and water quality, land use and other planning activities and foster cooperative approaches to address regional challenges. They are guided by governing bodies, primarily composed of representatives of the major local governments in the region, and at times representatives of other sectors and citizens.

Most regions have a single regional council responsible for these planning activities. In California and other states, a few regions have divided up regional planning responsibilities among regional councils of governments, air quality management districts, and county transportation commissions. A couple of regions have consolidated regional planning responsibilities into comprehensive regional governance mechanisms that also have regional service-delivery responsibilities (see Problem-Solving/Service-Delivery #3).

Regional planning councils have been in existence long enough that they are now entering their third era, according to their historians.

The years from the late 1940s to the mid-1960s were an era of *voluntary cooperation*. Regional planning councils were mostly voluntary associations of local governments, responding to local needs and concerns and driven by a desire for intergovernmental cooperation to achieve goals that could not be achieved by local governments working alone. The number of regional planning councils grew to approximately 175 during this period.

From the mid-1960s to the early 1980s, regional planning councils were driven by *national and state government incentives and requirements,* including state mandates for creating sub-state regions and national requirements for areawide plans as a precondition to receiving funding from dozens of national government programs. Regional planning councils were even required to review and comment on local applications for national government funding as A-95 clearinghouses. Some regional councils even experimented with developing regional capital improvements programs to integrate and rank the relative importance of capital facilities. (National Association of Regional Councils, 1976)

The number of regional planning councils grew to more than 670 during this period. According to Pat Atkins, the prevailing etiquette for regional planning councils during this era included:

- stay with the feds,
- maintain a low profile,
- provide comprehensive planning assistance only,
- don't compete with the public sector governments, and
- don't compete with the private sector businesses.

The years from the early 1980s to the present could be described as an era of *strategic localism.* Regional planning councils have made a number of changes to respond to reduced national and state government funding. They have attempted to modify their relationships with their members, shifting from conducting regional comprehensive planning, for which there is little funding available except for transportation and air and water quality planning, to meeting the local service delivery needs of their members, including pursuing any national and state government funding available. They have also made other adaptations to survive, including directly delivering services for state and local governments and assisting in developing intergovernmental agreements.

The national government proportion of regional planning council budgets has declined from 3 out of every 4 dollars (75 percent) to less than half their budgets (45 percent), some of which has been replaced with increased state and local government funding. Many of the planning activities of regional planning councils have been divided up among their members, further contributing to a decline in the average size of their staffs from twenty-two to seventeen, in the national programs they administer from four to two-and-a-half, and in their budgets to approximately $1 million. According to Bruce McDowell of ACIR, many of them are "disappearing into the background static of regional governance." (Committee for Enterprise Development Symposium)

It is not surprising, then, that the number of regional planning councils has declined to approximately 530, with many holding on to life by their "fingertips." Again, according to Pat Atkins, the new etiquette for regional planning councils includes:

- go with the states,
- market your agency,
- pick a few things to do well,
- invite competition, and
- be innovative. (Atkins, 1992 and 1993; University of Oregon)

In addition to topical regional planning processes, regional planning councils are increasingly initiating holistic regional strategic planning or visioning processes, focusing especially on economic competitiveness. The Metropolitan Washington Council of Governments, for example, sponsored the Partnership for Regional Excellence, which convened approximately 200 community leaders and recommended developing regional agreements on land use, transportation and environment, leading to the preparation of a new regional plan. (Dodge, Interstate Study Commission, 10–11) Similarly, the Atlanta Regional Commission and Association of Central Oklahoma Governments recently sponsored even more participatory regional strategic planning processes called Vision 2020 and Central Oklahoma 2020, respectively. (West and Taylor)

Regional planning councils also have some influence over the implementation of their plans.

They make the primary recommendations for the use of national and state transportation funds and developing strategies for achieving air and water quality standards, subject to state and national government approval and enforcement. They also attempt to influence the implementation of their own regional plans. The San Diego (California) Association of Governments, for example, encourages local governments to follow a self-certification process to assure consistency of their plans, policies and ordinances with the regional plan and offers conflict resolution procedures for resolving interjurisdictional conflicts. (Sulzer)

Regional planning councils serving as regional growth management boards generally have the most defined implementation responsibilities (see Equitable #3, Chapter 5).

Many regions have informal or formal sub-regional planning councils as well. The largest regions — Chicago, Los Angeles and New York — have sub-regional planning organizations to provide for more local participation in sub-regional planning processes as well as facilitate coordination of regionwide planning processes. Regions with large numbers of local governments, such as the Pittsburgh region, have sub-county councils of governments to foster intergovernmental cooperation among neighboring groups of ten to twenty jurisdictions.

Regional planning councils are also being created in other countries to foster intergovernmental cooperation among local jurisdictions. With the infusion of Eurodollars into regional economic development in the European Common Market countries, regional planning councils are being created in Birmingham, England, Frankfort, Germany, and Valencia, Spain, for example, to design economic development strategies. (van den Berg)

Accomplishments

Regional planning councils have offered the one ongoing institutionalized resource for addressing crosscutting challenges in most regions of the country. They have guided regional transportation and air and water quality and even growth management planning. They have developed working relationships among local government leaders, who have collectively become an influential constituency for addressing regional challenges in many regions. Many of the regional councils have also responded to the needs of their member governments and assisted them in conducting planning processes and securing national and state government funding.

Strengths and Shortcomings

The major strength of regional planning councils is their experience and professional resources for guiding problem-solving processes to address regional challenges. Their major shortcoming is their vague, and often weak, powers and authorities.

Even though they have existed for two to three decades in most regions, regional planning councils still have mixed support from community leaders and citizens and unpredictable year-to-year funding. Many of them justly deserve "football-without-laces" awards for being the longest-suffering, most vaguely empowered regional governance mechanisms. As a result of this mixed support, community leaders and citizens often turn to other regional problem-solving mechanisms or create new ones, such as multi-sector regional alliances (see Problem-Solving #5). Moreover, regions with multiple, and especially competing, regional planning organizations can complicate addressing regional challenges in a timely and effective manner.

Finally, the major strength of regional planning councils with implementation responsibilities, such as regional growth management boards, is that they can provide a "throttle" on outrageous local action in developing regions. Besides, by negotiating the preparation of guidelines, such as for acceptable and unacceptable development, and offering mediation and conflict resolution services, they can help overcome conflicts between communities that threaten regional development gridlock.

Potential

Regional planning councils have emerged as a major regional problem-solving resource, but they often need to have their roles, responsibilities and relationships clarified and possibly their memberships broadened to meet the emerging challenges of this century and the next.

Clarify roles, responsibilities, and relationships and empower regional planning councils. Regional planning councils are in transition, possibly to some new form of regional problem-solving mechanism — one that provides neutral, timely regional information to community leaders and citizens, convenes community leaders and citizens to develop strategies to address emerging regional challenges, mediates differences among members on the implementation of these strategies, and delivers services to individual and groups of members.

Unfortunately, the transition is complicated by the variety of publicly sponsored entities carrying out regional planning responsibilities. In California, for example, state legislation has been proposed to create regional development and infrastructure agencies to assume responsibility and powers of transportation planning agencies, air quality management districts, councils of governments, and water quality districts. (Atkins, "From the Mauling to the Malling of Regionalism," 1993, 5) As part of conducting a regional governance examination (see Strategic #2, Chapter 4), the range and activities of regional planning organizations could be examined to determine overlaps, and outright competition, in regional planning responsibilities.

Most important, the regional planning councils could be examined to determine if they have the requisite powers and authorities to carry out assigned responsibilities. Regional planning councils are jointly empowered by state and local governments; both delegate some of their planning powers and authorities in order to be able to address challenges that emerge at the regional level — super-local and sub-state — between them. It might be useful to convene state and local government officials to negotiate the powers and authorities that they could provide to regional planning councils for carrying out their regional problem-solving responsibilities, possibly in the form of a community charter (see Problem-Solving/Service-Delivery #2). Moreover, they could negotiate an approach for monitoring the effectiveness of regional planning councils in carrying out these responsibilities and make adjustments as necessary.

For example, regional planning councils empowered to implement regional growth management programs have been ceded such a combination of state and local government powers and authorities, including preparing regional growth management plans and assuring local compliance with the plans. Similar authorities for land use and infrastructure planning have been provided to the regional planning councils in Portland, Oregon, and Minneapolis/St. Paul, which are part of regional planning and service districts (see Problem-Solving/Service-Delivery #3).

Regional planning councils also could be empowered to administer processes for siting controversial regional facilities. Frank Popper of Rutgers University suggests assigning points to various classes of facilities, such as community-based correction half-way houses and solid waste disposal plants and distributing the points to all communities (neighborhoods, municipalities, counties) within a region. Communities would be obligated to accept such facilities if they had unused points but could trade equivalent projects. One community could offer a coal-fired power plant in exchange for three half-way houses in another community. The regional planning council would establish the point values, assign points to communities, and oversee the transactions. To assure equity in unwanted facilities, it could subtract points for existing unwanted facilities or assign no points to communities already overburdened with such facilities. (Popper)

In a variation on this approach, John O'Looney of the University of Georgia at Athens recommends creating a marketplace for unwanted regional facilities. He suggests assigning development rights for unwanted regional facilities to communities; the communities, in turn, could sell the development rights and be compensated for accepting unwanted facilities. Neighborhoods that have already been the location of a number of unwanted facilities would not need to accept any development rights, helping locate such facilities equitably within a region. (O'Looney)

Finally, regional planning councils could be authorized to conduct regional impact analyses on major development projects, such as major jobs centers, solid waste disposal plants, or new transit corridors. A regional planning council could assess the overall impact of the proposed project on sound regional development, as well as its benefits and costs for individual community institutions and residents, such as jobs created and taxes generated versus infrastructure, environmental or other costs. It could make recommendations on the overall desirability of the development as well as for assigning benefits and costs among impacted communities, possibly as a condition of its approval.

Regional planning councils will never be fully effective unless they are provided the state and local powers and authorities to permit them to address emerging regional challenges.

Expand the geographic scope and diversify the membership of regional planning councils. Many regional planning councils have not expanded as their regions have become urbanized; even the Metropolitan Council of Minneapolis/St. Paul has remained at the same seven counties while the metropolitan statistical area has grown to thirteen counties. Regional planning councils need to encompass urbanizing areas if they are to shape further regional growth.

Most regional planning councils are dominated by elected officials from their member jurisdictions. Most also have nonpublic members; a few have many. One such is the Board of Trustees for the Ohio-Kentucky-Indiana Regional Council of Governments, which designates approximately one-third of its more than one hundred members as at-large citizen members, drawing a sizable proportion of its members from outside the public sector.

Options for including representatives of all sectors affected by regional challenges on regional planning councils include:

- adding enough nonpublic members to the governing boards of regional planning councils to be representative, but not adding so many as to threaten elected officials' majorities,
- exchanging members with organizations in other sectors, such as regional chambers of commerce, academic research institutes or citizens leagues, or
- directly electing citizen representatives to regional planning councils.

The proposed Metropolitan Board for the St. Louis region, for example, would be empowered to examine regional challenges and submit to the electorate recommended strategies for addressing these challenges, including recommendations for financing the strategies. Its proposed strategies would need to be approved at the ballot box by a majority of the voters in both the city and county of St. Louis. The members of the board would be elected from sub-regional districts of approximately equal population.

The proposed Southern California Regional Council would have a governing body composed of elected officials selected by their peers and citizens elected from districts of approximately equal population. The

Regional Council would consolidate the responsibilities of various regional planning councils so as to coordinate comprehensive planning for the Los Angeles region. A thirty-two-member Regional Advisory Council would provide for nonpublic sector input into regional planning.

Contacts

- Intergovernmental agreements: International City/County Management Association, Washington, D.C., 202-289-ICMA
- Regional planning councils: National Association of Regional Councils, Washington, D.C., 202-457-0710

Problem-Solving #2
Private Regional Problem-Solving Mechanisms

Privately initiated regional problem-solving mechanisms have focused most of their attention on addressing regional economic development and related challenges.

The most prevalent form of private regional problem-solving mechanisms are regional chambers of commerce or growth associations, which pursue the interests of their primarily business members. Most of them have grown out of central city chambers of commerce, as the interests of businesses have become more regional, and now exist in many regions across the nation. Other business leadership groups and business research institutes have been established in some regions as well.

Given the interests of their members, these groups often take the lead in conducting regional economic development and related problem-solving and planning activities

Some sponsor regional economic development strategic planning processes. The Dayton Area Chamber of Commerce, for example, raised funds to conduct the Challenge 95 regional planning process and established a Challenge 95 Leadership Network to oversee its implementation, in the Dayton region. (Challenge 95 Leadership Network) The Greater Baltimore Committee sponsored a regional visioning process to develop a life sciences vision for the Baltimore region. (Greater Baltimore Committee, *Baltimore: Where Science Comes to Life,* 1991)

Some design and oversee regional marketing programs. The Greater Denver Chamber of Commerce's Metro Denver Network electronically shares information on business prospects in the region. The Metro Denver Network provides information on business prospects to eight major county government and local chamber participants which in turn provide information through local networks of economic development organizations. All participants are connected by electronic databases, bulletin boards, and e-mail and a system for tracking individual prospects. Participants are governed by an operating agreement and code of ethics; unacceptable actions can lead to expulsion from the network.

The Denver Metro Chamber of Commerce solicited approximately $11 million in corporate pledges to support the Denver Metro Network and other activities over the past decade, including campaigns for a new regional convention center and airport. The Denver Metro Network is governed by a board composed of its participants and corporate supporters. Similar networks are being developed in other regions throughout the state of Colorado.

Similar marketing efforts in other regions include the Trade Development Alliance of Seattle (Wallis, 1994, 23–4; National League of Cities, 1993, 13), New Cleveland Campaign and Greater Cleveland Marketing Partnership (Wallis, 1994, 23–4), Forward Hampton (Virginia) Yards (National League of Cities, 1993, 15), Carolinas Partnership (National League of Cities, 1993, 16), Penn South West (Pittsburgh, Pennsylvania), and the Greater Washington Initiative (Behr).

Some sponsor other related regional planning activities, such as tax studies and public works improvement programs. Build Up Greater Cleveland, staffed and partially financed by the Greater Cleveland Growth Association, addresses infrastructure needs in the Cleveland region by preparing and annually updating a community capital investment strategy that monitors public works needs, conducting an extensive public works education program, applying its good offices to the resolution of public works management issues, and lobbying for additional public works financing. Over the past decade it has attracted more than $1 billion in new public works financing.

Some sponsor regional leadership programs, such as in the Atlanta (Georgia), Dayton (Ohio) and Winston-Salem/Greensboro/High Point (North Carolina) regions (see Empowering #1, Chapter 6) or regional leadership discussions, such as through the Potomac Conference of the Greater Washington Board of Trade, which periodically convenes community leaders to discuss timely regional challenges.

In addition, other business leadership groups, usually with more limited memberships, take the lead in conducting regional problem-solving activities. The Allegheny Conference on Community Development in the Pittsburgh region has been sponsoring regional economic development planning activities since its founding in the late 1940s; its latest plan recommends a Regional Economic Revitalization Initiative for reinvigorating manufacturing in the region. (Allegheny Conference on Community Development) Similarly, in the Cleveland Region, Cleveland Tomorrow has taken the lead in conducting regional economic development planning and promoting specific downtown development projects. (Wallis, 1994, 23–24)

Finally, business research institutes, in the form of economy leagues or think tanks, exist or are being created in some regions. Some of the economy leagues that were created to reform local governments earlier in the century have broadened their agendas to address regional challenges. For example, the Western Pennsylvania Division of the Pennsylvania Economy League conducted research on an assets district (see Equitable #2, Chapter 5) for the central county in the region. Recently, a privately sponsored think tank, the Allegheny Institute, was created to conduct public policy research on various regional challenges, such as the future of the Pittsburgh Pirates.

Private regional problem-solving mechanisms are primarily organized as nonprofit 501(c)(6) or 501(c)(3) organizations. They depend upon contributions of their members and community foundation support, and, at times, state and local government support, for conducting their regional problem-solving and planning activities.

Accomplishments

Private regional problem-solving mechanisms have made significant contributions to addressing economic development and related regional problem-solving and planning processes.

Strengths and Shortcomings

The major strength of private regional problem-solving mechanisms is the knowledge, discipline, funding, and clout that business leaders bring to regional problem solving. The major shortcoming is the all too often exclusiveness of the problem-solving processes, given the reluctance of many business leaders to participate in open discussions with other community leaders and especially citizens.

Potential

Private regional problem-solving mechanisms are already achieving their potential in regions with established regional chambers of commerce or growth associations and other regional business leadership organizations. In fact, they often have more clout than other regional problem-solving mechanisms, especially on regional economic development topics, because of their ability to develop a consensus among their members and market their recommendations to the public and other sectors of the community that are not as well organized or financed.

Many of the private regional problem-solving mechanisms are losing their clout, however, because of their leaders' preoccupation with personal business concerns and the growing impact of the academic and nonprofit sectors on regional economic competitiveness. The major employers in the Pittsburgh region, for example, which made its reputation in heavy manufacturing, are mostly local colleges and universities and hospitals.

To preserve their clout, and more important, to make their problem-solving processes equitable and empowering, private regional problem-solving mechanisms are beginning to reach out to other sectors and are inviting them to participate in their planning processes. Some are beginning to invite representatives of other sectors to participate on their governing bodies or to exchange members with other regional problem-solving mechanisms.

Private regional problem-solving mechanisms could broaden citizen involvement in their planning processes for addressing regional challenges, add representatives of citizen regional problem-solving mechanisms (see Problem-Solving #4) to their governing boards, or foster the creation of academic and other research institutes to advise community leaders and citizens on regional challenges (see Problem-Solving #3). Such actions would mimic those being taken by world class businesses to be more directly responsive to their customers by placing them on their boards of directors.

Contacts

- American Chamber of Commerce Executives, Alexandria, Virginia, 703-998-0072
- National Council for Urban Economic Development, Washington, D.C., 202-223-4735
- ✓ Dayton Area Chamber of Commerce, Dayton, Ohio, 513-226-8231
- Greater Baltimore Committee, Baltimore, Maryland, 410-727-2820
- Denver Metro Chamber of Commerce, Denver, Colorado, 304-534-8500
- Greater Cleveland Growth Association, Cleveland, Ohio, 216-621-3300
- St. Louis Regional Commerce and Growth Association, St. Louis, Missouri, 314-231-5555
- Greater Washington Board of Trade, Washington, D.C., 202-857-5900
- Allegheny Conference on Community Development, Pittsburgh, Pennsylvania, 412-281-1890
- Cleveland Tomorrow, Cleveland, Ohio, 216-574-6276
- Pennsylvania Economy League, Western Pennsylvania Division, Pittsburgh, Pennsylvania, 412-281-1890

Problem-Solving #3
Academic Regional Problem-Solving Mechanisms

Academic regional problem-solving mechanisms have historically focused on addressing the urban challenges in central cities, but today some are shifting at least some of their attention to addressing region-wide challenges.

The most prevalent form of academic regional problem-solving mechanisms are college or university research institutes and public service programs.

Academic research institutes and public service programs conduct neutral, professional research on urban and regional challenges and provide information and staff support for regional problem-solving processes, such as regional strategic planning processes or annual leadership symposia. Many of these institutes and programs had their origins in examining the urban challenges to central cities, usually the ones in which the institutions are located. Although most of these institutes and programs were initiated by individual institutions, the national government supported academic urban observatories in a number of central cities in the 1960s and 1970s and the state of Ohio has supported an Urban University Program at eight of its universities for the past fifteen years.

Most of the current institutes and programs are supported by a mixture of internal and especially external funding sources, including contracts with public agencies, grants from state governments and foundations, and endowments from wealthy alumni.

The research institutes are set up either as institution-wide centers, such as the Center for Greater Philadelphia at the University of Pennsylvania, or under a school of public or urban affairs, such as the Urban Center in the College of Urban Affairs at Cleveland State University. Some are established as public service programs, often tied to the life of a particular regional problem-solving process and answerable to a regionally sensitive president or professor. Governors State University, for example, initiated, generated funding for, and is providing staff support for the Regional Action Project 2000+, a strategic planning process in the southern part of the Chicago region.

As the regional implications of urban challenges emerged in the last couple of decades, some existing centers and programs have shifted their agendas (and sometimes their names) and new centers have been created to address regional issues.

- The Institute of Portland Metropolitan Studies, Portland State University, defines its role as a catalyst for responding to regional challenges. It is developing a set of tools for providing regional governance information to "potential collaborators and partners," including a Metropolitan Clearinghouse, a Metropolitan Briefing Book, a *Metroscape* newsletter, and an electronic Metropolitan Newsnet, and sponsors an annual leadership symposium (see Empowering #2, Chapter 6). (Seltzer)

- The Center for Greater Philadelphia, at the University of Pennsylvania, orchestrated a Year of the Region program that included publication of reports and editorials, forums and conferences for community leaders and citizens, and community meetings and talk shows (see Prominent #5, Chapter 3). It also sponsors an annual Southeastern Pennsylvania Legislators' conference to discuss and select priority regional initiatives for state legislature action, such as creating a regional port authority.

- The Urban Center, at Cleveland State University, conducts research on various aspects of regional economic competitiveness and sponsors annual Summits on Regional Competitiveness. It supports collaborative efforts such as Build Up Greater Cleveland (see Problem-Solving #2) and a regional geographic information system and offers training for public works professionals region-wide through its Public Works Management program.

- The Center for Urban and Public Affairs, at Wright State University, provided staff support for a regional strategic planning process, called Challenge 95, and sponsored an international Symposium on Regional Cooperation.

- The Taubman Center for State and Local Government, at Harvard University, recently convened academics from other institutions for an informal dialogue on the evolution of regional governance. It also sponsors the annual Ford Foundation funded Innovation in American Government awards.

Two collaborative groups of colleges and universities, the Urban Affairs Association (UAA) and the North American Institute for Comparative Urban Research (NAMICUR), organize conferences on urban and regional issues. UAA sponsors annual conferences to share research on urban affairs; NAMICUR sponsored a conference in 1994 on "Metropolitan Governance without Metropolitan Government."

Accomplishments

Academic research institutes and public service programs have conducted research and provided staff expertise on regional challenges to other regional problem-solving mechanisms involved in regional strategic planning and other problem-solving processes. Efforts that they support have successfully developed and implemented action plans for addressing numerous regional challenges.

Strengths and Shortcomings

The major strength of academic research institutes and public service programs lies in the neutral, professional resources they can provide for addressing regional challenges. The major shortcoming is the limited resources of these institutes and programs: usually only a few part-time faculty members, professional staff, and student interns. It is also often difficult to interest academicians in addressing regional challenges in a timely manner, given their teaching and other academic demands.

Potential

Academic regional research institutes and public service programs have considerable potential that could begin to be realized with a couple of actions.

Focus more attention on regional challenges. In part, the dearth of models of regional governance comes from lack of academic interest in regionalism over the past couple of decades, after a flurry of activity in the 1950s and 1960s. Victor Jones, who wrote the classic text on metropolitan governments in 1942, commented in the 1950s that until research was done to "supplement the administrative and structural studies of metropolitan communities with studies of the metropolitan organization and relationships of attitude and opinion-forming agencies," the failure of reform proposals was likely to continue. Such research was rarely undertaken. (Jones, 129–133)

Existing institutes and programs, especially those that focus on urban affairs, could expand their regional affairs activities, if not shift priority attention to regional affairs, especially given that addressing almost any major urban challenge requires a regional strategy. Even awards programs, such as the Innovation in American Government awards, administered by the Taubman Center at Harvard University, could recognize regional governance excellence, in addition to national, state and local government excellence.

New academic institutes and programs could be launched with a focus on regional affairs. In fact, colleges and universities that primarily educate students and conduct research in their regions are beginning to define themselves as metropolitan universities. A number of them have signed a "Declaration of Metropolitan Universities" and are publishing a journal on metropolitan universities. Creating a regional public service-research institute or program would help reinforce their identity as metropolitan institutions.

Formalize relationships with other regional problem-solving mechanisms. Academic regional research institutes or public service programs rarely take the lead in sponsoring regional problem-solving processes, except for the regional strategic planning processes mentioned above. But they can sponsor regional governance initiatives, such as the annual summits or conferences of regional leaders mentioned above, and provide professional support for regional problem-solving mechanisms, such as the staff support provided by the Morrison Institute at Arizona State University to help establish the Valley Citizens League in the Phoenix region. Developing ongoing relationships with regional problem-solving mechanisms helps provide the professional resources needed by these mechanisms to address complex regional challenges and, in turn, it is hoped, helps make the case for supporting academic regional research institutes and public service programs.

Contacts

- Institute of Portland Metropolitan Studies, Portland State University, Portland, Oregon, 503-725-5170
- Center for Greater Philadelphia, University of Pennsylvania, Philadelphia, Pennsylvania, 215-898-8713
- The Urban Center, College of Urban Affairs, Cleveland State University, Cleveland, Ohio, 216-687-2135
- Center for Urban and Public Affairs, Wright State University, Dayton, Ohio, 513-873-3888
- Taubman Center for State and Local Government, Harvard University, Cambridge, Massachusetts, 617-495-0557
- Metropolitan Universities: Transaction Publishers, Rutgers, The State University, New Brunswick, New Jersey, 201-932-2280

Problem-Solving #4
Citizen Regional Problem-Solving Mechanisms

Citizen-initiated regional problem-solving mechanisms — regional civic organizations or RCOs— have emerged in a small number of regions as citizen interest has grown in addressing regional challenges.

RCOs are nonpartisan, independent and open membership organizations that conduct studies of emerging regional challenges and educate and encourage citizens and community leaders to address them. Almost all of them give priority attention to regional governance reform.

Often called citizens leagues, forums or councils, they have been created in various regions over the past century, usually as nonprofit 501(c)(3) organizations. Some of the earliest, such as the Citizens League of Greater Cleveland, were created to reform municipal governments. Many have sprung up in the last decade to oversee the implementation of regional planning processes, such as the Valley Citizens League (Phoenix), or to provide a citizens voice in addressing regional challenges, such as the Citizens League of Southwestern Pennsylvania (Pittsburgh).

The most common activities of RCOs are:
- organizing citizen study committees, study circles and summits to explore emerging regional challenges and recommending strategies for citizen action, including developing regional governance strategies,
- holding citizen seminars ("speakouts," as one citizens league calls them) and publishing newsletters to educate residents on timely topics, and
- providing technical assistance to citizen-based organizations dealing with regional challenges.

One citizens league, with an affiliated institute that conducts research on regional challenges, is set up as a nonprofit 501(c)(6) organization to conduct a candidate rating program for local government elected offices.

RCOs range in size from less than 250 to more than 2,000 individual members and from less than a dozen to more 500 corporate members. They have budgets from under $100,000 to over $1,000,000 annually; consequently, staffs range from none to more than two dozen individuals. Corporate member contributions and foundation and other grants provide the primary support for most of the RCOs, but individual membership dues and other income have become increasingly important, especially for newer RCOs. (Dodge, 1990)

Over the past few years, Healthy Communities programs have emerged as new form of RCOs. Created as a joint effort of the National Civic League and the U.S. Public Health Service to develop innovative approaches to tackling issues related to the overall health and quality of life in communities, they now exist in more than 150 communities, especially in Colorado. While most of the programs focus on bringing stakeholders together in individual communities, many are addressing topics that cut across communities and entire regions, such as the Central Oklahoma 2020 regional strategic planning process in the Oklahoma City region. (Norris, 280; National Civic League, *1995 Healthy Communities Action Project*; *Doing Democracy,* Summer, 1995)

Other models of citizen-based organizations that serve multiple communities exist across the country and might offer models for regional civic organizations.

- The Citizens Budget Initiative of Southwestern Pennsylvania brings citizens together across the Pittsburgh region to discuss and develop positions on the national government budget.

- At the state level, The North Dakota Consensus Council, Inc., a nonprofit organization, sponsors public-private forums on timely issues statewide and guides the development of state policy and legislation.

- Similarly, Georgia Healthy Decisions, a nonprofit corporation conducts statewide focus groups and surveys as well as open-ended public discussions. The results are turned over to voluntary regional boards that act as catalysts to "share the results with policymakers, media, business leaders and the health care industry." (*The Public Innovator,* October 27, 1994)

- Finally, "faith-based organizations" are bringing congregations together across regions to organize citizens to address economic, social and racial disparities, such as Communities Organized for Public Service (COPS) and the Metro Alliance in the San Antonio (Texas) region. (*Doing Democracy,* "Citizens Discover Economic Solutions")

Accomplishments

RCOs have offered one of the few opportunities for ongoing citizen involvement in regional decision making, and they have made substantial contributions to improving regional governance. The Citizens League of Minneapolis/St. Paul conducted some of the initial examinations and helped create the Fiscal Disparities Program (see Equitable #2, Chapter 5) and Metropolitan Council (see Problem-Solving/Service-Delivery #3). According to Stephen Forman, former Director of the Municipal League of Seattle-King County, citizen leagues "create inclusive but strategically focused coalitions around specific issues that can substitute for broad consensus."

RCOs often provide the catalyst for addressing a topic that is too politically charged for community leaders to address, such as intercommunity fiscal disparities. They have also played a role in building relationships among regional governance mechanisms, such as convening meetings of the directors of regional service-delivery mechanisms. (Citizens League of Greater Cleveland, 1992)

Strengths and Shortcomings

For all of their accomplishments, RCOs, not counting the Healthy Communities programs, only exist in a couple of dozen regions and even then often lead hand-to-mouth existences. Their history is strewn with the wreckage of organizations that have only survived for a few years; few have had an ongoing impact on regional governance.

Potential

The potential of RCOs has been repeatedly touted over the past few decades. In 1975, a group of mostly privately sponsored urban affairs groups, called the Metropolitan Affairs Nonprofit Corporations or MANCs recommended creating regional citizens organizations as the "basic ingredient" in strengthening the regionwide community. They suggested that these organizations take a generalist approach, have a regional perspective, be concerned with process, take a long-term view, and be independent. Moreover, it recommended that they conduct in-depth analyses, have broad contact with community leaders and organizations, and engage in what they called "information marketing" of a regional agenda. (Metropolitan Affairs Nonprofit Corporations, 516)

Finally, the MANCs recommended that the regional citizen organizations have a professional staff, the strong commitment of community organizations and the financial support of the private sector. More recently, Neal Peirce recommended that RCOs, which he refers to as "metropolitan partnerships," receive significant backing, "up to $1 million to get launched and budgets of several hundreds of thousands of dollars afterward. They need such funds to attract and hold large memberships, not only from the policy elites but from every class, income, racial and geographic group across a metropolitan area, and to effectively use sophisticated tools of communication." (Peirce, 322)

With this type of mandate and at these levels of support, RCO s could launch most of the regional governance initiative options, especially developing regional citizenship skills (see Empowering #1, Chapter 6) and the other Empowering and Equitable initiatives, and even take the lead in developing Strategies for Achieving Regional Governance Excellence (see Strategic #2, Chapter 4).

A proposed RCO in the Washington, D.C., region, tentatively called a Washington Regional Alliance, might offer a model for future RCOs. It would conduct examinations of emerging regional challenges, but it would also attempt to address their implications for particular communities. Rather than assemble regionwide study committees, it might consider using techniques like study circles that bring small groups of communities together to develop collaborative strategies (see Empowering #4, Chapter 6) and interactive videoconferencing to test and endorse them.

The Washington Regional Alliance would probably involve representatives of community-based organizations as well as citizens in its activities, thereby creating a membership of individuals and organizations. If it is able to attract substantial front-end funding (up to $1 million), build a membership of a couple thousand in the first few years, and have a couple of victories, it could provide a model for launching successful RCOs for the 21st century.

Contacts

- Citizens League of Greater Cleveland, Cleveland, Ohio, 216-241-5340
- Citizens League, Minneapolis/St. Paul, Minnesota, 612-338-0791
- Valley Citizens League, Phoenix, Arizona, 602-241-9886
- Citizens League of Southwestern Pennsylvania, Pittsburgh, Pennsylvania, 412-462-5533
- Washington Regional Alliance, Washington, D.C., 301-652-4019

Problem-Solving #5
Multi-Sector Regional Problem-Solving Mechanisms

Multi-sector initiated regional problem-solving mechanisms — often called multi-sector or regional alliances or partnerships — have been the focus of greatest experimentation in regional decision making over the past decade, from convening affected interests to address a particular regional challenge to creating regional alliances to develop regional visions and economic competitiveness strategies.

Part of the appeal of regional alliances is their potential to develop into ongoing mechanisms for bringing community leaders from all sectors and citizens into regional decision making. Regional alliances could become the "holding companies" that identify emerging regional challenges, convene the appropriate community leaders and citizens, guide the design of strategies for addressing the challenges, and assure their timely implementation. (Richman and Oliver, 20) They might function like Mister Rogers of children's television. That is, they could be mechanisms that behave like benevolent but influential "puppeteers" who assemble the appropriate community leaders and citizens (the "puppets") in decision making processes (the "stage") and continue to influence their behavior (pull their "strings") as necessary to address regional challenges. (Dodge, 1988)

Regional alliances are jointly sponsored by some or all of the interests affected by a regional challenge. They tend to be more inclusive than publicly or privately initiated regional problem-solving mechanisms and attract more leaders than citizen-initiated regional problem-solving mechanisms. As a result, they also tend to be less cohesive, exercise the vaguest of problem-solving powers, and survive only long enough to address a particular regional challenge, if that long. Few ever have the opportunity to evolve as "Mister Rogers" mechanisms.

Regional alliances are also usually jointly financed by some or all of the interests affected by a regional challenge. In addition, community foundations and major businesses have been a primary source of funding for regional alliances. Regional community foundations are even being established to support regional alliances and strengthen regional decision making, such as the Foundation for the National Capital Region in the Washington, D.C., area.

Regional alliances tend to provide the venues in which the various sectors interact to address particular problems, a regional "united nations" bringing together disparate local interests to address cross-cutting challenges. Although the interactions are not always up to the quality of Olympic competitions, the importance of finding winning multi-sector strategies is critical to future regional competitiveness and quality of life.

Regional alliances carry out a variety of activities.

Regional Strategic Planning and Visioning: Community leaders and citizens in many regions have conducted regional strategic planning or visioning processes to design future visions for their regions, including identifying competitive niches in the global economy, and to develop strategic initiatives for beginning to achieve the visions. Among these are Atlanta Vision 2020, Central Oklahoma 2020 (Oklahoma City), and Regional Action Project 2000+ (Chicago).

Most of these processes have been guided by a temporary regional alliance, a steering committee composed of a broad cross section of community leaders, which in turn actively involves other community leaders and citizens in stakeholder workshops, task groups, community forums and even electronic town meetings. Generally, these processes are staffed by one of the other regional problem-solving mechanisms, most commonly a regional planning council (see Problem-Solving #1).

Some states have established programs for assisting in the development of regional strategic planning or visioning processes, especially if they focus on economic competitiveness, as does the State of Oregon Regional Strategies Program. (National Council on Urban Economic Development, 48–49) A number of these regional strategic planning processes are reported on in *Shaping a Region's Future: A Guide to Strategic Decision Making for Regions.* (Dodge, 1995)

Some regions continue, or modify, the regional alliances to oversee the implementation of the strategies resulting from the strategic planning and visioning processes. For example, the Challenge 95 Leadership

Network, composed of public, private and other sector leaders from the six counties in the Dayton region, oversaw the implementation of Challenge 95, a regional strategic plan. The Leadership Network established five committees that oversaw the priority economic development, education, environment, human relations/human needs and technology/innovation strategic initiatives. The county governments and the Greater Dayton Chamber of Commerce provided annual contributions to support launching the Challenge 95 initiatives. The Center for Urban and Public Affairs at Wright State University provided a secretariat for the Leadership Network; the co-chairs and members of each subject area committee contributed technical support to their committees.

Similarly, a number of initially citywide strategic planning and visioning efforts have expanded to address regional challenges. Chattanooga Venture, for example, periodically holds community dialogues and develops an agenda of regional goals, the most recent called Vision 2020, and guides its implementation by groups of community organizations and individuals. Chattanooga Venture has a governing board of approximately 60 community leaders and a small staff.

A few of these regional alliances have been institutionalized to guide regional strategic planning and visioning processes, such as the Regional Plan Association in the New York region. It produced long-term plans for the region in the 1920s and 1960s and recently released a new plan to guide the region into the next century.

Regional Leadership Consensus Building: Some ongoing regional alliances — composed of public, private, and usually academic, nonprofit and civic leaders — have been created to develop a consensus on regional challenges.

Some of these organizations have existed for decades and address regional challenges as they emerge. The Metropolitan Planning Council in the Chicago region, for example, which has a board of approximately fifty community leaders, and a fifteen-person staff, is pursing a broad-based Regional Cooperation Initiative. The Detroit region's Metropolitan Affairs Corporation, which has a board composed of approximately forty community leaders, is pursuing regional economic development and related issues, and has staff provided, under contract, by the Southeast Michigan Council of Governments. Both alliances are financed by business, foundation and individual contributions.

The Greater Indianapolis Progress Committee (GIPC) identifies regional challenges, divides its membership into task forces to develop strategies for addressing them, and works with local governments and others for their implementation. It has hundreds of members and a governing board of approximately seventy-five members. Over the past three decades, it has involved more than 5,000 individuals in its task forces, which have addressed topics from creating Unigov, the consolidated central city-county government (see Problem-Solving/Service-Delivery #2), to examining the economy of Central Indiana. It generates funding for implementing its strategies from businesses and foundations and has a small staff.

Some of these ongoing regional alliances are newer and have been developed to address particular regional challenges. The Southwestern Pennsylvania Growth Alliance, for example, develops annual legislative agendas among public, private and academic leaders in the Pittsburgh region and coordinates lobbying for state and national government action. (The Southwestern Pennsylvania Growth Alliance)

Today, there is growing interest on the part of community leaders and citizens in creating new regional alliances that not only include all sectors and can address any regional challenges, but can do so systematically and interactively. The Greater Triangle Regional Council in the Research Triangle of North Carolina, for example, is composed of approximately three dozen of the most senior public, private, academic and other community leaders. Its purpose is to:
- "set strategic long-term directions for the region,
- consider ventures needed to achieve success,
- identify resources needed to undertake the ventures, and
- muster the teamwork needed to see that the ventures are implemented."

The council is an independent organization that:
- "sets goals and develops long-term strategies;
- accomplishes its goals by fostering support, enlisting the participation and contributions of others, and coordinating their efforts;

- focuses on 'win-win techniques' to share resources so that all communities share in the benefits and burdens of change;
- demonstrates the features, advantages, and benefits of the ventures it supports in order to garner the participation of others in the region; and
- may sponsor ventures, but works with and through other organizations and local governments that operate programs or deliver services."

The initial regional challenges addressed by the Regional Council are solid waste management, at-risk middle school students and future regional growth. Funding has been provided by business contributions but might shift to a voluntary dues structure. Staff support is provided by the Triangle J Council of Governments. (Greater Triangle Regional Council; *Regional Reporter,* 6)

Regional Economic Development: Regional alliances have been created to develop broad strategies as well as address specific economic development challenges.

On one hand, Piedmont Triad Partnership, an ongoing regional alliance in the Greensboro/Winston-Salem/High Point region of North Carolina conducts a range of activities to make the region prominent to community leaders and citizens and market the region in other regions in this country and abroad. (See Empowering #3, Chapter 3.)

On the other hand, the Fort Drum Steering Council, a temporary regional alliance, was created to address a particular economic development challenge — the massive expansion of an army base in the Watertown, New York, region. The council had a twenty-three member governing body composed of community representatives from the three impacted counties and established ten task forces to develop strategies to address various aspects of the challenge, including coordinating implementation of infrastructure improvements, social services and local land use regulations. (Dodge, "Regional Problem Solving in the 1990s," 1990, 8)

Downtown development partnerships also have been created to foster the development of, and increase community life in, downtowns of regions. With the demise of national and state government funding, central city downtowns realize that they have to build working relationships with their suburban neighbors, if they are to be a healthy "core" of the region.

Regional Social Development: Regional alliances — from traditional United Ways to new mechanisms — have been created to address social development challenges.

For example, almost all regions have United Ways, ongoing regional alliances, which have been experimenting with a number of different approaches to addressing regional social service challenges for the past few decades. Regional United Ways have been created in many regions to coordinate the fund-raising and planning activities of county and central city United Way efforts. Many have also experimented with community problem-solving task forces, such as the Community Initiatives Committee of the United Way and Community Chest of Greater Cincinnati. These task forces, composed of community leaders and citizens, develop common strategies to address emerging crosscutting social challenges. Some support independent regional problem-solving mechanisms, such as Jacksonville Progress, Inc., to address intercommunity and regional social challenges. (United Way of America, 1–5)

New types of regional alliances are being created as crosscutting social challenges affect a broader range of providers and consumers. Social service agencies, along with the Atlanta Regional Commission and United Way, have created the Alliance for Human Services to coordinate social service problem solving in the region. (Harry West, National Academy of Public Administration conference) Similarly, the arts and cultural agencies in the central city and county in the Dayton region have created the Montgomery County Arts and Cultural District to develop cooperative strategies and spend $1 million annually in sales tax revenues. (Dodge, Montgomery County Leadership Network, 1992)

Intergovernmental Cooperation: Various forms of regional alliances have been created to foster intergovernmental cooperation.

During the 1980s, for example, the Intergovernmental Cooperation Program provided a regional alliance for Pittsburgh's public, private, civic and academic organizations to foster intergovernmental cooperation. It focused on identifying opportunities and designing strategies for cooperation; it generally used its members to guide the implementation of strategies. Its projects included establishing a Local Government Academy to train municipal officials, sharing sewer cleaning and repair equipment and public works activities, developing a shared computer network among sub-county councils of governments and local governments, and initiating the development of a countywide 911 emergency communications system. (Dodge, 1985)

Finally, the Community Cooperation Task Force, a temporary regional alliance composed of public, private, and academic leaders in the Dayton region, designed and oversaw the implementation of the economic development/tax sharing program called ED/GE. (See Equitable #2, Chapter 5)

Megalopolis Cooperation: Megalopolises are areas with economic or other significance beyond the central city and surrounding suburbs and growth areas of individual regions; they sometimes include neighboring regions, states, and even parts of nations.

The Mon Valley Tri-State Network, for example, is a regional alliance that brings community leaders together in a super-Pittsburgh region that includes parts of the states of Pennsylvania, West Virginia, and Maryland. Projects include a Leadership Academy to train economic development professionals to pursue collaborative strategies, develop common riverfront development strategies for the entire Monongahela River watershed, and foster greater cooperation among colleges and universities.

A number of multi-state and international regional alliances have been established to address common economic development concerns. The Cascadia Transportation/Trade Task Force is developing Pacific Rim markets, a regional stock market, and a high-speed train system for an area stretching from Portland, Oregon, to Vancouver, British Columbia. The Transboundary Initiative for Collaborative Problem Solving brings midwestern Canadian and U.S. public and private leaders together. Similar alliances have been created along the Rocky Mountains (Rocky Mountain Trade Corridor), along the U.S.-Mexico border (Camino Real Economic Alliance), across the old South (Mid-South Common Market), in the Buffalo-Toronto super-region (Niagara), along the northern Red River between Minnesota and Manitoba (Red River

Trade Corridor), and in the Austin-San Antonio super-region (Greater Austin-San Antonio Corridor Council) to foster trade and economic development. (National League of Cities, 1993 and 1995)

Accomplishments

Multi-sector regional problem-solving mechanisms or regional alliances have been able to assemble community leaders and citizens to address some of the most demanding regional challenges, such as developing a future vision or economic competitiveness strategy for the region. At times, they have collectively energized community leaders and citizens to address crosscutting challenges that had previously defied resolution by the most conscientious efforts of individual sectors.

Strengths and Shortcomings

Multi-sector regional alliances are almost inevitably caught in a conundrum: the participants need to "lose" some of their individual independence to "gain" collective success in addressing regional challenges.

Each sector and its organizations need to be willing to cede some of their individual powers and authorities to the regional alliances in return for the collective clout — political influence, special expertise and access to resources — needed to address complex, crosscutting challenges. Regrettably, the regional alliances that have the greatest success are viewed with the greatest suspicion and often have their powers and authorities reduced or revoked as a reward for their accomplishments.

Not surprisingly, the half-life of regional alliances is quite short; most never survive addressing their first regional challenge; few are ever institutionalized with a predictable ongoing source of funding. At best, they seem to enjoy a love-hate relationship with their participants.

Potential

Multi-sector regional problem-solving mechanisms or alliances, at their best, are developing cooperative strategies for addressing regional challenges as well as experimenting with regional decision making for the 21st century.

Most important, experimentation with regional alliances needs to continue to be fostered in the future.

- Single sector initiated regional problem-solving mechanisms could broaden their membership or exchange members with other sector organizations to improve their capacity to address multi-sector regional challenges.

- Periodic meetings of directors or board chairs of regional problem-solving or service-delivery mechanisms, such as have been convened by the Citizens League of Greater Cleveland, could also be held to increase awareness of multi-sector regional challenges. (Citizens League of Greater Cleveland, *The Performance of Special Purpose Government in Greater Cleveland,* 1992)

- Predictable funding sources could be provided for multi-sector regional problem-solving mechanisms. Funds might come from regular public, private, and community foundation contributions or from a dedicated tax to create a regional governance fund to support strengthening regional decision making (see Strategic #5, Chapter 4).

- Temporary regional alliances could be recycled, or institutionalized, to address related regional challenges.

- Single-county regional alliances, such as the Montgomery County Leadership Network in the central county in the Dayton region, could be expanded to regional alliances.

New types of regional alliances need to be tested. The Bank of America, in its report, *Beyond Sprawl,* recommends creating alliances for sustainable communities:

Past efforts to reduce sprawl have been hampered because little constituency exists beyond groups of government reformers, some local government leaders, community groups, and conservationists. But, as this report suggests, many other players in California's future will also find themselves increasingly stifled by sprawl. Political alliances must be forged between environmentalists, inner city community experts, farmers, and suburbanites to improve the quality of life in all our existing communities and protect our resources. (Bank of America, 11)

Contacts

- ✓• Atlanta Vision 2020: Atlanta Regional Commission, Atlanta, Georgia, 404-364-2500
- • Central Oklahoma 2020: Association of Central Oklahoma Governments, Oklahoma City, Oklahoma, 405-848-8961
- • Regional Action Project 2000+: Governors State University, Chicago, Illinois, 708-534-6360
- ✓• Chattanooga Venture, Chattanooga, Tennessee, 615-267-8687
- • Greater Indianapolis Progress Committee, Indianapolis, Indiana, 317-327-3860
- • Regional Plan Association, New York, New York, 212-980-8530
- • Southwestern Pennsylvania Growth Alliance, Pittsburgh, Pennsylvania, 412-281-1890
- • Greater Triangle Regional Council, Research Triangle, North Carolina, 919-558-9320
- • Rocky Mountain Trade Corridor, 406-443-8316
- • Camino Real Economic Alliance: El Paso Chamber of Commerce, El Paso, Texas, 915-534-0591
- • Mid-South Common Market, 901-575-3515
- • Niagara, 716-852-2762, extension 365
- • Red River Trade Corridor, 218-281-8459
- • Greater Austin-San Antonio Corridor Council, 512-245-2535
- • Piedmont Triad Partnership, Greensboro, North Carolina, 910-668-4556, 800-669-4556
- • Mon Valley Tri-State Network, Morgantown, West Virginia, 302-293-2552
- • Cascadia Transportation/Trade Task Force, Seattle, Washington, 206-672-4224
- • The Transboundary Initiative for Collaborative Problem Solving, Bismark, North Dakota, 701-224-0588
- • Metropolitan Planning Council, Chicago, Illinois, 312-922-5616
- • Metropolitan Affairs Corporation, Detroit, Michigan, 313-961-2270

Service-Delivery #1
Intergovernmental Service-Delivery Arrangements

Many intercommunity, and even regional, services are delivered by local governments.many central city governments still provide services, such as zoos, museums, arenas and stadia, or regional celebrations and festivals that serve regional populations. Even the smallest of jurisdictions provides services that are intercommunity or regional in nature, such as solid waste collection, though frequently on an insufficient and piecemeal basis, until intercommunity solutions are developed voluntarily or mandated by state and national governments.

When local governments voluntarily enter into informal and formal arrangements with their neighbors, they substantially improve their capabilities to deliver intercommunity and even regional services. Such voluntary arrangements among local governments have grown over the past few decades in every region, nationally. Examples of two or more local governments jointly delivering almost any major public service, including the most controversial, such as public safety services, can be found in almost any region. Even school districts cooperate in delivering bus transportation and maintenance services, just as county governments cooperate in delivering jail and solid waste disposal services.

These intergovernmental service-delivery arrangements include:

- informal, often unwritten, cooperation, to share materials, equipment and even personnel, such as for construction projects,
- mutual aid agreements, which permit neighboring police and fire departments to respond to emergency situations or to pursue offenders into neighboring jurisdictions,
- intergovernmental service contracts, which permit one local government to deliver services to others in return for a fee or provision of another service (for a list of examples, see International City/County Management Association, 1992),
- joint administration compacts, which permit two or more local governments to deliver a service together that would be more expensive to provide individually,
- councils of governments, which not only permit member municipalities to raise common problems, discuss potential solutions, and

design strategies but provide a mechanism for delivering cooperative services (see Problem-Solving #1),

- transfers of functions, which permits a local government to take
responsibility for providing a service, temporarily or permanently,
such as a county for municipalities in the county,

- functional consolidations, which permit two or more local governments to deliver a service through a jointly created service board,
and

- a special district or authority, which is a legally separate entity
created by two or more local governments to deliver a service (see
Service-Delivery #3 and 4).

Most of these arrangements are made directly by the participating
governments. Some, however, are negotiated and administered by
councils or associations of governments. In southern Montgomery
County, Ohio, for example, nine jurisdictions created Gov-Tech to
monitor cable services and develop cooperative arrangements. In Allegheny County, Pittsburgh, sub-county councils of governments involve more than 100 of the 130 jurisdictions in cooperative activities,
such as joint purchasing of materials, sharing of equipment and personnel, joint dispatching of public safety services, and joint service-delivery arrangements. A countywide association of jurisdictions, the
Allegheny League of Municipalities, has developed purchasing pools
for municipal insurance and lobbies for the common interests of its
members.

The vast majority of these arrangements are among a few neighboring
local governments within a single county. The obstacles to expanding
these cooperative arrangements seem to grow exponentially with each
additional local government, in part due to the difficulty in agreeing on
common service and reimbursement standards. Intergovernmental
service-delivery arrangements are rare at countywide, much less regional levels, as well as for the delivery of the most controversial public
services.

One of the rare exceptions involves library services in the Pittsburgh
region. The Allegheny County Library Association (ACLA), composed of
the independent public libraries in the central county in the region, is
establishing an electronic information system to integrate the catalogs

of individual library holdings and is distributing $5 million a year in regional asset district funding to improve library services. ACLA is currently preparing a plan to guide the future development of library services countywide.

The rationale developed in 1974 and 1983 by the Advisory Commission on Intergovernmental Relations for entering into these arrangements is still valid in the 1990s.

ACIR's 1974 rationale cited economic efficiency, equity, political accountability and administrative efficiency. Its 1983 rationale cited the ability of cooperative arrangements to address the lack of qualified equipment and personnel, achieve economies of scale, eliminate service duplication, respond to the feeling that it is more logical to organize service beyond jurisdictional or area limits, take politics out of service delivery, respond to funded or unfunded state or national government mandates, and respond to citizen demands for cooperative service arrangements. (ACIR, 1974, 1983; Stouffer, 2)

Since 1983, little has happened to make those abilities any less necessary or desirable.

The examples of intergovernmental service-delivery arrangements that are most extensive and, thereby, have some potential applicability regionwide usually involve the major governments in the region, such as:

Joint efforts of central cities and counties to sort out service-delivery responsibilities: After years of battling over "annexation, joint agency operation and funding, and economic development," newly elected executives for Jefferson County and the City of Louisville, Kentucky, entered into an agreement in 1986 called the Louisville and Jefferson County Compact. The Compact provides for sharing various revenues, such as occupational taxes, and defining the respective responsibilities of the governments for more than a dozen activities, some of which are consolidated for joint operation under the compact. In addition, the city government agreed to a moratorium on annexation and the county government agreed to assume a greater share of urban services and discourage any annexations by suburban governments during the 12-year term of the agreement. The Compact is not a single

document, but a series of ordinances, and has institutionalized cooperation between the two governments. (Dodge, Greater Baltimore
Committee, 1991, 10; Smith, 17)

In a more informal manner, the City of Pittsburgh /County of Allegheny
Cooperative Services Program has created task forces, composed of
representatives from government, business, labor, and civic agencies,
to develop cooperative agreements between the two governments. Each
year, the program, which is administered by the Western Division of
the Pennsylvania Economy League (see Problem-Solving #2), intends
to address approximately half a dozen timely topics for cooperation.
(Pennsylvania Economy League, 1994)

In a similar manner, the Mandan-Bismark-Burleigh-Morton Joint
Service Network has been established by the cities, counties, and school
and park districts in the Bismark, North Dakota, region to "concentrate
on government functions and services that might be better provided
together rather than separately." Initial examinations include investment pooling, computer networking, solid waste education, joint administrative activities, and a regional visioning process. The Network's
first two years were funded by the North Dakota Advisory Commission
on Intergovernmental Relations; continuing activities are being funded
by the eight participating jurisdictions, which also provide technical
support to the working groups. (Mandan-Bismark-Burleigh-Morton
Joint Service Network)

To offer an alternative to city annexation of county land, the State of
Virginia has authorized local governments to enter into voluntary
arrangements that are beneficial to the orderly growth and continued
viability of counties, cities and towns. These agreements can include
"fiscal arrangements, revenue and economic growth sharing, dedica-
tion of all or any portion of tax revenues to a revenue and growth
sharing account, boundary line adjustments, acquisition of real property and buildings and joint exercise or delegation of powers as well as
modification of specific annexation, transition or immunity rights as
determined by the local governing body." Such arrangements have been
entered into in lieu of annexations between Charlottesville and Albe-
marle County and Franklin and the Isles of Wright and Southampton.
(Dodge, Greater Baltimore Committee, 1991, 5)

Service-Delivery #1

County government delivery of municipal services: Probably the most famous example of county government delivery of municipal services is the Los Angeles County Contract Services, or "Lakeland" Plan (so named because Lakeland was the first municipality in the county to purchase a package of services covering almost all of its municipal responsibilities). Los Angeles County now provides as many as 40 or more services to almost all of the more than 80 municipalities. It provides additional services, such as for fire, library, and street lighting and maintenance services, through special taxing and assessment districts. Most services are provided uniformly across the county, but individual municipalities may purchase additional services under a General Services Agreement that most of the municipalities have executed. Service charges are based on actual costs and recalculated on an annual basis. Municipalities retain policy, planning and budgetary control over the contract services. Similar programs exist in other California counties, Hennipen County, Minnesota, and other counties across the nation.

Accomplishments

The Louisville and Jefferson County Compact has institutionalized cooperation between the two governments, according to Ron Vogel of the University of Louisville.

> Many community leaders treat the compact as sacred, although it is doubtful that many members of the community are even aware of the existence of the compact...There are a number of reasons — easing of the county's fiscal crisis, intangible psychological benefits of compact, fear of renewal of annexation battles and economic competition — that suggest that the compact will endure not only until 1998, but failing another consolidation effort, in all likelihood the compact will be renewed (perhaps with revisions) into the next century. (Vogel)

The Los Angeles County Contract Services Plan provides cost-effective services to municipalities and helps compensate county government for the loss of property taxes in incorporated areas by keeping county departments at full strength. County delivery of municipal services also changes the mindset of county government employees, since they are now delivering services to cities that can cancel them at any time, not to a captive audience of county taxpayers. Similarly, municipal officials are constantly making comparisons between purchasing county government services or delivering their own. The plan also provides an alternative to political consolidation that retains the flexibility to make changes in service delivery as conditions warrant.

Strengths and Shortcomings

According to Ron Vogel, the benefits of the Louisville and Jefferson County Compact include increasing the efficiency and equalizing the costs of services provided through joint agency operation and reducing city-county economic competition and conflict over annexation. Its shortcomings include continuing struggles over: the equity of tax sharing arrangements; providing matching funds for joint agencies in budget cutbacks, complicating the lives of staff who serve two masters; and coordinating city-county community development priorities. (Vogel, 26)

One sometimes cited strength of intergovernmental service-delivery arrangements is that they pave the way for regional service-delivery arrangements. Regrettably, except for central city-county cooperation and some intercounty cooperation, such as the examples above, this initiative appears to have limited applicability to regional challenges for which the number of public sector interests, as well as other community interests, grow astronomically. A lot of hopes for regional cooperation have been based on "growing" intergovernmental cooperation incrementally, from a few municipal governments to the entire county and region, and have been all too predictably dashed after very few "increments."

Intergovernmental service-delivery arrangements appear to work best when the issues are clearly understood and the potential terms of a deal or arrangement can be negotiated among a relatively small group of local governments.

Potential

The potential for intergovernmental service-delivery arrangements is considerable among groups of small and large local governments in most regions. Given the number of local governments in many regions, intergovernmental service delivery provides some flexibility in delivering services that are either inefficient or impossible to deliver by individual communities. It also helps prepare government officials and citizens for negotiating strategies for addressing emerging regional challenges.

Intergovernmental service-delivery arrangements, however, do not usually suffice for the delivery of regional services, except in conjunction with one or more of the other regional service-delivery mechanisms.

Contacts

- Allegheny County Library Association, Pittsburgh, Pennsylvania, 412-672-6247
- Louisville and Jefferson County Compact: City of Louisville, Kentucky, government, 502-574-3061; Jefferson County government, 502-574-5754
- City of Pittsburgh/County of Allegheny Cooperative Services Program: Western Pennsylvania Division of the Pennsylvania Economy League, Pittsburgh, Pennsylvania, 412-281-1890
- Mandan-Bismark-Burleigh-Morton Joint Services Network: City of Bismark government, 701-222-6471
- Los Angeles County Contract Services Plan: Los Angeles County government, 213-974-1234

Service-Delivery #2
Other Than Public Regional Services

In some cases, private, academic, nonprofit, and civic organizations deliver intercommunity and regional services, at least on a piecemeal basis, often as part of publicly financed privatization efforts. Private firms offer some or all of the solid waste collection and disposal services and other public works services or deliver water, sewer, cable television, electric and other public franchise services. Colleges and universities sometimes offer regional data collection and processing services and provide a home for small business development centers. Nonprofit organizations operate regional cultural facilities and offer the majority of social services in many regions.

The delivery of primarily publicly financed services tends to shift back and forth between public and private service deliverers over time, related, of course, to whether it is possible to make a profit on their delivery. Public transit services were almost all private up to a couple of decades ago, but now they are predominantly delivered by single- or multiple-service authorities (see Service-Delivery #3 and #4), but interest is growing in private delivery of some services, especially those that can be financed with toll receipts. The delivery of sewer, water, and solid waste collection and disposal services has similarly vacillated between public and private service deliverers over time.

Some argue that the best way to guarantee high quality publicly financed services is to prevent a monopoly of either public or private service delivery, either by having a mix of both, or holding the threat of changing from one to the other over the heads of the current service delivers.

Most recently, a new breed of multi-sector service deliverers, often depending on a mixture of public, private, and other financing, seems to be springing up to deliver regional services. In the Austin, Texas, region, for example, a nonprofit agency has been established to share the cost of constructing and operating a fiber-optics communications network. Participants include the City of Austin, Austin Independent School District, Travis County, the University of Texas and Austin Community College. (Lemov)

In many regions, transportation systems are especially fertile ground for nonpublic, multi-sector service delivery. Long a predominately public system, now private and other sectors are becoming more active in its delivery. Some regions envision a much more market driven system in the 21st century, with a mixture of public, private, nonprofit and other service delivers. For example:

- In the Seattle region, the State of Washington selected developers to design, finance, construct, and operate six critical components of the regional transportation system. Though most are consortia of private planning and construction firms, a couple are driven by civic agencies. Given that the financing of these facilities involves tolls, state government has now empowered citizens to petition (5,000 signatures) for a public advisory vote on these projects. (Reinhardt; Capell, 63–64)

- In the Washington, D.C., region, the Toll Road Corporation of Virginia is designing, financing, constructing, and will soon operate the Dulles Greenway toll road. Once the bonds are retired and a profit is realized, the road will be turned over to the State of Virginia. (Dodge, Interstate Study Commission, 1994, 16)

- In the Los Angeles region, the Southern California Association of Governments is creating a public/private partnership, called the Southern California Economic Partnership, to deploy new technologies that could create new jobs as well as reduce transportation costs. Five technologies have been selected for initial development: zero emission vehicles, alternative fuel vehicles, smart shuttle transit which is electronically demand responsive, intelligent vehicles highway systems which are also electronically demand responsive, and telecommute-teleservices marketing and communications to facilitate movement of information as opposed to people. Industry clusters are being assembled around each of these technologies. Some of the product development responsibilities will be assumed by individual and consortia of businesses and some might require establishing public-private consortia, such as ComSat, at least until they have survived the product development phase and are self-supporting. (Dodge, Interstate Study Commission, 1994, 37)

Accomplishments

Private, academic, nonprofit, civic and multi-sector regional services have been an important component of regional service delivery. As market considerations are increasingly introduced into the delivery of public services, such as in transportation, nonpublic mechanisms might become more attractive delivers of regional services.

Strengths and Shortcomings

The major strengths of nonpublic delivery of regional services are attracting nonpublic technical expertise and financial resources and introducing competition into the delivery of public services. The major shortcoming can be assuring the availability of cost-effective and even subsidized services for distressed communities and their citizens.

Potential

Private, academic, nonprofit, civic and especially multi-sector delivery of regional services has considerable potential. In fact, it might even be more flexible to have nonpublic service deliverers, especially if they can be encouraged to be responsive to the special needs of distressed communities and their citizens. To avoid the fragmented delivery of regional services, however, some type of regional service delivery coordinating group (see Service-Delivery #5) could be considered.

Contacts

- Toll Road Corporation of Virginia, Sterling, Virginia, 703-707-8870
- Southern California Economic Partnership: Southern California Association of Governments, Los Angeles, California, 213-236-1800

Service-Delivery #3
Regional Single-Service Authorities

Regional single-service authorities, or special purpose governments, are the most common form of regional service-delivery mechanisms in most regions of the nation.

Of the more than 33,000 single-service authorities, approximately 10 percent have a regional mandate for providing:

- water treatment services, such as the Metropolitan Sanitary District of Greater Chicago or Metropolitan St. Louis Sewer District (Goodman, 188);

- water supply services, such as the Metropolitan Water District of Southern California, which distributes water from the Colorado River (Goodman, 188);

- air pollution control services, such as the South Coast Air Quality Management District in the Los Angeles basin;

- transportation services, such as the Washington Metropolitan Area Transportation Authority and Metropolitan Washington Airports Authority in the Washington, D.C., region;

- industrial development services, such as the Regional Industrial Development Authority in the Pittsburgh region;

- port services, though most port authorities deliver other types of regional services as well (Service-Delivery #4); and

- parks, housing and urban redevelopment, solid waste management, and other services.

Collectively, regional single-service authorities hire more than 400,000 employees, expend more than $15 billion annually, and often have importance comparable to that of general purpose municipal and county governments. Most of the regional single-service authorities charge fees and use revenue financing; some, such as the transit authorities, depend upon subsidies as well, in the form of annual government contributions, dedicated tax funding, or even the surpluses from other operations. (National Academy of Public Administration, 1980, 58; Cisneros, 1995, 8)

Regional single-service authorities began to spring up when annexation was no longer a strategy for addressing crosscutting challenges, to "fill cracks in the patchwork system of American local government." Among the first were authorities created in the Boston region to handle sewage (1889), parks (1892), and water supply (1895). Some are established by local governments, with appropriate state enabling legislation; others are established and funded directly by state governments. Most provide only a single service or a collection of related services and have governing bodies composed of local or state government officials. (National Academy of Public Administration, 1980, 62)

Recently, other regional problem-solving mechanisms have begun to examine the roles and responsibilities of regional single-service authorities, both individually and in relation to one another and local governments. The Citizens League of Greater Cleveland, for example, has prepared a number of reports on their special purpose governments and developed guidelines for their operations, covering such matters as their governing board composition and selection, board-management roles and relationships, board size and term length, compensation of board members and board policies. It secured compliance by some of the authorities to these guidelines as well as convened periodic meetings of their directors to forge closer working relationships. (Citizens League of Greater Cleveland, 1989, 1992)

Some regional single-service authorities have also had success as regional problem-solving mechanisms. Regional authorities for water and sewer service and, at times, transit have had considerable success in addressing new crosscutting challenges, especially when the strategies for addressing earlier challenges have established precedents. It is often easier, for example, for a regional single purpose authority to assume leadership for developing the second exclusive busway or third sewage treatment plant than it is to deal with such challenges *de novo* or to address a challenge that has implications outside the mission of the authority, such as intergovernmental financing or management of inter-modal (transit, highway, airport) transportation activities.

Accomplishments

Regional single-service authorities have made it possible to deliver services that could not be easily provided by any local general purpose government or nonpublic entity. They have provided the flexibility at the local level to respond to the changing demands of community leaders and citizens for quality services.

Strengths and Shortcomings

According to the National Academy of Public Administration, the advantages of regional single-service authorities include:
- bypassing restrictions on local government financing,
- receiving federal government support, such as in housing and urban redevelopment,
- overcoming limitations on the powers of local governments, such as in contracting, and
- addressing challenges that cut across governmental jurisdictions. (National Academy of Public Administration, 1980, 63)

Moreover, regional single-service authorities are often created "to insulate (the delivery of critical services) from political machinations of government." (Wallis, 1994, 11)

The disadvantages of regional single-service authorities include:
- lack of political accountability, to either the electorate or local government governing bodies,
- lack of accountability to state and federal governments,
- increasing fragmentation of regional service delivery, "not one of them is entrusted with the whole" (Peirce, 318), and
- sometimes, increased costs of creating separate public entities. (National Academy of Public Administration, 1980, 65)

Potential

The potential of regional single-service authorities appears to be in their modification. In most regions, they have been so much the preferred approach to delivering intercommunity or regional services that their sheer numbers are causing concern.

The National Academy of Public Administration has long recommended conducting examinations (as in the Cleveland region) of regional single-service districts, including collecting information on their operations and considering a range of structural changes to reduce the number and independence of regional single-service authorities, including:

- consolidation of like authorities into larger entities,
- consolidation of related special districts into multi-purpose ones (see Service-Delivery #4),
- abolition of special districts with obsolete functions,
- merger of special districts with general purpose units of government, such as the merger between the Municipality of Metropolitan Seattle service district and King County government, and
- transformation of independent special districts to more closely resemble dependent public agencies, by limiting funding alternatives or increasing local officials' roles in their operation. (National Academy of Public Administration, 1980, 67–71)

Contacts

Examples of regional single-service authorities can be found in almost all regions of the nation, and especially in the multi-county regions.

Service-Delivery #4
Regional Multiple-Service Authorities

Regional multiple-service authorities, or special purpose governments, are similar to regional single-service authorities, but much rarer. The most common form is the regional port or development authority, which generally provides transportation, economic development, and other services in addition to providing port facilities.

Port authorities have been traditionally associated with the almost 200 deep draft ports dispersed along the Atlantic, Gulf, Pacific, and Great Lake coasts. In the past two decades, however, port authorities have been increasingly seen as economic development mechanisms, leading to increased economic development activities in established port authorities and the creation of new authorities, including some in inland locations. The combination of real estate, financing, and taxing powers available to port authorities has made them an attractive addition to the arsenal of economic development tools.

The range of port authority activities is mind-boggling. Port authorities develop land and buildings; provide economic development services and financing; buy, lease, and sell property; provide air and water pollution control works; and establish foreign trade zones and promote tourism. They operate a wide range of facilities: airports, bridges, tunnels, canals, locks, commuter rail, transit and bus systems, inland river terminals, industrial parks, business incubators, world trade centers, terminal and shortline railways, shipyards, commercial vehicles, dredges, utility lines, and other public recreational facilities.

Port authorities are typically empowered to exercise eminent domain, conduct studies and develop plans, levy facility charges, issue bonds, sue and be sued, apply for government and foundation grants, and enter into agreements. Some can levy property taxes, such as to finance and subsidize operations and provide funds necessary for budget activities. Many are given police powers and a few can exercise regulatory powers.

The Delaware River Port Authority in the Philadelphia region, for example, operates four major toll bridges crossing the Delaware River, the PATCO rail transit system and port and related facilities on the

Pennsylvania and New Jersey sides of the river. In 1992, the port authority compact was modified by the two states, with Congressional approval, to unify the ports of the Delaware River, pursue economic development activities throughout the "port district," and expand its geographic scope to cover additional counties, for a total of fourteen, including inland counties, in the region. The Authority is governed by a Board of Commissioners, most of them appointed by the governors of the two states. The Authority is self-sufficient, covering the losses on the PATCO rail transit system from the surpluses on the toll bridges. (Dodge, Interstate Study Commission, 1994, 42–43)

In the St. Louis region, the Bi-State Development Authority operates the bus system and MetroLink rail system, a general aviation airport, and the passenger transportation system in the Gateway Arch and finances various port facilities and economic development projects, such as in the vicinity of MetroLink stations. The Authority is governed by a Board of Governors, appointed by the governors of the two states. The Authority is self-sufficient, except for small grants for the Gateway Arch operations and substantial subsidies for transit operations from state and local governments in the region. (Dodge, Interstate Study Commission, 1994, 43)

The Port Authority of New York and New Jersey is the largest of its kind, covering seventeen counties with a population of 15 million and having an annual budget of $2.7 billion (1994) and more than 9,000 employees. The Port Authority operates the three major regional airports and general aviation airports, a number of the major toll bridge and tunnel facilities, the PATH rail transit system, bus stations, various port facilities, industrial parks and the World Trade Center. It is an innovator in such new technologies as electronic traffic management and electronic toll collection. The Port Authority is governed by a Board of Commissioners appointed by the governors of the two states. The Port Authority is self-sufficient, using the airport surpluses to cover the losses on the PATH transit system, but is facing future fiscal crises. (Dodge, Interstate Study Commission, 1994, 43–44)

Port authorities located in single-state regions, such as the City of Tulsa-Rogers County Port Authority (Oklahoma) or the Toledo-Lucas County Port Authority (Ohio), are usually created by state enabling legislation, as opposed to requiring an interstate compact and the approval of the U.S. Congress, and they usually have governing bodies appointed by local government officials.

Some regional multiple-service authorities have also been successful as regional problem-solving mechanisms. Regional port and development authorities have had considerable success in addressing new crosscutting challenges, such as taking the lead in developing strategies for addressing an economic development opportunity or threat, especially if it is directly related to its mission or a similar challenge it previously addressed.

For example, the Port Authority of New York and New Jersey convenes the top executives of the major New York and New Jersey transportation providers, including the separate regional planning agencies in the two states, in informal forums two to three times a year. These meetings have led to the creation of informal working groups to examine regional challenges, such as a recent one on the movement of goods. In addition, the Port Authority convenes staff members from the transportation providers on a monthly basis to share plans and projects and support the informal working groups. The Port Authority also hosts periodic conferences on transportation challenges and is beginning to hold conversations with state and local governments to prepare a new vision for the future of the region and itself. (Dodge, Interstate Study Commission, 1994, 44)

Accomplishments

Port and development authorities have provided regions with the capacity to provide needed transportation and port facilities as well as to finance and coordinate the implementation of economic development strategies, using an almost unique combination of powers.

Strengths and Shortcomings

Interviewees in a recent study indicated that the strengths of port authorities include:
- operating like businesses,
- providing unique combinations of land, building, and facility assets and financing tools for economic development,

- filling a vacuum, especially in areas without other economic development staff,
- being independent from day-to-day politics of public and private entities,
- serving as a neutral forum to coordinate developing economic development strategies,
- having professional governing boards, and
- having potential to be the "best mechanism for long-term investment."

Interviewees also indicated that the shortcomings of port authorities include:

- having less opportunity to generate income without revenue-producing services, such as port facilities,
- having limited political clout,
- providing too slow a return, including political, to compete with the more immediate demands for government and foundation subsidies,
- being fiscally constrained by bad investments,
- having difficulty in protecting client confidentiality in a public entity, and
- "when strong, provide mechanisms that still need to be complemented with other public, private and community economic development efforts; when weak, can leave other economic development activities hanging." (Dodge, Montgomery County Leadership Network, 1992)

Potential

There is considerable potential for expanding regional single-service authorities to multiple-service authorities or creating new regional multiple-service authorities.

Some of the most active discussions involve creating regional multi-modal transportation authorities. These might be similar to the ones that exist in various states, such as the Maryland Transportation Authority, which operates seven toll facilities — two tunnels, four bridges and fifty miles of turnpike — throughout the state. Such an authority was considered by the Interstate Study Commission for the Washington, D.C., region — the Washington Metropolitan Area Transportation Authority or WashTrans — to finance and deliver regional highway, bridge, transit and airport facilities and services. A similar authority was considered with the primary responsibility for assessing alternative approaches and pursuing strategies for financing regional transportation facilities and services — TransFund. (Dodge, Interstate Study Commission, 1994, 37)

Some of the discussions involve combining single regional services into a multiple-service authority. For example, in the Richmond region, a regional multiple-service authority — the Richmond Metropolitan Government — has been proposed to handle water, sewer, solid waste and transportation facilities and services. (McCormack, 1995)

Contacts

- Delaware River Port Authority, Camden, New Jersey, 215-925-8780
- Bi-State Development Authority, St. Louis, Missouri, 314-982-1594
- Port Authority of New York and New Jersey, New York, New York, 212-435-7000
- City of Tulsa-Rogers County Port Authority, Catoosa, Oklahoma, 918-266-2291
- Toledo-Lucas County Port Authority, Toledo, Ohio, 419-243-8251

Service-Delivery #5
Regional Service-Delivery Coordinating Groups (new)

Regional service-delivery coordinating groups could foster dialogue among regional service providers, coordinate the delivery of existing regional services, and help implement strategies for delivering new regional services. In general, regional service-delivery coordinating groups could focus on making service delivery effective and flexible to changing service needs.

Such groups are a relatively new type of regional decision-making mechanism.

A few informal coordinating committees have been created. One, made up of the staff directors of the regional service-delivery mechanisms in the Cleveland region, operated for a couple of years (see Service-Delivery #3). Another, drawn from the board chairs and staff directors of the regional transportation providers in the New York City region, operates on an ongoing basis (see Service-Delivery #4).

A more formal group, the Forum on Cooperative Urban Services (FOCUS) brings elected officials and staff from more than thirty city, county, and special purpose governments together to address mutual service-delivery responsibilities in the Portland, Oregon, region. FOCUS was formed to develop joint recommendations on a new charter for Metro, the regional planning and service district (see Problem-Solving/Service-Delivery #3) and lobby for its approval by the electorate. It has continued to meet monthly to discuss regional challenges, especially those related to managing growth. FOCUS conducts analyses of new service-delivery arrangements, such as integrating the activities of agencies responsible for managing drinking, sanitary, and surface water, and has even prepared a handbook to guide community leaders and citizens in developing collaborative service-delivery arrangements. FOCUS is governed by a ten-member steering committee, contracts for staff support from local consulting firms, and authorizes one of its members to handle fiduciary responsibilities. It communicates its recommendations to its members as well as to the Metropolitan Policy Advisory Committee of Metro, which includes some of the FOCUS members. Members contribute from $1,100 to $9,900 a year, based on their population, to support the operations of FOCUS. (Julie Hammerstadt, Institute of Portland Metropolitan Studies)

Similarly, the Capitol Region Partnership provides a "permanent formal forum to enable independent regional organizations to take collaborative action ... within the Hartford [Connecticut] region." The major regional planning, sanitation, transit, water and sewer, and economic development organizations are members; in addition, the regional chamber of commerce in an ex officio member. Members have developed a long-range plan with thirteen action projects and meet regularly to oversee its implementation. The directors meet monthly, the directors and board chairs meet quarterly, and the full boards meet annually. (Capitol Region Partnership, 1996)

Informal and formal groups have also been created to bring particular types of service providers together. Build Up Greater Cleveland, for example, brings public works agencies in the region's central county together to develop joint capital improvement plans and service-delivery arrangements (see Problem-Solving #2). Staff directors of transportation agencies are often brought together on special committees for regional transportation planning processes. For the most part, however, they focus their attention on divvying up transportation facility and operations resources, as opposed to finding common approaches for improving existing service delivery or handling new service-delivery responsibilities. In addition, directors of regional public and private service-delivery mechanisms have formed coordinating groups to oversee the implementation of particular projects, such as among regional authorities and public and private utilities in the implementation of regional geographic information systems.

Accomplishments and Strengths and Shortcomings

The informal regional service-delivery coordinating groups have already had some success in exchanging information, identifying common concerns, examining these concerns and even launching joint projects such as electronic toll collection demonstrations and geographic information systems. The more formal regional service-delivery coordinating groups are beginning to address more demanding agendas for improving regional service delivery.

Potential

The potential for regional service-delivery coordinating groups is practically unlimited. They could provide an important complement to regional problem-solving mechanisms.

A regional service-delivery coordinating group could be convened to guide the implementation of strategies to address new regional challenges or to examine changes in existing service-delivery arrangements to make them more effective. The group could be composed of directors and board members of regional service-delivery organizations, possibly with a rotating chair every six months to a year.

The regional service-delivery coordinating group could respond to requests from regional problem-solving mechanisms or develop its own agenda of common issues to address. Task groups of service providers, along with community leaders and citizens, could develop proposals for group action. The coordinating group could make recommendations to regional problem-solving and service-delivery mechanisms, and local, state and national governments, as well as make reports on its examinations to community leaders and citizens.

The costs of staff support for regional service-delivery coordinating groups could be shared among the participants; logistical support could also be provided by the current chair of the coordinating group. Staff support could be supported through member dues or provided through other regional decision-making mechanisms, such as a regional planning council (see Problem-Solving #1), an association of governments (see Service-Delivery #1), or a single or multiple-service authority (see Service-Delivery #3 and 4).

Contacts

- Citizens League of Greater Cleveland, Cleveland, Ohio, 216-241-5340
- Port Authority of New York and New Jersey, New York, New York, 212-435-7000
- FOCUS Portland, Portland, Oregon, Greg Chew, 503-228-7352
- Capitol Region Partnership: Capitol Region Council of Governments, Hartford, Connecticut, 203-522-2217

Problem-Solving/Service-Delivery #1
Empowered Counties and Central Cities

Counties have emerged as the major units of local government in many regions, empowered to provide a mixture of state mandated, locally demanded and regionally needed problem solving and service delivery. Central cities that have been empowered to annex surrounding growth areas also serve as regional problem-solving and service-delivery mechanisms.

Counties divide up regions in various ways. Some include central cities and a considerable amount of the surrounding developed area, such as Allegheny County (Pittsburgh, Pennsylvania) did until the last decade. Others divide up a central city and surrounding areas like pieces of a pie, as do Clackamas, Multnomah, and Washington Counties in the Portland region. Still others provide part or all of the "donut" surrounding the central city or county, as do the Maryland and Virginia counties surrounding Washington, D.C.

In regions where the central city and surrounding developed areas are substantially contained in single urban counties, county governments are often leading efforts to develop strategies for addressing regional challenges (regional problem solving) as well as delivering regional services (regional service delivery). In regions that include more than a single urban county, the number of counties is usually sufficiently small (from two to ten) that they can coordinate activities and collectively serve as regional problem-solving and service-delivery mechanisms.

County governments were originally conceived as administrative units of state governments to deliver election, judicial and other state-mandated services. Over the past few decades, they have emerged as the only units of local government that cover all or even a substantial part of the geographic area affected by regional challenges. Counties with unincorporated areas have had increasing demands from residents to provide "municipal" services in developing areas. As a result, county governments often must wrestle with the conflicting demands of state, local, and now regional challenges.

County governments have also been asked by municipalities to assume services, resulting in the transfer of public health, housing, special public safety services, community and economic development, and other municipal responsibilities to county governments. Some county governments have even assumed the responsibilities of countywide service authorities. King County Washington, for example, was combined with the previously independent Municipality of Metropolitan Seattle, which delivered sewage treatment, transit and other services.

County governments also often offer municipal services on a contract basis to municipalities, such as the "Lakeland" plan in Los Angeles County (see Service-Delivery #1). Finally, county governments have often been the logical choice to take on new crosscutting responsibilities such as public transit and a widening array of social services. In many regions, county governments have become the major local governments, in terms of the range of their activities and the size of their budgets.

If counties had not existed before the last couple of decades, they would probably have had to be invented by now.

Without them, regional service delivery would have had to depend almost exclusively on special authorities or piecemeal delivery by municipal governments. Even where they barely exist, such as in New England states, interest is growing in breathing life into them to address regional challenges, such as the effort to strengthen Cumberland County in the Portland (Maine) region.

Many urban and rural counties have responded to these new demands by instituting considerable changes in their capacities and capabilities. Many have wrested broadened powers and authorities from state government and adopted home rule charters to remove themselves from state government "micro-management." Most of the larger ones have replaced the commission form of government with either an elected county executive or professional county manager and county council or legislature. Some have attempted to differentiate responsibilities with their municipalities; Multnomah County, Oregon, developed an agreement with its largest cities — Portland and Gresham — to annex all of the unincorporated areas of the county so as to avoid duplication in the delivery of municipal services.

Not that this has been an easy process. Allegheny County, Pennsylvania, for example, has repeatedly rejected reforms, including creating a federated government with the City of Pittsburgh and adopting home rule charters to change the commission form of government.

The growing importance of counties has not diminished the regional importance of central cities. Many of them continue to take the lead on regional strategic planning and visioning processes, such as the recent Strategic Choices process initiated by Austin, Texas. (City of Austin Government) Many central cities also deliver a wide range of regional services, such as sewer and water services, as well as provide museum, park, arena, stadium, convention, and other facilities and the locus for regional festivals and celebrations.

In fact, central cities that have continued to annex surrounding growth areas, such as Columbus, Ohio, or Albuquerque, New Mexico, serve as both regional problem-solving and service-delivery mechanisms. At times, but not recently, consideration has even been given to assigning extraterritorial powers to central cities in this country, similar to those originally assigned to Metro Toronto. At one time, Toronto had planning control over an area of 480 square miles beyond the 240 square miles for which it had service delivery responsibility. As these outlying areas began to develop, however, fears of their annexation by Metro Toronto led to establishing four surrounding, relatively independent, regions.

Accomplishments

Counties provide an already existing local government that can serve as a regional problem-solving and service-delivery mechanism. Many of the larger counties have responded to the opportunity and strengthened their capacities and capabilities, and now actively take the lead in addressing regional challenges. Central cities have taken the lead in regional problem solving and service delivery as well, when, like counties, they contain a substantial part of the developed and even undeveloped areas of the region.

Strengths and Shortcomings

The major strength of counties is that they are often the only general purpose governments with the geographic scope to address regional challenges. They also often have the seasoned personnel to address crosscutting challenges. The major shortcoming of counties is that they often lack the powers and authorities, resources, and leadership to address regional challenges.

Sometimes counties have legal and fiscal limitations that inhibit undertaking new responsibilities. In spite of the increasing numbers of counties eligible for home rule charters, many are still treated like administrative units of their states and have little flexibility in financing their activities beyond the regressive and often inflexible property tax. As a result, when faced with the choice of financing the delivery of a critical existing service or examining a newly emerging regional challenge, they commit their resources and energies to the former.

Finally, counties are often distrusted by other units of government, either because they are viewed as competitors for resources to address emerging challenges, regional and otherwise, or because of a history of unwillingness of county leaders to become involved in addressing regional challenges until obligated to do so by state or national government legislation.

Potential

The potential future of counties and central cities as regional problem-solving and service-delivery mechanisms is being compromised by development patterns. As growth expands beyond county boundaries and central city annexation, the ability of either to influence growth or address other regional challenges is diminished, except through city-county and intercounty cooperation. But counties and central cities can still strengthen their capacities and capabilities to be effective partners in addressing regional challenges with other county governments and sectors. Moreover, they can address the county or city level aspects of regional challenges, such as intercommunity or interneighborhood disparities, and develop problem-solving and service delivery approaches that have regional application.

Contact

- National Association of Counties, Washington, D.C., 202-393-6226

Problem-Solving/Service-Delivery #2
Municipal/County Government Modifications, Federations and Consolidations

The relationship between municipal and county governments has provided almost endless opportunities for strengthening, and weakening, regional problem solving and service delivery. Municipalities can be incorporated, combined, and even disincorporated; central cities can actively annex their surrounding communities; and central cities and urban counties can create federated or consolidated governments. All of these options change the relationships among local governments and, thereby, have an impact on regional decision making.

Municipal Modification

Municipalities are incorporated out of unincorporated county areas. State legislatures set conditions for municipal incorporation, such as minimum sizes for different classes of local governments or processes to be followed and citizen approvals required. Some consideration has been recently given to tightening the conditions for incorporation in various states, so as to discourage the proliferation of local governments, such as by increasing the minimum sizes for new municipalities, requiring separation from existing local governments to allow annexation of in between areas, or limiting annexation authority to larger municipalities.

Municipal combinations are often considered and rarely accomplished. They do occur in many regions every five to ten years but at such a slow pace as to hardly put a dent in the growing number of municipal governments. Some municipalities get as far as conducting feasibility studies, often with community foundation or other financial support, of the fiscal and legal impacts of consolidation, but fail to take into consideration community officials' political resistance and citizens' fear of change to a larger unit of government. Considerably greater success has occurred in other countries, especially those with unitary government systems that can mandate local change. Great Britain, for example, has considerably reduced the number of municipalities by creating unified local authorities, and Sweden has reduced the number of its municipalities from 2,500 to only 260. (Thomas, Clarke, 1994, 20)

Confluence St. Louis tied municipal incorporations and combinations together in its recommendations for strengthening regional governance, in a report entitled "Too Many Governments?" The report recommended incorporating all of St. Louis County and clearly dividing responsibilities between municipalities and County government and enlarging, merging, and forming municipalities in St. Louis County until each municipality has a population between 25,000 and 75,000.

A similar model was followed for creating the metropolitan governments in many of the Canadian provinces, including Metro Toronto.

Municipal disincorporation or dissolution has been suggested as an approach to specifically deal with distressed communities. Frank Lucchino, the controller for Allegheny County (Pittsburgh region), has proposed allowing distressed municipalities to disincorporate and become the responsibilities of neighboring municipalities (through merger in whole or in parts) or county government (through county government delivery of municipal services), thereby sharing the cost of their public services across more affluent communities of the county. (Lucchino)

Finally, boundary review commission have been established in twelve states (Alaska, California, Iowa, Michigan, Minnesota, Missouri (St. Louis County), Nevada, New Mexico, Oregon, Utah, Virginia, and Washington) since the 1960s, often with the purpose of managing regional development in rational ways. Most have focused their attention on the establishment, consolidation, annexation, and dissolution of municipal governments and resolving boundary conflicts, but a few are beginning to take a more regional perspective in their examinations.

In half the states, commissions operate state wide; in the other half, they operate at the county level (California) or the regional level (Oregon). Most of the commissions have the authority to approve or deny proposals, subject to judicial appeal or popular referendum. (Advisory Commission on Intergovernmental Relations, 1992; Dodge, Greater Baltimore Committee, 1991, 10)

The Portland, Oregon, Metropolitan Area Local Government Boundary Commission, for example, reviews and approves boundary changes of cities and eight types of special districts. Over time, the Boundary Commission has become a "major force in implementing land use planning by testing boundary changes against plans for land development and the provision of public services." The members are appointed by Metro, the regional planning and service district (see Problem-Solving/Service-Delivery #3) in the Portland region. (Abbott, Carl)

Central City Annexation

Central city or larger municipal annexation can have an impact on regional decision making.

Between 1950 and 1990, four-fifths of the nation's central cities expanded their boundaries by 10 percent or more; they annexed more than 12,000 square miles and more than doubled in area. Four out of five of the annexations took place in the Sunbelt, but the largest single expansion was far to the north: Anchorage, Alaska, grew from 12 to almost 1,700 square miles. (Rusk, 1993, 10; Cisneros, 1995, 5)

Until the early decades of this century, many cities were annexed by other cities; ten of the largest fifty cities in 1850, most of them adjacent to major eastern cities, such as Boston, New York and Philadelphia, disappeared by 1900. (Rusk, 1993, 54) The city of Allegheny was annexed by Pittsburgh in 1907, the last of over a dozen successful annexations by Pittsburgh. By the early decades of this century, new suburban municipalities in many regions began using their growing clout in state legislatures to prevent additional annexations of other incorporated municipalities by central cities. Some central cities, however, continued to grow, especially in the southwest, until Houston and San Diego are now larger in land area than New York, and Dallas is larger than Chicago. (Goodman, 193)

Central City-County Government Federations and Consolidations

Rodney Kendig observed, in *The American County* in February, 1972, a rare governmental phenomenon that was being nurtured by the rapid suburbanization of the 1960s and 1970s:

Emerging from the cocoon of dust and disuse, the city-county consolidation butterfly now flits across the local government landscape. Once chased by academicians and occasionally landed by an isolated community here and there, city-county consolidation is now pursued like the rarest of butterflies by scores of communities and noticed with more than passing curiosity by additional dozens of local governments.

Similar interest in central city-county government consolidation or federation has reemerged in the 1990s, this time being driven by concerns about economic competitiveness with other regions and fiscal disparities between central cities and surrounding suburbs.

Thirty central city-county consolidations have been created over the past two centuries, half of them in the decades noted by Kendig. Consolidated governments range in population from a few thousand to millions, but most of the recent ones have been under 200,000 in population. The recent consolidations are also equally divided between mayor-council and council-manager forms of government.

Two successful consolidations occurred in the 1980s, and three have taken place thus far in the 1990s — two in Georgia, between the City of Athens and Clarke County, and the City of Augusta and Richmond County, and one in Louisiana, between the City of Lafayette and Lafayette Parish. Consolidation efforts continue, including recent attempts in the city and county of Sacramento, California, Tallahassee and Leon County, Florida, and ongoing efforts in Charlotte and Mecklenburg County, North Carolina, Knoxville and Knox County, Kentucky, Kansas City and Wyandotte County, Kansas, and Las Vegas and Clark County, Nevada. The National Association of Counties compilation of city-county consolidations appears on the following page.

Consolidations initially resulted from city government annexation of primarily unincorporated surrounding counties, as in New Orleans, Boston, Philadelphia, San Francisco, and multiple counties in New York City. Starting with Baton Rouge in 1947 and continuing to the present day, consolidations are now resulting from the combination of central cities and usually partially incorporated surrounding counties into entities called cities — such as Jacksonville (the Consolidated City of Jacksonville government [Duval County, Florida]) and Virginia

Consolidated County Governments in the United States

September 1990

Consolidated Government, State	Population	Date(s)
New Orleans-Orleans Parish, La.	559,770	1805
Boston-Suffolk County, Mass.	722,794	1821
Nantucket Town-Nantucket County, Mass.	5,660	1821
Philadelphia-Philadelphia County, Pa.	1,815,808	1854
San Francisco-San Francisco County, Ca.	664,520	1856
New York City (5 boroughs), N.Y.	7,481,613	1874/94/96
Denver-Denver County, Co	484,531	1902
Honolulu-Honolulu County, Hawaii	705,381	1907
Baton Rouge-East Baton Rouge Parish, La.	310,922	1947
Newport News-Warwick City, Va.*	138,760	1952/1958
Hampton-Elizabeth County, Va.	125,013	1952
Nashville-Davidson County, Tenn.	446,541	1962
Virginia Beach-Princess Anne County, Va.*	213,954	1962
Chesapeake-South Norfolk-Norfolk County, Va.*	104,459	1962
Jacksonville-Duval County, Fla.	562,283	1967
Indianapolis-Marion County, Ind.	782,139	1969
Carson City-Ormsby County, Nev.*	24,928	1969
Juneau-Greater Juneau, Alaska	16,749	1969
Columbus-Muscogee County, Ga.	160,103	1970
Sitka-Greater Sitka Borough, Alaska	6,111	1971
Lexington-Fayette County, Ky.	186,048	1972
Suffolk-Nansemond City, Va.*	49,210	1972/1974
Anchorage-Greater Anchorage Borough, Alaska	161,018	1975
Butte-Silver Bow County, Mont.	43,034	1976
Anaconda-Deer Lodge County, Mont.	15,101	1976
Houma-Terrebonne Parish, La.	101,600	1984
Lynchburg City-Moore County, Tenn.	4,510	1988
Athens-Clarke County, Ga.	78,800	1990

* independent cities that are historically city-county consolidations

Source: National Association of Counties, Research Department
Two consolidations have occurred since the list was compiled: Augusta-Richmond County, Ga., and Lafayette City-Lafayette Parish, La. in 1996.

Beach (City of Virginia Beach) and other consolidations in Virginia — or unified governments — such as the Metropolitan Government of Nashville and Davidson County, Tennessee; Unigov (Consolidated Government of Indianapolis and Marion County, Indiana); and the Unified Government of Athens/Clarke County, Georgia.

Most of the early consolidations required only state government legislative approval. In the past three decades, however, all consolidations except one — Indianapolis-Marion County — have been approved by local referenda, sometimes following state legislative action. Many of the consolidation attempts have failed at the polls; 46 out of 62 were rejected between 1949 and 1979, and another 24 out of 25 between 1983 and 1992 alone. (National Academy of Public Administration, 1980, 75-6; Durning) Two of the recent consolidation attempts were covered by the Voting Rights Act of 1965 and required U.S. Department of Justice approval as well, which was successfully secured in Athens-Clarke County and in Augusta-Richmond County, Georgia.

City-county consolidations have both mayor-council and council-manager forms of government. Elected executives are called metropolitan county or metro mayors; appointed ones managers or chief administrative officers. Many of the independently elected city and county officials continue under the consolidated governments with some combination where duties overlap, such as between elected county sheriffs and appointed city police chiefs.

Legislative bodies are called metropolitan or metro councils, city-county councils, councils or commissions. They vary in size — from ten plus the mayor in the City of Virginia Beach government to forty plus the mayor in the Metropolitan Government of Nashville and Davidson County — usually to help guarantee minority and neighborhood representation from central cities. They all have some legislators elected by district; many also call for some at-large or super-district members, to balance regional and local perspectives.

Other incorporated municipalities located in the geographic area of the consolidated governments rarely opt to become part of the consolidated governments and generally continue as independent jurisdictions, receiving county level services from the consolidated government and directly delivering their own municipal services. Residents in these incorporated municipalities only pay for the general services of the consolidated governments at a general services tax rate, whereas residents in unincorporated areas pay for municipal services as well at an additional urban services rate.

School and special districts are generally not merged into the consolidated governments. An exception is the merger of city and county school districts in the Nashville-Davidson County, Tennessee, consolidation. After consolidation, somewhere between a few and dozens of general and special purpose local governments remain within the geographic area of the consolidated governments.

Central city-county consolidation is also referred to as a *one-tier consolidated government,* since typically county and municipal services are delivered by the same level of government. In addition to those mentioned above, similar single-tier governments exist in smaller regions in Canada, such as Edmonton, Calgary, Winnipeg, and London. The creation of Unicity in Winnipeg in 1972 was probably the most dramatic, involving the consolidation of twelve municipalities and the Corporation of Greater Winnipeg and resulting in a governing body with fifty-one members. (Sancton, *Governing Canada's City-Regions*)

There are also a few formal *two-tier federated governments* that differentiate county (areawide) from municipal (local) government responsibilities by state statute. The best known example in this country is between Dade County (which is defined as a metropolitan county) and the City of Miami and the other two dozen municipalities in its midst.

Metropolitan Dade County provides fire services (except in a few municipalities), library services (except in a few municipalities), special police services, waste disposal (but not collection), some housing and redevelopment services, airport and seaport services, and traditional county health, hospital, and court services countywide. It is governed by a seven-member commission, including an elected mayor, and operates as a council-manager government. Miami and the other municipalities continue to deliver police services and some housing and redevelopment services and to control local zoning decisions. A few unincorporated areas are considering incorporation to control police and zoning, but thus far they have been unwilling to absorb the higher tax rates generally associated with incorporation (the unincorporated county tax rate is generally lower than that of municipalities). Similarly, a few incorporated areas in Miami are considering disincorporation to take advantage of Dade County's lower tax rate. Over the years since creating the metropolitan county government, there has been some volatility in new incorporations and disincorporations; coincidentally, the current number of municipalities is approximately the same as at its creation in 1957.

Similar two-tier statutory relationships exist in other countries. The Ontario provincial government established Metro Toronto in the early 1950s and reduced by half — from thirteen to six — the number of local authorities within the developed part of the region at that time, in part by annexations in the early years of Metro. The Metro Council, composed of the mayors of the six municipalities and twenty-eight councilors elected by districts, serves as both the executive and legislative body. For the most part, Metro Toronto has dealt with the most critical regional challenges, particularly expanding roads, sewers, water mains and public transportation, while local authorities have retained responsibility for police, fire, public health and public welfare services. Some responsibilities are shared among the local authorities, such as street construction, road maintenance, traffic control, public assistance, and zoning and planning. Metro Toronto does not have taxing authority, but it is empowered to raise and apportion bond funding among the local authorities. Two-tier governments have been replicated in the most populated Canadian provinces, especially Ontario and Quebec, almost provincewide. (Stein)

Across the Atlantic, the Rotterdam (Netherlands) region is currently considering reducing by more than half — from twenty-six to ten or twelve — the number of municipalities in the region, including dividing up the City of Rotterdam, and creating a new regional administrative structure. Given the failure of an earlier port authority, the "Rijnmond," to develop solid working relationships between levels of government, the new "urban-regional" government is being designed to carry out municipal, provincial, and national government tasks, requiring the ceding of authorities from all three levels of government. (van den Berg; German Marshall Fund)

State statutes governing local governments also generally differentiate county and municipal government responsibilities, creating the informal, but often vague and overlapping, two-tier local government system that exists in most U.S. regions today. Sometimes local governments attempt to clarify their respective responsibilities without creating a two-tier government. Portland and Gresham have entered into an arrangement with Multnomah County, Oregon, to annex the remaining unincorporated areas in the county and deliver municipal services, thereby freeing county government to deliver only countywide services.

Finally, a couple of *three-tier government systems* have been created between city and county governments and third-level regional planning and service districts (see Problem-Solving/Service-Delivery #3).

According to interviewees in a recent study, the factors influencing recent consolidation efforts include:

- Race and class variations across central city and balance of county: heterogeneity makes consolidation more difficult.
- Capacity of city and county governments: both equally strong makes consolidation more difficult.
- Efficiency/financing of government services: community leader and citizen perception of relative efficiency of governments and fiscal disparities of city and county populations can influence consolidation.
- Government scandals/crises: often critical to attracting community leader and citizen interest for consolidation efforts.
- Economic impact: consolidation efforts can benefit from community official and citizen concerns for regional economic competitiveness.
- Political impact: increased political clout of consolidated government, concerns of eliminating city or county government elected officials, and number and attitudes of other local governments in county can help or hurt consolidation efforts.
- City-county consolidation process: the process followed by charter commissions can affect the outcome of consolidation efforts. (Dodge, Montgomery County Leadership Network, 1992)

Accomplishments

The municipal modifications that probably have had the greatest positive impact on regional decision making have been those in Canada and other countries that divided up the central city and region into a small number of relatively large municipalities. Such modifications tend to remove the political threat of central cities, provide appropriately sized municipalities for the delivery of public services, and keep the number of municipalities small enough to develop working relationships for regional problem solving and service delivery.

The continuing march of municipal incorporations complicates regional decision making. Municipal combinations and disincorporations are sufficiently rare to have little impact on regional decision making.

Annexations by central cities continue to have a substantial impact on regional decision making where they can still be accomplished, generally in the southern and western part of the country. The more the central city contains the developed, and developing, parts of the region, the more it can behave as a regional problem-solving and service-delivery mechanism. In many regards, whoever shapes growth controls the governance of regions.

Henry Cisneros, the Secretary of the U.S. Department of Housing and Urban Development, summed up the positive economic impacts of city-county consolidations and federations: all "superannexations" (as he calls city-county consolidations and federations) are "fiscally sound, unified governments with strong credit ratings, and all are successful communities with rates of economic growth well above their competitors." (Cisneros, 1995, 5)

Without question, the consolidation or federation of the two major local governments in a region has an impact on regional decision making, especially in developing a consensus public position for addressing regional challenges. City-county consolidations do not eliminate all local governments, but they often diminish the differences between the two primary public protagonists and fix responsibility for public involvement in regional decision making. City-county federations, however, do not appear to have the same impact on diminishing differences, as the rocky history of relationships between Dade County and its municipalities indicates.

Strengths and Shortcomings

The strengths of central city-county consolidations include:

- Reducing service inequities between central city and suburban governments.
- Reducing the number of government departments; from 77 to 9 in the Metropolitan Government of Nashville and Davidson County, 49 to 10 in the Consolidated City of Jacksonville Government, and 28 to 6 in the Consolidated Government of Indianapolis and Marion County. Yet some critics argue that the conflicts continue within, as opposed to between, departments. (Sancton, *Governing Canada's City-Regions,* 32)
- Facilitating regional planning, especially visioning and transportation planning and economic development marketing.
- Fostering contested elections, due to the attraction of new candidates.
- Freeing major local governments from some state legislative oversight.
- Securing community leader and citizen acceptance, given the few changes made in consolidated government charters after initial adoption.

The shortcomings of central city-county consolidations include:

- Little evidence, except anecdotal, that greater efficiencies and economies of scale actually occur, although there is some evidence that consolidation results in greater service integration and slows down the growth of government budgets.
- Mixed record of comprehensive planning, balancing suburban/central city development needs, and dispersing low-income housing. Some consolidated governments have been focused on downtown development, such as Unigov (Indianapolis/Marion County), at least in the initial years; some have focused on suburban development, such as Unicity (Winnipeg, Manitoba). (Sancton, *Governing Canada's City-Regions,* 24, 95)

- Failure to redraw boundaries as development occurred outside consolidated government boundaries. Indianapolis-Marion County now only contains 59 percent of the population in its ten-county region; Nashville-Davidson County, 50 percent of its six-county region; and Jacksonville-Duval County, 70 percent of its five-county region. (Rusk, 1993, 95)

Similarly, Metro Toronto is beginning to fray around the edges as development leaps into the surrounding regions of Halton, Peel, York, and Durham. While the Ontario provincial government played a key role in creating Metro Toronto, it has also complicated its implementation. Metro Toronto originally contained most of the population of the region, and it was given planning control over the 480 square miles that surrounded the 240 square mile area in which it exercised service delivery responsibilities. Fear of annexation led to stripping Metro Toronto of this extraterritorial planning authority and creating the surrounding metro regions. Now Metro Toronto includes only slightly more than half of the region's population.

To address inter-regional challenges, the Province of Ontario has established an Office of the Greater Toronto Area. It acts as a secretariat for the Greater Toronto Co-ordinating Committee, which is composed of senior staff members from metro and municipal governments throughout the region. Together, they are experimenting with what has become a new type of three-tier government — municipal, regional, and provincial. (Stein, 11–13)

Even Unicity (Winnipeg, Manitoba) has gone from containing almost all (99.1 percent) of the region's population at its founding in 1972 to 85.4 percent in 1991, in part due to the succession of the Headlingly area. Similar to Toronto, the provincial government has created a Capital Region Committee, composed of provincial and local government officials, to address regional challenges, but it has met infrequently in its first few years. (Sancton, *Governing Canada's City Regions*, 26)

Finally, city-county consolidations depend upon attracting visionary regionalists to serve on their governing bodies and as their executives. Strong, well-liked mayors who served long terms made a significant difference in the acceptance and accomplishments of Unigov (Indianapolis/Marion County). A visionary regionalist chair similarly helped prevent the Metro Toronto Council from being dominated by the parochial interests of its local elected official members. (Vogel, 3; Dodge, Montgomery County Leadership Network, CCC-C1, 2)

Andrew Sancton summed up the advantages and disadvantages of Canada's two-tier governments in Governing Canada's City Regions:

> The general advantages and disadvantages of two-tier government are well known. Their great strength in their ability to centralize some government functions while at the same time decentralizing others. This provides a degree of integration at the centre while enabling the constituent units to protect their identity and to experiment with innovative types of responses depending on local conditions and preferences. The main weaknesses of two-tier systems are that they produce endless discussions about which level should be doing what and generate frequent complaints about apparent duplication, overlap and lack of coordination. (Sancton, *Governing Canada's City Regions*, 57)

Potential

With two possible exceptions, municipal modifications will probably continue to make few contributions to regional decision making.

First, municipal combinations could be facilitated by state government. The California Constitution Revision Commission, for example, recommends community charters that would allow voters to create new intercommunity structures to deliver some or all of the services now provided by cities, counties, special authorities, school districts and counties, thereby increasing service delivery flexibility and possibly reducing the number of local governments. Incentives for creating community charters would include the ability to propose local taxes with the vote of the people and relief from state regulation. (CCRC News)

Second, allowing municipal disincorporation could provide a last chance, or even a veiled threat, for dealing with the service inequities in the most severely distressed communities (See Equitable #2, Chapter 5). Municipal disincorporation doesn't directly deal with underlying economic disparities and can politically disenfranchise residents of these communities, but it might offer the only option if regional tax sharing or municipal combinations are unacceptable for dealing with equity and empowering concerns.

Annexations of current and future regional growth areas by central cities and larger municipalities could continue to have a major impact, especially where surrounding growth areas are unincorporated.

Central city-county consolidations or federations could continue to have an impact on regional decision making, by bringing together a region's two major local governments. Unfortunately, the two governments alone no longer shape growth, which has now moved beyond the boundaries of the central county in many regions. To achieve the same results, the city-county consolidation of today has to have extraterritorial planning authority, similar to that originally given to Metro Toronto by the Province of Ontario, or involve consolidation with other counties in the region.

Contacts

- Confluence St. Louis, St. Louis, Missouri, 314-533-3123
- Office of the Greater Toronto Area, Toronto, Ontario, Canada, 416-314-6400
- Consolidated Government of Indianapolis and Marion County (Unigov), Indiana, 317-327-3610
- Consolidated City of Jacksonville government, Florida, 904-630-2703, 904-630-1377
- Metropolitan Government of Nashville and Davidson County, Tennessee, 615-862-6000
- City of Virginia Beach, Virginia, 804-427-4242
- Unified Government of Athens/Clarke County, Georgia, 706-613-3150
- Metropolitan Dade County, Miami, Florida, 305-375-5311

Problem-Solving/Service-Delivery #3
Regional Planning and Service Districts

There are a few examples of regional districts that combine regional planning councils and the delivery of regional sewer, transit or other services. The most touted examples in this country are the Metropolitan Council in the Minneapolis/St. Paul region and the Metropolitan Service District, or Metro, in the Portland, Oregon, region. A similar example is the Greater Vancouver Regional District in the Vancouver, British Columbia, region of Canada.

The Metropolitan Council (Minneapolis/St. Paul region):   The Metropolitan Council was created by the Minnesota state legislature in 1967 to adopt regional development plans and policies and to coordinate the activities of other regional service delivery agencies, including appointing their members and reviewing their capital budgets, as well as local governments, including reviewing their projects of "metropolitan significance." It covers seven counties, approximately 200 municipalities, and 100 special districts. For most of its life, it has had primarily a planning and policy development (problem solving) role, albeit with strong review and even control authorities. There were a few exceptions, such as directly administering a metropolitan housing and redevelopment authority and open space program.

In 1994, however, the state legislature reconstituted the Metropolitan Council as a public corporation and political subdivision of the state to assume operating responsibilities for transportation (regional transit board and metropolitan transit commission) and sewage treatment (metropolitan waste control commission). The Metropolitan Council continues to have the power to require local compliance with its plans, including using the courts to override provisions of local government plans that are inconsistent with the regional plans. In addition, the Metropolitan Council has expanded access to funding, including regional property taxes to finance its own and subsidize transit operations and fees to finance its waste control operations. It also has authority to use bond financing, but must obtain general authority from the State legislature to issue them.

The seventeen members of the Metropolitan Council are appointed by the Governor, sixteen from separate geographic districts and an at-large chair, all of whom serve at the pleasure of the governor and receive annual salaries. Given the new operating responsibilities, a regional administrator position was created, to be filled by the Council. Also, Council members are being divided into committees to oversee their environment, community development, and transportation responsibilities. Planning and operational groups will report to each of these committees. The transportation advisory board (planning agency), metropolitan transit commission (operating agency) and regional transit board (coordinating group), for example, report to the transportation committee.

Compared to particular regional problem-solving and service-delivery mechanisms, the Metropolitan Council combines an empowered regional planning council (see Problem-Solving #1) with a regional multiple-service authority (see Service-Delivery #4), such as a regional port authority. It comes closest to the regional approaches tried in other countries, such as the two-tier governments in Canada, which also resulted from strong state, or provincial, government action. Given that Minneapolis/St. Paul is the only major and dominant region in Minnesota, it is probably not surprising that the state legislature behaves, at times, like a regional governing body.

The Metropolitan Council was the first model — and continues to be one of the most innovative models — of a regional planning and service district empowered by and accountable to state government but expected to earn the respect of, and coordinate, local governments to guide the sound development of the region. (National Academy of Public Administration, 1980, 88; Naftalin; Dodge, Interstate Study Commission, 1994, 45; and various reorganization documents)

Metro (Portland, Oregon, region): The Metropolitan Service District was created by the Oregon state legislature in 1977 and approved by the voters in the three central counties of the Portland region the following year. Originally, Metro was a consolidation of the regional planning council and the Metro Service Council, which was responsible for solid waste disposal, and the Washington Park Zoo, which had been administered by the Portland Zoological Society.

Although legislation enabled it to add additional regional responsibilities, with voter approval of a revenue base, none was added until it built and began operating the Oregon Convention Center in 1986. In 1990, Metro took over responsibility for the facilities managed by the Portland Exposition-Recreation Commission (center for performing arts, civic stadium and exposition center) and in 1994 several regional parks, cemeteries and marine facilities from Multnomah County.

In 1992, voters approved a new charter with the following ambitious preamble:

> We, the people of the Portland area metropolitan service district, in order to establish an elected, visible and accountable regional government that is responsive to the citizens of the region and works cooperatively with our local governments; that undertakes, as its most important service, planning and policy making to preserve and enhance the quality of life and the environment for ourselves and future generations; and that provides regional services needed and desired by the citizens in an efficient and effective manner, do ordain this charter for the Portland area metropolitan service district, to be known as Metro.

Metro is required by the charter to produce a future vision (Region 2040) and regional framework plan by 1997, including amending the urban growth boundary required by the state growth management program (see Problem-Solving #1). The home rule charter also requires Metro to adopt ordinances to assure consistency of local government plans with the regional framework plan, including adjudicating differences and requiring changes in local land use standards and procedures, as necessary.

Metro's unique contribution to a regional planning and service district is its elected Metro Council and Executive Officer. Starting with a seven-member board composed of local elected officials, it shifted to an elected board of a dozen councilors in 1977 as a result of state enabling legislation. The 1992 charter reduced the size of the council back to seven, all of whom are elected by district. To maintain its ties to local government, the Metropolitan Policy Advisory Committee of Metro, which guides the Region 2040 regional planning process and recommends growth management policy, is primarily composed of local elected officials. These officials have also created a separate coordinating group, called Focus on Cooperative Urban Services (FOCUS), which develops joint recommendations for Metro consideration (see Service-Delivery #5).

The new charter also authorizes Metro to levy property, sales and income taxes, with voter approval, as well as continue to use the taxes and fees already collected in its various operations. The charter requires voter approval before issuing general obligation bonds. The new charter also calls for election of a Metro Auditor to monitor its fiscal activities. (Metro, *Passport to Metro Regional Services,* 1994–1995; 1992 Metro Charter; Abbott, Carl)

Greater Vancouver Regional District (Vancouver, British Columbia, region): The Greater Vancouver Regional District was established in 1965 to take over the functions of separate authorities for delivering sewage, water, health and hospitals, and industrial development services and regional planning responsibilities. Its activities have grown to include affordable housing, regional parks, air quality control, and 911 emergency communications as well as providing personnel and labor relations services to its member municipalities.

The Greater Vancouver Service District is not seen as a regional government, but as a "tidying up" of the existing system and creating a framework for increased municipal cooperation for "reasons of economy, effectiveness and fairness." As a result, it, and two dozen counterparts throughout British Columbia, look more like regional planning councils (see Problem-Solving #1) with some regional service responsibilities than like the two-tier governments in other Canadian regions.

The Greater Vancouver Regional District has a twenty-nine-member board of directors, with weighted voting, composed primarily of members of the eighteen municipal councils and two electoral areas in the region. It is an extremely flexible mechanism. It can provide different services in different municipalities; in fact, members can decide to opt out of district functions. It can change its boundaries to accommodate potential growth areas as well as enter into arrangements with adjoining regional districts to conduct planning processes or deliver regional services.

Little controversy has resulted from the establishment of regional districts, especially after their land use planning powers were stripped in 1984. However, the Greater Vancouver Regional District was able to prepare a regional development plan — the Livable Region Strategic Plan — that focuses on developing regional towns to prevent urban sprawl and minimize commuting as well as protect an environmentally sensitive region from too rapid growth. (Sancton, *Governing Canada's City Regions*, 65–70, and organization documents)

Accomplishments

The Metropolitan Council, Metro, and Greater Vancouver Regional District have each had successes and failures in addressing regional challenges.

The Metropolitan Council succeeded in creating a regionwide sewer system and blocking the construction of an unneeded airport. It has had, however, a mixed record in siting new facilities: It was left out of recent decisions on the siting of the Metrodome stadium, World Trade Center, a horse racing track in the suburbs, and a new landfill. Metro went from early failures, such as proposing a technically correct but politically unacceptable approach to storm water runoff, to assuming responsibility for the Washington Park Zoo and siting, constructing and operating the Oregon Convention Center. (State of California)

These regional planning and service districts demonstrate that single mechanisms, with appointed or elected government bodies, can develop strategies for addressing regional challenges and guide their implementation, in collaboration with others.

Strengths and Shortcomings

The major strength of regional planning and service districts is their capacity to design, guide, and even help implement, strategies for addressing regional challenges. Moreover, they can focus regional decision making and make it prominent enough to capture and sustain community leader and citizen interest in addressing regional challenges.

The major shortcomings of regional planning and service districts are the major obstacles to creating them. One obstacle is attracting regional "pioneers" to support regional planning and service districts, and once created, to serve on their governing bodies. Attracting visionary regional thinkers (appointed or elected) is critical to determining whether the district is a force for cooperative regional action or divisive parochial reaction.

Another obstacle is striking a balance between state and local government interests, to secure the state powers and authorities and local government cooperation needed to succeed at regional decision making. Each of the modifications in the authorities of the Metropolitan Council and Metro has wrestled with this balance. The last change in the Metropolitan Council, for example, extended its powers (including more control by local citizens) but retained gubernatorial appointments (to continue state control of its membership).

A third obstacle is finding the patience to build community leader and citizen support for creating the districts. All of the regional planning and service districts went through gestation periods lasting decades, and since their creation they have often been the subjects of new studies and continuing modifications. Given their experimental nature, it is not surprising that they have gone through such an evolutionary process. What is amazing is that they have survived and emerged stronger with each transformation.

Potential

Regional planning and service districts have considerable potential for other regions, nationally. In fact, a recent study by the Metro Forum, a regional leadership alliance (see Problem-Solving #5) in the Denver, Colorado, region, recommended creating an "umbrella regional planning and service agency" for the Denver region. The proposed agency, the report said,

.... should have the capacity to set regional policy, formulate regional plans, resolve interjurisdictional conflicts, provide services, as appropriate, generate financial resources, and ensure that regional policies and plans are successfully implemented. The regional services identified for further consideration include water supply, transportation, tax equity and regional revenue sharing, health care, environment (air and water supply), solid waste, and open space.

The regional planning functions of the Denver Region Council of Governments would be transferred to the proposed agency, and possibly some service delivery responsibilities of existing regional single-service authorities (see Service-Delivery #3). The proposed governing body would have elected or appointed members from districts or at large. (Metro Forum)

Andrew Sancton, author of *Governing Canada's City-Regions,* suggests that the regional planning and service delivery districts, such as the Greater Vancouver Regional District, might even offer a more flexible regional governance mechanism for those Canadian regions that have already created consolidated or federated governments. He notes that the structural solutions for the "super-region" of Toronto all have shortcomings: maintaining the status quo of five contiguous regions, each divided into municipalities, and strengthening the Greater Toronto Coordinating Committee to coordinate their activities; consolidating all municipalities with each of the five regional governments; or abolishing the five regional governments and replacing them with a single new one. (Sancton, 96–97)

Given the histories of the three examples above, regions that have already wrestled with modifying their regional planning councils (see Problem-Solving #1), have already established regional single and even multiple-service authorities (see Service-Delivery #3 and #4), and have experimented with various regional problem-solving mechanisms, including regional alliances (see Problem-Solving #5) are probably prime candidates for considering regional planning and service districts, especially if they continue to have difficulty developing timely responses to emerging regional challenges. Creating such districts could be facilitated by state governments if they enacted enabling legislation to create intercommunity or regional charters, as the California Constitution Revision Commission recommends (see Problem-Solving/Service-Delivery #2).

Given that regional planning and service districts come closest to behaving like metropolitan governments in multiple-county regions, they will probably only receive consideration after other mechanisms for addressing regional challenges are not working effectively enough for community leaders and citizens. And then their implementation will probably be evolutionary. In fact, the initial interactions could be some form of the combination of a regional planning council (see Problem-Solving #1) and a regional service delivery coordinating group (see Service-Delivery #5).

The National Academy of Public Administration suggested guidelines for designing a regional planning and service district, based on the recommendations of study commissions in the Minneapolis/St. Paul, Portland, and Tampa Bay regions:

- A directly elected regional council should be created (two commissions suggested a 15 member board, and one a 29-member board).
- Council members should be chosen from single member districts, ranging in population from 50,000 to 75,000.
- The regional council should be headed by an executive, the office to be filled through an at-large election in one instance, and in the other two plans, to be appointed by the elected council.
- The voluntary council of governments approach (see Problem-Solving #1), should not be used, yet the existing COG should be built upon to develop the new regional government.
- The existing municipal or county governments should not be merged or abolished, at least in the short term.
- Each of the reorganization plans would result in a three-tier system of local government: municipalities, counties and elected regional council.
- Each of the proposed multi-county agencies would be responsible for a limited but important set of functions considered regional in character. All three study commissions agreed that the following seven services should, in whole or in part, be provided at the regional level: comprehensive planning; land use planning; sewage treatment and disposal; water treatment and supply; water distribution; and public transportation.

While the role of direct service provider was envisioned for the regional agency in these seven areas, the major emphasis was placed upon

Problem-Solving/Service-Delivery #3

planning, coordinating and policy making. (National Academy of Public Administration, 1980, 86–87)

Contacts

- The Metropolitan Council, Minneapolis/St. Paul, Minnesota, 612-291-6359
- Metro, Portland, Oregon, 503-797-1700
- Greater Vancouver Regional District, Vancouver, British Columbia, Canada, 604-432-6200

Chapter 8
Making Regional Governance a State and National Priority

I am not an advocate for frequent changes in laws and constitutions. But laws and institutions must go hand in hand with the progress of the human mind. As that becomes more developed, more enlightened, as new discoveries are made, new truths discovered and manners and opinions change, with the change in circumstances, institutions must advance also to keep pace with the times.

— Thomas Jefferson, Letter to Samuel Kercheval, July 12, 1816

As much as individual communities cannot resolve crosscutting and regional challenges without involving their neighbors, neither can many regional governance initiatives reach their full potential without involving state and national partners.

Partners, state and national, governmental and nongovernmental, are critical to implementing initiatives across all five components of regional governance excellence.

First, the only elected officials representing most regions are those that hold state or national government office, especially some members of state legislatures and the U.S. Congress and governors and presidents.

If they respond to their regional constituencies, and use the bully pulpit of their offices, these officials can contribute to making regional governance prominent. If their message of regional interdependence is reinforced by the actions of state and national government agencies — as well as national and sub-national organizations representing the private, academic, nonprofit, foundation and civic sectors — they can dramatically change community leader and citizen attitudes, and behavior, almost overnight.

Second, state and national governments often support, and sometimes create, regional problem-solving and service-delivery mechanisms.

The national government has supported regional planning councils to address transportation, air and water quality, health care, aging, and other challenges, as well as regional authorities to provide sewer and water, transit, and even housing and redevelopment services. State governments have supported many of the same regional problem-solving and service-delivery mechanisms, usually providing the enabling legislation for their establishment, from regional planning councils (see Problem-Solving #1, Chapter 7) to regional planning and service authorities, such as the Metropolitan Council in the Minneapolis/St. Paul region (see Problem-Solving/Service-Delivery #3, Chapter 7).

Some regional problem-solving and service-delivery mechanisms are even financed and administered as state agencies, generally with governing boards of local representatives. The State of New York, for example, creates regional mechanisms in areas that have fragile environments or stagnant economies. The Tug Hill Commission helps local governments in upstate New York's Tug Hill plateau address their environmental concerns and develop management plans to shape their futures. (Coe) A bit further north, the Development Authority of the North Country has financed critical infrastructure projects and coordinated planning for economic development in the Watertown area.

Third, other state and national organizations often help breathe life into regional decision-making mechanisms.

Regrettably, all too many regional problem-solving or service-delivery mechanisms tend to be ineffective, unless deals can be negotiated between state and local government officials. Sometimes private, academic, nonprofit, foundation, civic, or other nongovernmental organizations can provide neutral technical assistance, such as "elder statespersons" who can convene participants in negotiating the deals for empowering regional decision-making mechanisms. In addition, they can often provide the front-end financial assistance to implement the agreements negotiated to make regional decision-making mechanisms work. Even the national government can play a critical role in facilitating these discussions, especially when regions cut across state boundaries.

Finally, a two-decade-old proposal indicates the importance of involving public and nonpublic partners in strengthening regional governance.

In 1975, a group of regional private and civic-sponsored problem-solving mechanisms, called the Metropolitan Affairs Nonprofit Corporations, recommended that local, state and national private and foundation sectors provide sustained philanthropic support for regional citizen organizations to build citizen understanding and involvement, and that local, state and national governments support regional coordinating bodies and provide incentives for improving "regional productivity." They even recommended convening a national conference to develop a ten-year agenda of regional productivity initiatives to be implemented in time for the Bicentennial of the Constitution. (Metropolitan Affairs Nonprofit Corporations, 518–525)

Such bold state and national initiatives, in partnership with community leaders and citizens, are needed now more than ever to strengthen regional governance; to improve our ability to compete globally and flourish locally in the 1990s. Having focused national government assistance on the cities in the 1960s and 1970s, and on the states in the 1980s, it would be appropriate to focus what's left of this largesse on regions for the 1990s and beyond.

The effectiveness of the federal system in the 21st century will be substantially determined by our efforts to improve regional governance during the balance of the 20th century.

This chapter suggests state and national initiatives to assist community leaders and citizens who are pursuing regional governance excellence. Particular initiatives are especially directed at making regional governance prominent, strategic, equitable, empowering and institutionalized, and are so noted.

Any of the initiatives could be undertaken by almost any state and national organization, governmental and nongovernmental; a couple, however, are particularly targeted at state and national governments or national foundations and are also so noted. Contacts for initiatives and organizations cited are given in the references at the end of the book.

State/National #1
Expand State and National Organization Agendas for Fostering Regional Governance Excellence (Prominent)

The number of national organizations helping their members to address regional challenges is expanding almost as quickly as the challenges. These organizations include:

- public sector interest groups, such as the Council of State Governments, Development District Association of Appalachia, International City/County Management Association, National Association of Counties, National Association of Development Organizations, National Association of Regional Councils, National Conference of State Legislatures, National Council for Urban Economic Development, National Governors Association, National League of Cities, and U.S. Conference of Mayors;

- other sector interest groups, such as the American Chamber of Commerce Executives, American Planning Association, American Society for Public Administration, Committee for Enterprise Development, International Downtown Association, National Academy of Public Administration, National Civic League, United Way of America, and Urban Affairs Association as well as national associations of Metropolitan Universities and regional associations of grant makers; and

- national citizen-based organizations, such as the Association of Community Organizations for Reform Now (ACORN) Common Cause, Industrial Areas Foundation, and League of Women Voters.

Some national and state level organizations have helped to develop the tools that are used in regional problem solving and service delivery and provide services to promote their use; the services range from periodic newsletters and training to technical assistance and "how to" publications. At the national level, these include the following, with excerpts from their purposes and a note about their publications:

- Center for Living Democracy ("supporting role of regular citizens in solving America's toughest problems;" newsletter, *Doing Democracy*)

- Institute for the Study of Civic Values ("developing neighborhood social contracts and other activities to help the poor gain self-sufficiency;" no publication)
- The Lincoln Institute of Land Policy (focuses its attention on the use and taxation of land, which in recent years has become more regional, leading to examining intergovernmental tax policy and regional growth management, both in the United States and Latin America; newsletter, *LandLines*)
- National Institute for Dispute Resolution ("advances the field of conflict and dispute resolution;" newsletter, *NIDR News*)
- Program for Community Problem Solving ("promote an understanding and application of effective processes for solving community problems;" manual, *Pulling Together, A Planning and Development Consensus-Building Manual*)
- Study Circles Resource Center ("promoting small-group, democratic, participatory discussions on social and political issues;" newsletter, *Focus on Study Circles*)

At the state level, The North Dakota Consensus Council, Inc., provides community leaders and citizens with "forums and assistance to use consensus processes for building agreement on public policy issues important to North Dakotans." A few multi-state organizations, such as the Center for the New West, have also provided assistance in regional decision making. In addition, various state governments and associations of governments are sponsoring futures examinations that involve exploring roles of regions, such as the Georgia Futures Commission, sponsored by the Georgia state legislature, and the 1996 Horizons Task Force, sponsored by the Kentucky League of Cities.

A few national organizations have taken the next step and pursued special activities to foster regional governance excellence.

- The International City/County Management Association (ICMA) has created a Regionalism Task Force. Task Force member Tim Honey, city manager of Boulder, Colorado, has prepared a paper to guide Task Force activities, including proposing that ICMA serve as an information resource on regionalism, sponsor an annual regionalism symposium, advocate regionalism with local government officials, and encourage state associations to pursue regionalism initiatives. A track at the annual ICMA conference is being devoted to regionalism. The ICMA has a part-time staff member supporting Task Force activities.

- The National Academy of Public Administration, whose membership includes some of the nation's most seasoned public administrators, has conducted various analyses of regional governance, including devoting the agendas of a couple of its semi-annual meetings to the topic and co-hosting a symposium on regional governance with delegations of community leaders from various regions, nationally.

- The National Association of Regional Councils has established the Institute for The Regional Community to bring national organizations with regional agendas together to pursue collaborative initiatives. It publishes a quarterly journal, *The Regionalist,* in cooperation with the Institute of Community and Area Development at the University of Georgia. It also plans to hold annual conferences on the regional community, publish a regional community books series and create a national clearinghouse on regionalism called RegionSource. The Institute has a part-time consulting director, Pat Atkins.

- The National Civic League has focused on regional issues for the past decade, including issuing a policy statement on the importance of regional governance. It has also recently launched the Alliance for National Renewal, led by John Gardner, founder of Common Cause and the Independent Sector, to bring national and other organizations together to creatively involve citizens in community problem solving at the local level. More than 110 organizations have joined the Alliance and are developing individual and collective efforts to foster national renewal, which are reported on in the Alliance's publication, *Kitchen Renewal.*

- The National League of Cities has developed the view that the U.S. economy is a "common market" of local economic regions, and these regions require regional governance. They have applied these ideas in publications, training workshops, policy development, and conferences. *Nation's Cities Weekly* carries special reports and articles on regional collaboration, including a recent eight-part series titled "The Metropolitan Perplex." Forthcoming publications include a manual on regional strategic planning, *Shaping a Region's Future.*

National foundations also are increasingly supporting regional prob-lem-solving mechanisms. The Annie E. Casey Foundation, for example, recently developed a jobs initiative that recommends creating regional intermediary agencies to coordinate job training and placement activi-ties in selected regions. The Kellogg Foundation is supporting a re-gional economic development training academy in the Pittsburgh region.

Last, but not least, national and state government agencies sponsor activities to foster regional governance excellence.

The national government has experimented with various approaches to help community leaders and citizens address regional challenges, from categorical grants-in-aid and the grand designs of the War on Poverty and Great Society of the 1960s to the revenue sharing and grant consolidation and national urban policy of the 1970s, to the New Federalism, budget reductions and regulatory cutbacks of the 1980s, to the New Covenant of the 1990s. (Harrigan, 358)

In addition, the Advisory Commission on Intergovernmental Relations has conducted research on regional governance topics for decades, but its inadequate funding does not allow it to either conduct examinations or promote its recommendations for improving regional governance. The U.S. Department of Housing and Urban Development (HUD) spon-sors occasional conferences on regional topics and publishes the journal *Cityscape* on urban and regional topics. HUD Secretary Henry Cisneros also publishes periodic essays on regional topics.

At the state level, for example, the State of Virginia provides grants to regional planning district commissions, and the State of Pennsylvania provides small grants for intercommunity cooperation, including sup-porting sub-county councils of governments, as do departments and advisory commissions on intergovernmental relations in other states.

State and national organizations could:

Expand regional governance agendas. The potential exists for all of these organizations to expand their activities to promote regional governance excellence, including pursuing the initiatives presented in this chapter. Equally importantly, other national, state and multi-state organizations could consider activities; Sister Cities International, for example, could sponsor a "Sister Regions" program. Finally, new national and state organizations are emerging or could be created by other regional problem-solving and service-delivery mechanisms, such as the recently created National Association of Regional Planning Councils, representing regional social service planning organizations (see Problem-Solving #1, Chapter 7), or the Regional Civic Organizations, representing citizens leagues and other regional civic organizations (see Problem-Solving #4, Chapter 7).

Hire regional governance experts. An excellent initial action for these organizations would be to hire a regional governance expert on a full- or part-time basis.

Such an individual could survey the regional governance needs of members and clients of the organization, review existing activities that respond to regional governance needs, suggest new or modified activities that better respond to these needs, lead task groups to secure resources and implement these activities. Moreover, this individual could build partnerships with other organizations interested in pursuing similar activities. Most important, this individual could educate members, clients, and other staff members on the importance of regional governance and help build member support for pursuing initiatives to strengthen regional governance.

State/National #2
Focus Initial State and National Organization Activities on Making Regional Governance Prominent (Prominent)

An excellent place for state and national organizations to begin is sponsoring activities to make regional governance prominent. State and national, governmental and nongovernmental, organizations could:

Use the organizational bully pulpit. First, and foremost, the leaders of organizations could speak out on regional challenges and the need to foster regional governance excellence. Using the largest bully pulpit, the White House, President Bill Clinton recently issued an executive order enhancing intergovernmental partnerships (E.O.#12875) directed at reducing unfunded national government mandates on state and local governments and increasing flexibility in waiving national statutory and regulatory requirements on state and local governments. (International City Management Association, 1993) Others could do likewise, and repeatedly, to educate members of their organizations and the general public on the importance of strengthening regional governance.

The potential of national and sub-national organizations to use the bully pulpit is almost endless. Regrettably, few organizations have had regional governance experts on their staffs, making it difficult for their leaders to speak knowledgeably and convincingly on the topic. Even when they do, such as the intergovernmental experts on White House and other staffs, they tend to have backgrounds in state and local government relations, not regional and neighborhood decision making.

Host regional governance symposia and develop, promulgate, and promote effective regional decision-making policy. Three of the organizations mentioned above, the National Academy of Public Administration, the National Association of Regional Councils, and the National Civic League, sponsored a roundtable on "city-states" for teams of community leaders from approximately a dozen regions. The National Civic League developed a policy statement on regionalism as a result of sponsoring dialogues on regionalism and regional civic organizations at its national conferences. (National Civic League, 1989)

Again, the potential for national and sub-national organizations to sponsor symposia and policy statements on regional governance is almost endless. In fact, given the few offered, there is probably little risk of scheduling conflicting symposia, or even policy statements, with other organizations.

Sponsor recognition awards for regional governance excellence. Some national and state recognition awards touch on regional governance. At the national level, the All-America City and Community Program of the National Civic League is increasingly attracting applications from groups of communities and even entire regions, some of which are selected for designation as All-America Communities. At the state level, the Pennsylvania State Department of Community Affairs gives awards for intergovernmental cooperation, generally to groups of municipalities or councils of governments.

The potential to modify or create new recognition awards is almost endless. Existing awards, such as the Innovations in American Government Award (Harvard University/Ford Foundation) or the Exemplary State and Local (EXCL)Awards Program (Rutgers University), could be modified by adding or focusing awards on regional governance excellence, or new awards could be provided for regional governance excellence, by national, sub-national, or state organizations.

State/National #3
Provide State and National Government Assistance for Preparing Regional Visions and Action Plans (Strategic)

State and national governments could influence the attitudes of community leaders and citizens if they offered more incentives for inter-community, and especially regional, cooperation.

The national government has already influenced the behavior of community leaders and citizens by requiring regional planning for transportation funding. The most recent iteration of these planning requirements, in the Intermodal Surface Transportation Efficiency Act (ISTEA), even requires public involvement in determining future land use patterns, to assure meeting future transportation needs in the most efficient manner. Most important, these plans are required before receiving the tens of billions of dollars made available each year to finance highway, transit, bike, and other transportation systems.

State and national governments could:

Require regional visions and action plans and offer assistance for their preparation. Regional visions and action plans could replace or at least tie together community-by-community plans. Such regional approaches have already been initiated for community and economic development planning by the U.S. Departments of Housing and Urban Development and Commerce.

At the state level, the State of Connecticut has already enacted legislation to develop voluntary fair-share housing compacts. The Capital Region Fair Housing Compact on Affordable Housing (Hartford region) has proposed providing between 5,000 and 6,400 units of affordable housing throughout the region over the next five years. The compact was developed by a committee of community leaders and ratified by the participating local governments. To help assure its regionwide impact, the state legislature also passed zoning legislation to allow developers to challenge denial of development permits in communities that have not met their fair share housing obligations. (Wallis, 1994, 29)

Make regional planning requirements more holistic. To avoid the plethora of planning requirements and, consequently, duplicating and overlapping plans, state and national government planning assistance could be consolidated and targeted on developing more holistic regional visions and action plans, such as for economic competitiveness and quality of life.

Such plans could be used to guide collaborative regional initiatives. They also would permit national and state governments to stop requiring customized *plans* and allow them to buy into, and support, dynamic ongoing strategic planning *processes* that guide the use of local, state and national resources.

For example, the Community Viability Fund, proposed by the U.S. Department of Housing and Urban Development, included strategic planning and urban design grants that could be used to support holistic regional visions and action plans. In addition, the transportation planning processes spurred by ISTEA are beginning to integrate transportation planning with land use and environmental planning to guide future development.

It is interesting that the launching of a multi-billion dollar regional economic development program by the European Community has resulted in the preparation of regional plans, often by newly created regional planning councils, and new regional relationships between community leaders and citizens and the European Community. (Shutt, 1994)

Similarly, state governments also are providing support for regional economic development planning and marketing activities, such as the state support for public/private partnerships in each region of North Carolina.

Provide guidance for regional planning and visioning processes. State and national government, and nongovernmental organizations could provide guidance for regional visioning processes. For example, the National Civic League could sponsor the development of new models for regional governance, building upon its experience in developing model city and county government charters.

An excellent initial action for state and national governments would be to grant waivers for planning requirements to regions that conduct holistic regional strategic planning processes, regularly monitor their progress in implementing action plans, and periodically update their visions and strategies.

Needless to say, a key component, not a secondary consideration, of these visions and action plans should be strategies for making regional governance prominent, strategic, equitable, empowering, and institutionalized.

State/National #4
Provide Foundation Support for Conducting a National Demonstration of Regional Governance Examinations and Establishing Regional Governance Funds (Strategic)

Community foundations already support regional strategic planning efforts, some of which include explorations of regional governance. For example, the John D. & Catherine T. MacArthur Foundation and Chicago Community Trust are supporting a regional visioning process in the southern part of the Chicago region.

National and community foundations could:

Sponsor a national demonstration of regional governance examinations. Community foundations could collaborate with each other and national foundations to launch a national regional governance demonstration in which they would facilitate conducting regional governance examinations (see Strategic #2, Chapter 3) in a sample of regions. Conducting these examinations in tandem would let the participating community leaders and citizens share information and experiences, and assist each other in conducting these prototype efforts. As the examinations are being completed, the consortium of national and community foundations could analyze the experience and prepare reports and provide training for community leaders and citizens in other regions interested in conducting regional governance examinations.

In addition to foundations, regional research institutes and public service programs at metropolitan and other colleges and universities could assist in developing new models for regional governance for consideration by community leaders and citizens.

Provide seed money for establishing regional governance funds. In addition, the consortium of national and community foundations could help create regional governance funds in each of the regions conducting regional governance examinations to provide seed money for launching priority initiatives for strengthening regional governance (see Strategic #5, Chapter 3).

These regional governance funds could be modeled after those instigated by the Public Education Fund to finance innovations in individual and groups of school districts. The Ford Foundation and community foundations provided seed money to create the local education funds which was matched with contributions from businesses and other local sources.

Moreover, the Public Education Fund demonstrations led to creation of the Public Education Fund Network by the local education funds to provide an ongoing conduit for sharing information and experiences and providing assistance (Public Education Fund Network). A similar Regional Governance Fund Network could emerge from a national demonstration to support regional governance funds.

State and national governments could also provide tax and other financial incentives to facilitate implementing Strategies for Achieving Regional Governance Excellence (SARGEs). David Rusk suggests offering financial incentives for consolidating central city and county governments, such as deductions for taxes paid to consolidated governments, tax exemptions or even credits for holders of consolidated government bonds, and direct assistance to consolidated governments. (Rusk, 108–109) Designing such incentives might better be tied to implementing the action plans emerging from regional governance examinations (Strategic #2), however, as opposed to dictating the desired forms of regional governance.

An excellent first step for national and community foundations to focus attention on the importance of regional governance would be to sponsor a national demonstration of regional governance examinations.

State/National #5
Prepare and Dialogue on National Reports on the State of Regional Governance (Strategic)

Presently, only the National Urban Policy Report prepared by the President comes close to providing a periodic report that touches on the state of regional governance. The 1995 report refers several times to the importance of regional participation in addressing urban challenges, such as:

> Because metropolitan regions represent the new geography of opportunity for tens of millions of Americans, national urban policies must encourage metropolitan-wide approaches to economic development,

and

> The problems of central cities cannot be solved in isolation from the resources and opportunities of their metropolitan regions. (U.S. Department of Housing and Urban Development, 1995, 5, 57)

Regrettably, these reports do not focus on regional governance and are published irregularly.

Considerable benefit could accrue from publishing a periodic report on the state of regional governance, both to provide a report card on past and present regional governance initiatives and to share thoughts on a vision and action plan for the future improvement of regional governance. If it is to be a national government document, the President could designate a working group to be responsible for its preparation, possibly staffed by the Advisory Commission on Intergovernmental Relations.

The state of regional governance report could express the national government's thoughts on regional governance; present the results of national government initiatives to strengthen regional governance, such as using federal "sticks and carrots" to foster competitive regionalism; and suggest future national government initiatives. The report could be released in conjunction with a White House Conference on Regional Governance that would bring national, state, and community leaders and citizens together to develop strategies for improving regional governance.

Reports on the state of regional governance also could be prepared by other national organizations, such as the National Academy of Public Administration or National Association of Regional Councils, alone, collectively or in collaboration with the national government. For example, the state and local government interest groups could designate a working group to prepare a periodic report and test its conclusions and recommendations in a national conference. Any of these approaches would help broaden the scope of the report by including the regional governance initiatives of other national and state organizations.

Finally, national foundations could finance a nationally respected college or university regional research institute to prepare a periodic report, with appropriate input from a wide range of national, state, regional and local participants, possibly also in conjunction with a national conference.

The potential is wide open for any one or group of the above to begin preparing one or more regular reports on the state of regional governance. An excellent initial action would be to coordinate the resources of state and national organizations to provide the critical mass needed to conduct the first of what it is hoped will become regular reports on the state of regional governance.

State/National #6
Provide State and National Government Assistance on a Regional Basis to Address Intercommunity Disparities (Equitable)

An American Assembly dialogue on regional challenges in 1993 concluded:

> The federal government should also "level the playing field" within metropolitan areas by the use of incentives or sanctions that foster a fairer distribution by the states of metropolitan-wide tax collections. Such a redistribution could:
> * help unite cities and suburbs as interdependent thriving metropolitan areas...
> * promote racially and economically integrated private and public housing throughout the metropolitan area that is both affordable to the poor and uplifting to families moving to independence...
> * redress the imbalance between highway and mass transit funding to make mobility of people, not vehicles, the goal...
> * promote region-wide economic development and planning, [and]...
> * equalize tax incentives for investment in industry, commerce and housing among cities, suburbs and nonmetropolitan areas. (American Assembly, 6)

Regrettably, national and state government assistance to address regional challenges is shrinking and even disappearing.

Various approaches, like those of the American Assembly, are now being suggested for offering regional incentives for addressing intercommunity disparities. They include:

- Reorganizing public housing on a regional basis, to provide scattersite housing, and pursuing aggressive fair housing and fair employment practices compliance.

- Creating regional improvement zones that connect distressed and affluent communities within a region. Regional improvement zones could be modeled after the Empowerment Zone/Enterprise City program, jointly sponsored by the U.S. Departments of Agriculture and Housing and Urban Development, and offer financial assistance coupled with greater flexibility in its use.

- Providing a system of nonprofit regional housing partnerships, border-to-border across states, that would support the development of local public, private, and nonprofit entities to provide affordable housing in all communities.

- Focusing the use of regional revenues on disparities. The proposed State of Minnesota Housing Disparities Act earmarks taxes on homesteads valued over $150,000 in the Minneapolis/St. Paul region for meeting affordable housing needs in wealthier suburbs (one-third) and redevelopment projects in the central city and inner suburbs (two-thirds). This legislation is coupled with a proposed Comprehensive Housing Choice Act that requires the Metropolitan Council for the Minneapolis/St. Paul region to encourage the reduction of housing barriers to maintain affordable housing throughout the region.

- Offering incentives to regions that initiate regional tax sharing and other approaches to address intercommunity disparities, such as special economic development funding as was done for the Economic Development/Government Equity program in the Dayton region (see Equitable #2, Chapter 5).

- Offering state public education assistance on a regional basis, since it represents a substantial proportion of the operating and capital budgets of local school districts.

Former Connecticut Governor Lowell Weicker proposed to divide the state into six regions and ask the communities and school districts in each to devise a way to equalize the racial ratio within the region. This legislation was defeated in the state legislature, but substitute legislation that encouraged school districts to develop cooperative initiatives, such as regional magnet schools, for addressing inter-district and regionwide public education challenges, was passed. (*New York Times*)

Texas state law offers the richest school districts various ways to assist their distressed neighbors, including merging tax bases with an adjacent distressed district, sending money to the state to redistribute to distressed districts, establishing and financing programs to educate students in distressed districts, transferring nonresidential property to the tax rolls of distressed districts, and outright consolidation with distressed districts.

The Pennsylvania State Department of Education proposed dividing up poor districts and assigning parts to adjacent districts. Pennsylvania, like other states, also has passed distressed school district legislation to appoint oversight boards or financial receivers and provide special assistance for bankrupt school districts. (Thomas, Clarke, 1994, 10, 30)

- Expanding tax incentives for urban economic development, including restoring the Historic Rehabilitation Tax Credits.
- Offering priority consideration or bonuses in all national and state government assistance for regional applications. Regionwide applicants for assistance could receive first consideration or be eligible for bonuses over single jurisdiction applications.
- Modifying government programs as well as public policies that adversely impact racial and economic segregation.
- Locating state and national government facilities in the distressed communities of regions, as an incentive for developing cooperative strategies for addressing intercommunity distress. State and national government agencies contemplating new or relocated facilities could be required to file regional impact statements that analyzed the impact of these facilities on intercommunity distress.

A variety of approaches could be combined into a "Competitive Regionalism" initiative for reversing intercommunity disparities.

The national government could trade funding flexibility — such as combining assistance into block grants or granting waivers and allowing greater discretion in using assistance — for a couple of critical conditions. The first could be to require community leaders and citizens to develop regional strategies for using the assistance to assure equal economic opportunity for all areas of the region, especially the distressed city neighborhoods and pockets of suburban poverty. The second could be to require community leaders to bring city and suburban organizations and citizens together in collaborative processes for developing and implementing these regional strategies.

Similarly, state governments could launch their own version of a Competitive Regionalism initiative, building on regional strategic planning and economic development efforts, such as the State of Oregon Regional Strategies Program or the proposed State of Virginia Regional Development Incentive Fund. Or they could make their public education and other local aid resources available on a regional basis, not school district by school district, local government by local government.

Both national and state efforts could encourage community leaders and citizens to assume collective responsibility for providing an "equal opportunity playing field." In addition to flexibility, national and state governments could offer incentives for tax sharing and other programs for reducing economic, service and ethnic disparities, such as providing national income tax deductibility for regional tax sharing programs.

The Competitive Regionalism initiative could be initiated as a demonstration. It could require selected regions to develop a vision and five- to ten-year regional strategy for reducing disparities, involving community leaders and citizens regionwide. As a special incentive, five- to ten-year funding guarantees could be provided by national and state governments in substantial amounts, such as $10 to $25 million or more per region annually.

An excellent initial action would be a Competitive Regionalism initiative demonstration in a half dozen regions, nationally.

State/National #7
Create a National Clearinghouse on Regional Governance and Support Complementary Regional Clearinghouses (Empowering)

A number of organizations are considering the creation of clearinghouses on regional governance and other regional challenges. These organizations include the Institute for The Regional Community (National Association of Regional Councils) and International City/County Management Association (Regionalism Task Force) at the national level and the Institute of Portland Metropolitan Studies at Portland State University in the Portland, Oregon, region (see Empowering #2, Chapter 6).

Such clearinghouses could share information on regional governance models, examinations, and initiatives as well as any analyses of their strengths and shortcomings. They could track regional information, including data on regional decision making, and compile and analyze it, establish electronic databases and bulletin boards to share information, prepare monographs on topics such as initiatives for making regional governance empowering, and sponsor workshops and symposia on regional governance excellence. They could even prepare periodic reports on the state of regional governance.

The clearinghouses could monitor national and state government expenditures in regions or even conduct reviews of their impacts on regional problem solving and service delivery. They might even offer a mechanism for reviewing national and state government funding, especially for projects of regional impact, such as was once actively pursued under the aegis of a national government executive order on regional and state clearinghouses (E.O. #12372).

The potential for creating at least one effective national clearinghouse on regional governance is considerable. There might be merit in combining these initial efforts into a coordinated national clearinghouse on regionalism and generating the considerable front end and annual operating resources needed to make it effective. The clearinghouse could also assist in the creation of complementary clearinghouses in individual regions and facilitate exchanging information and conducting analyses of importance to individual regions or groups of regions. A national clearinghouse on regional governance could be sponsored or administered by the Advisory Commission on Intergovernmental Relations, thereby breathing life and regular funding into this important institution.

State/National #8
Provide Leadership in Negotiating Deals to Strengthen Decision Making in Individual Regions (Institutionalized)

Most of the significant experimentation in strengthening regional decision making has enjoyed the active involvement of state and local governments, a representative cross section of community leaders, and informed citizens. In one way or another, whether initiated top-down by public and private leaders or bottom-up by citizens, these interests have interacted, often repeatedly, in making critical regional governance improvements over the past few decades.

Why? Because every meaningful regional change means negotiating what each interest is to give up in order to gain the capacity to address crosscutting challenges. State and local governments need to cede some of their authorities to a reformulated or new mechanism; other community leaders and organizations need to accept a regional actor with real powers and authorities; citizens need to accept substituting some of their desire for local control with regional cooperation.

Everyone needs to become a bit more of a regional citizen, mutually responsible for the fate of all, and become comfortable with being part of a regional as well as a local community. Participating in and negotiating regional governance deals requires regional "pioneers" — regional entrepreneurs to take the lead, regional wizards to guide the processes and regional champions to support the strategies — and a "leap of faith" by all.

State and local governments could help to establish special committees or commissions to facilitate negotiating these regional governance deals, such as the State Commission on the Capital Region in the Albany/Schenectady/Troy region of New York (see Problem-Solving #1, Chapter 7). They could especially provide the experts and mediators to negotiate these deals as well as the front-end funding to begin implementing the resulting regional decision-making mechanisms.

For example, individuals could be identified who have successfully negotiated similar types of deals, trained in regional governance, and made available for negotiating regional governance deals. Or seed money could be made available for the initial critical years in launching a new regional problem-solving or service-delivery mechanism or other type of regional governance initiative. State and national organizations, such as advisory commissions on intergovernmental relations, could maintain lists of such individuals and sources of financial assistance.

Most important, participants in negotiating these regional deals could be assisted in weighing the benefits and costs of regional governance initiatives and prepared to negotiate their interests in these discussions.

For example, state and local governments need to determine what powers and authorities they are willing to cede, or at least temporarily transfer, to new regional decision-making mechanisms and what they expect back in tangible results in addressing regional challenges. Or if they wanted to help prime the pump for regional governance reform, state governments could even announce in advance what powers and authorities they are willing to cede to regions that establish effective regional governance mechanisms, including providing greater flexibility in the use of financial assistance and modifying or eliminating existing mandates.

The potential for assisting in negotiating regional governance deals is endless and might represent the most critical state and national resource needed for achieving regional governance excellence.

State/National #9
Hold Regional Governance Confabs
(Institutionalized)

At times, various organizations have suggested that something like a "constitutional convention" needs to be held to sort out regional governance challenges.

They especially note the current mismatch between the constitutional units of government — national, state and, through states, local — and regional challenges. Some have suggested that it might even be necessary to reconfigure state boundaries so as to better incorporate regions in their midsts, to create region-states. Their thinking is based on what appear to be the more productive relationships in states with single major regions or relatively self-contained regions (such as the Minneapolis/St. Paul region). For example, Roger Lewis, an academician and columnist for the *Washington Post,* suggests that the only approach that might make the Washington, D.C., area work effectively as a region is to create the 51st state of the Greater Washington Metropolitan Region. (Lewis, Roger)

Various national organizations have made attempts to sponsor "constitutional congresses." A few years ago, the National Association of Counties recommended convening representatives from all levels of government and nongovernmental interests in a County Congress to debate the future role of counties in the federal system. It suggested that other public interest groups sponsor similar "congresses," culminating in a national congress to debate and develop recommendations for strengthening the federal system. In such a debate, regional concerns and governance would be a central and probably pervasive theme. More recently, the National Governors Association attempted to hold a similar "congress of the states," only to have it undermined by the infighting of political interests that appear to have become more strident and ideological in the 1990s.

The potential of a national "constitutional convention" is problematic; however, history suggests that the last constitutional convention, in 1787, was the consequence of the Mount Vernon Conference held two years earlier to discuss regional challenges.

Rather, the potential of one or more regional governance confabs — to borrow a term from the late Donald Stone, public administrator *extraordinaire* — is more probable. The regional governance confabs could be sponsored by state and national, and regional, organizations to bring community leaders and citizens together to dialogue on regional governance and develop initiatives for state and national government legislative action to achieve regional governance excellence. Maybe it would be possible to hold a national regional governance confab, even a White House Regional Governance Confab, to sort through the initiatives developed in earlier confabs and develop consensus recommendations for state and national government legislative action.

State/National #10
Create a National Regional Governance Coordinating Mechanism

A national coordinating mechanism, a regional governance coalition, could facilitate dialogue among state and national organizations and assist them to pursue collaborative activities for fostering regional governance excellence. The organizations with the most active regional governance agendas could create such a mechanism.

On one hand, the mechanism could be an informal group, consisting of organizational representatives, that meets periodically. It could create working groups of representatives, as necessary, to develop integrated or joint activities, especially for the more challenging initiatives presented in this chapter, such as:

- issuing policy statements on the importance of and recommendations for strengthening regional governance,
- establishing a national clearinghouse on regional governance with the capacity to share information electronically,
- sponsoring recognition awards for regional governance excellence,
- providing technical assistance on strengthening regional governance, such as conducting seminars, workshops and training programs on regional governance, sponsoring user groups of community leaders and citizens pursuing Strategies for Achieving Regional Governance Excellence (SARGEs), and supporting the development of regional clearinghouses on regional governance,
- fostering the provision of financial assistance for strengthening regional governance, such as national and community foundations for preparing and implementing SARGEs, national government for a Competitive Regionalism initiative, and state governments for regional school aid, and
- conducting national conferences and preparing reports on the state of regional governance.

On the other hand, the mechanism could be more formal, providing a secretariat for facilitating dialogue and pursuing and even sponsoring collaborative activities identified by the representatives, such as preparing reports or hosting conferences on the state of regional governance.

Given the overlapping interests and limited resources to help community leaders and citizens strengthen regional governance, creating a regional governance coalition would be an excellent initial action for state and national organizations to take collectively.

Chapter 9
Putting It All Together: Achieving Regional Governance Excellence

Like an oyster, you start with one little piece of grit and you end up with a beautiful pearl, just by building and building.
    — District of Columbia participant in focus group on establishing a regional civic organization in the Washington, D.C. region

The first eight chapters of this book speculated on the future of regional governance, described its rising importance, recommended a framework for improving it and presented a range of initiatives — a "cafeteria of ideas" — for strengthening regional decision making and making regions work.

This last chapter closes with some thoughts for community leaders and citizens on using these materials to achieve regional governance excellence.

- Conduct initial explorations and hold symposia, but quickly conduct a holistic regional governance examination.
- Select regional governance initiatives that offer opportunities for regional governance preeminence.
- Set performance measures for individual regional governance initiatives and for achieving the overall future vision for regional governance excellence.
- Build the capacity to pursue regional governance excellence.

Conduct Initial Explorations and Hold Symposia, But Quickly Conduct a Holistic Regional Governance Examination

Chapters 3 through 7 presented three dozen initiatives for community leaders and citizens to consider for achieving regional governance excellence. More options undoubtedly exist or will be developed and tested over the remaining years of this century.

My strongest advice is not to pursue these initiatives on an ad hoc basis. Although each has merit, isolated implementation could complicate and even diminish a region's decision-making performance. It would be far more effective to convene a working group — composed of a sample of community leaders and citizens and supported by regional governance experts — and conduct initial regional governance explorations or hold regional governance symposia to inform other community leaders and citizens on the state of regional governance and the range of existing regional decision-making mechanisms (see Prominent #1 and #2, Chapter 3).

Most important, these introductory activities should be quickly followed up by conducting a regional governance examination. This would engage community leaders and citizens, and the organizations they represent, in designing a future vision that uniquely fits the region, selecting the regional governance initiatives most appropriate for pursuing the vision, and implementing a holistic Strategy for Achieving Regional Governance Excellence (SARGE). (See Strategic #2, Chapter 4).

Each SARGE should be crafted to build upon the existing network of regional-decision making mechanisms and their activities and select a set of regional governance initiatives that respect the particular needs, culture, and circumstances of the region. Conducting a regional governance examination could follow a more informal or formal approach.

A more informal approach for strengthening regional governance could begin by creating an informal working group to get the attention of community leaders and citizens and conduct an initial regional governance exploration or hold a regional governance symposium. The working group could then turn to the most likely existing regional problem-solving and service-delivery mechanism, or organize a collaborative effort among two or more mechanisms, to develop a SARGE and launch regional governance initiatives. To institutionalize an ongoing capacity to strengthen regional governance, a regional alliance (see Problem-Solving #5, Chapter 7) and regional service delivery coordinating group (see Service-Delivery #5, Chapter 7) could be created with state government and other state and national organization participation.

A more formal approach for strengthening regional governance could also begin by creating an informal working group to get the attention of community leaders and citizens and conduct an initial regional governance exploration or hold a regional governance symposium. The working group could then organize a regional renaissance committee to launch a year of the region campaign or sponsor a regional excellence day to build community leader and citizen interest. Simultaneously, the working group could organize a regional alliance, possibly staffed by one or more of the regional problem-solving and service-delivery mechanisms, to develop a SARGE and oversee launching regional governance initiatives. To institutionalize an ongoing capacity to strengthen regional governance, a problem-solving/service-delivery mechanism could be created, such as a regional planning and service district, (see Problem-Solving/Service-Delivery #3, Chapter 7) empowered by state government and managed by community leaders and citizens.

I believe that the implementation of a well-conceived SARGE will systematically strengthen a region's network of regional problem-solving and service-delivery mechanisms and make regional decision making more prominent, equitable, and empowering. I also believe that the process itself will reassure community leaders and citizens that they can work together and build the trust needed to make regional decision making work.

Select Regional Governance Initiatives that Offer Opportunities to Make Regions Preeminent

Although any of the three dozen types of regional governance initiatives can be considered for implementation as part of a SARGE , some will probably emerge as givens and others will offer debatable choices for achieving regional governance excellence.

More important, community leaders and citizens should select some regional governance initiatives that break new ground and offer the opportunity for preeminence in regional decision making, to become known as one of a handful of regions, nationally or even internationally, for pursuing particular types of experimentation in regional decision making. The regions that have established this reputation, such as the Minneapolis/St. Paul and Portland regions, are already reaping the returns in economic development and a high quality of life.

On the next three pages is a Regional Excellence Dozen, any combination of which, I believe, can make a region preeminent for its regional governance.

Set Performance Measures for Individual Regional Governance Initiatives and Achieving the Overall Future Vision for Regional Governance Excellence

Community leaders and citizens could use the measures, or benchmarks provided in Chapters 3 through 7, and presented on pages 368 –369, as well as new ones they develop, to assess the performance of regional governance initiatives in making regional governance prominent, strategic, equitable, empowering, and institutionalized. Community leaders and citizens could set specific expectations for individual initiatives and measure progress towards meeting them.

Moreover, these and other performance measures could be used to monitor progress toward achieving the future vision for regional governance excellence. Community leaders and citizens could monitor changes in the fiscal, economic, and ethnic gaps among communities or assess the year-to-year experiences of addressing regional challenges to monitor progress in building a seamless network of regional decision-making mechanisms. Community leaders and citizens could set specific expectations to be met by certain milestones, such as the turn of the millennium.

Finally, I suggest sharing the results of measuring performance region-wide, possibly in an annual report on the state of regional governance.

The Regional Excellence Dozen:
Regional Governance Initiatives
To Make Regions Preeminent

Prominent

Create the critical mass of activities needed to capture the attention of community leaders and citizens and make regional governance important to them.

1. **Sponsor an annual Regional Excellence Day (Prominent #5):** Keep building community leader and citizen interest in regional governance with an annual celebration, including activities such as presenting regional governance awards for outstanding performance (Prominent #4), reporting on progress in implementing regional governance initiatives (Strategic #4), holding open houses at regional governance mechanisms, sponsoring dialogues on emerging regional challenges, and recruiting community leaders and citizens to work on regional projects.

Strategic

Maintain momentum in improving regional governance, systematically.

2. **Institutionalize the SARGE process (Strategic #2):** Create an ongoing capacity to develop, implement, monitor and update the Strategy for Achieving Regional Governance Excellence (SARGE) including securing the pledges of community leaders and citizens to pursue priority regional governance initiatives (Strategic #3), providing regular reports on the state of regional governance (Strategic #4), and creating regional governance funds/foundations (Strategic #5).

Equitable

Educate community leaders and citizens on intercommunity disparities and reverse the widening service inequities, economic distress and racial segregation among communities.

3. **Offer regional interdependence dialogues for all community leaders and citizens regionwide (Equitable #1):** Educate small groups of citizens from different communities across the region on the threats and opportunities of regional interdependence and recruit graduates as facilitators for the next round of small groups; recruit a coalition of academic, community and religious groups to keep sponsoring new rounds of small groups until they are offered to all community leaders and citizens regionwide.

4. **Combine regional tax sharing and service-delivery modifications to guarantee basic public services to citizens regionwide (Equitable #2):** Generate adequate regional revenues, such as sharing some of the increased tax revenues resulting from new development, to guarantee basic public services in distressed communities; simultaneously, require service modifications, such as joint delivery by smaller distressed communities or between affluent and distressed communities, to assure effective use of the resources.

5. **Combine intercommunity linkage projects, shared development of regional projects and urban growth boundaries to create economic opportunities for all communities regionwide (Equitable #3):** Develop linkage projects between affluent and distressed communities, such as offering mobility to jobs in the former and redeveloping parcels in the latter; share benefits of regional employment centers and shopping malls across impacted communities; and establish urban growth boundaries to foster infill development, especially in distressed communities; overall, create an "equal opportunity playing field".

6. **Offer affordable housing to create mixed income communities regionwide (Equitable #4):** Require affordable housing in new housing developments, including subsidized units for the very poor, and convert public housing projects to mixed income projects, or tear them down.

Empowering

Develop regional citizenship, foster intercommunity relationships and empower citizens in regional decision making.

7. **Broaden regional leadership programs into regional citizenship programs (Empowering #1):** Broaden the curriculum of regional leadership programs to include followership and citizenship skills; open up participation to more community leaders and citizens; and channel graduates into assisting regional decision-making mechanisms and implementing SARGE regional governance initiatives.

8. **Create ongoing "Sister Community" relationships between affluent and distressed communities regionwide (Empowering #4):** Arrange Sister Community relationships between pairs of communities to exchange cultural and other groups, participate in regional interdependence small group discussions, and pursue joint activities in each other's communities, with the support of corporate, academic and other partners.

9. Establish citizen advisory boards or elect citizen representatives to regional governance mechanisms (Empowering #5): Either establish citizen advisory boards to review and comment on plans, budgets and other actions of individual regional problem-solving and service-delivery mechanisms or directly elect citizen representatives to an empowered regional planning council (Problem-Solving #1), regional alliance (Problem-Solving $5) or regional planning and service district (Problem-Solving/Service-Delivery #3) that has authority to develop regional plans, set urban growth boundaries, and possibly deliver regional services.

Institutionalized

Provide the range of regional decision making mechanisms needed to address regional challenges in a timely and effective manner.

10. Create at least one effective public, private, academic and civic regional problem-solving mechanism (Problem-Solving #1– 4): Each sector needs an effective regional mechanism to educate its members and develop positions on regional challenges as well as take the lead in addressing regional challenges, such as a regional planning council, regional chamber of commerce or growth association, college or university regional affairs research institute or public service program and regional civic organization; similar mechanisms could be created for labor, religious, and other sectors.

11. Institutionalize the capacity to launch regional alliances to address regional challenges (Problem-Solving #5): Build the capacity to turn to an existing regional problem-solving mechanism to sponsor a regional alliance representing all sectors of the region or create one or more ongoing regional alliances to address particular types of regional challenges as they emerge; expand the supply of regional "pioneers" — regional entrepreneurs to initiate regional alliances, regional wizards to guide their problem-solving processes, and regional champions to support the implementation of priority initiatives. (Empowering #1)

12. Create a regional service-delivery coordinating group (Service-Delivery #5): Convene regional service-delivery mechanisms regularly to guide implementation of new regional services and develop cooperative arrangements for delivery of existing regional services; such a group could be free-standing, attached to a regional planning council or regional alliance, or be part of a regional planning and service district.

Build the Capacity to Pursue Regional Governance Excellence

Given that regional decision making is the responsibility of a network of often very independent problem-solving and service-delivery mechanisms, some, if not most, community leaders and citizens can all too easily become ineffective pawns in this marketplace or, at times, battleground of powerful interests. Given that the regional governance network needs to be tweaked, if not continually prodded, into improvement, community leaders and citizens need to create the capacity to pursue regional governance excellence.

Performance Measures For Regional Governance Initiatives

Making Regional Governance Prominent

- Make regional governance as visible and important as the regional challenges that it is addressing.

- Make intercommunity and regional problem-solving and service-delivery mechanisms as visible and important as their local counterparts.

Making Regional Governance Strategic

- Design a consensus vision for the future of regional governance and develop a collaborative action plan for achieving regional governance excellence: a Strategy for Achieving Regional Governance Excellence (SARGE)

- Implement priority regional governance initiatives in the action plans.

- Prepare periodic reports and hold conferences on the state of regional governance.

- Regularly update future visions and action plans for regional governance excellence.

- Develop and experiment with new models for regional governance.

At a minimum, community leaders and citizens need to create the capacity to:

- examine regional governance and develop SARGEs,
- secure commitments and launch priority initiatives to improve regional governance,
- regularly monitor and report on the state of regional governance, and
- periodically update the SARGEs.

To whom can community leaders and citizens turn to provide them with this capacity, to guide and even take the lead in the pursuit of regional

---

Performance Measures For Regional Governance Initiatives

Making Regional Governance Equitable

- Pursue coordinated initiatives to address intercommunity fiscal, economic and racial disparity.
- Reverse the widening and begin to close fiscal, economic, and racial gaps among communities, regionwide.
- Create an "equal opportunity playing field" (basic quality services, equal economic opportunity, and racial integration) for all communities and populations in the region.

Making Regional Governance Empowering

- Enable citizen interaction across communities and regionwide.
- Empower citizen involvement in regional decision making.
- Build regional citizenship and a sense of regional community.

Making Regional Governance Institutionalized

- Experiment with regional problem-solving and service-delivery mechanisms that efficiently guide community leaders and citizens through equitable and enabling processes for effectively addressing the most pressing challenges.
- Build a "honeycomb network" of regional problem-solving and service-delivery mechanisms that interact seamlessly to provide regional governance excellence.

governance excellence? Some insights are provided by the histories of regions known for their willingness to experiment.

In the Canadian regions, the provincial and "metro" governments often take the lead in studying and modifying regional governance. The Greater Toronto Coordinating Committee, for example, has generated an excellent series of reports on governance in the Toronto region over the first half of the 1990s.

In the Minneapolis/St. Paul and Portland regions, state governments, which often serve as informal regional governments for the states' dominant regions, often take the lead to improve regional governance, in conjunction with local interests, such as a regional citizens organization (see Problem-Solving #4, Chapter 7) in Minneapolis/St. Paul, a regional service delivery coordinating group (see Service-Delivery #5, Chapter 7) in Portland, and regional planning and service districts (see Problem-Solving/Service-Delivery #3, Chapter 7) in both regions. Collectively they, like the Canadian regions, also are continually studying and modifying regional governance.

In the Dayton region, which also is continually experimenting with regional governance, a new ad hoc regional alliance (see Problem-Solving #5, Chapter 7) often takes the lead, in partnership with a regional chamber of commerce (see Problem-Solving #2, Chapter 7), university public service institute (see Problem-Solving #3, Chapter 7), or urban county (see Problem-Solving/Service-Delivery #1, Chapter 7).

In other regions, almost any of the regional decision-making mechanisms described in Chapter 7 have taken the lead to improve regional governance:

- regional planning councils (Problem-Solving #1) in the Atlanta and Oklahoma City regions,
- regional chambers of commerce and other business organizations (Problem-Solving #2) in the Denver and Pittsburgh regions,
- a university public service program (Problem-Solving #3) in the Chicago or university research institute in the Philadelphia regions,
- regional citizens organizations (Problem-Solving #4) in the Cleveland and St. Louis regions,

- regional alliances (Problem-Solving #5) in the Winston-Salem/Greensboro/High Point or Research Triangle, North Carolina, regions,
- a regional multiple-service authority (Service-Delivery #4) in the New York City region, or
- central city-county government federations and consolidations, such as Unigov in the Indianapolis/Marion County region. (Problem-Solving/Service-Delivery #2)

The most productive regional governance experimentation occurs in regions in which community leaders and citizens:

Focus on the region of the future: Community leaders and citizens from outlying growth areas, as well as from the already developed central cities and suburbs, get together regularly to explore the region of the future. They recognize that whoever shapes future regional growth determines who benefits from economic development and controls regional decision making.

Make regional governance improvement a priority: Community leaders and citizens are active catalysts for regional governance improvement. Moreover, they have made regional governance improvement the priority focus of at least one regional decision-making mechanism. Having one such mechanism is critical; having more than one can help guarantee an ongoing agenda of regional governance experimentation.

Continually examine regional governance: Community leaders and citizens never allow regional governance to gather moss, much less rest on its laurels. They have not necessarily conducted single organized regional governance examinations, such as a SARGE, but they are always examining some aspect of regional governance.

Engage state government officials in their deliberations: Few, if any, changes in regional governance can be successfully implemented without the participation, support, and sometimes ceding of powers and authorities by state governments. In fact, state governments often take the lead in initiating regional governance examinations and launching new regional governance initiatives.

Community leaders and citizens in these regions are beginning to think and act like regional citizens, to not just consider the communities in the region as *yours and mine,* but *ours.*

I suggest that community leaders and citizens use the topic of conducting a holistic regional governance examination to raise the question: Which existing, or possibly new, mechanism or mechanisms should make the pursuit of regional governance excellence its priority responsibility? Good times to explore options are while conducting initial explorations of regional governance (see Prominent #1, Chapter 3), holding periodic regional governance symposia (see Prominent #2, Chapter 3), or especially while designing a regional governance examination (see Strategic #2, Chapter 4). While a region is launching these initiatives, some existing mechanism might step forward or some new mechanism might be suggested to oversee the design and implementation of the SARGE and focus its priority attention on achieving regional governance excellence.

Most important, community leaders and citizens should charge this mechanism(s) to be inclusive of all community leader and citizen interests and empower it (them) to conduct the initial regional governance examination and oversee the implementation of its priority initiatives as well as be around long enough to update the SARGE in the future.

In addition to designating mechanisms to focus priority on regional governance, community leaders and citizens need to generate resources — technical experts and financial aid — to guide examinations and launch priority regional governance initiatives.

Historically, special funding sometimes has been appropriated for specific regional governance examinations, for example, through a special local or state study commission. Sometimes the resources of existing regional governance mechanisms, such as regional planning councils, single- or multiple-service authorities, or planning and service districts, have been tapped for specific examinations. Sometimes a stream of regional governance projects, such as ones undertaken by regional business organizations or regional civic organizations, has been supported by community foundations.

I suggest providing more predictable sources of funding for financing the development of SARGEs and the implementation of priority regional governance initiatives to build and sustain momentum towards achieving regional governance excellence. Therefore, it might be useful to establish regional governance funds (see Strategic #5, Chapter 4) to develop, monitor, and update SARGEs and to launch priority regional governance initiatives. These funds could be financed from a number of sources, among them earmarked regional taxes or matching state government funds.

Finally, community leaders and citizens need to develop the will power of their colleagues to achieve regional governance excellence.

Community leaders and citizens need to get beyond the propensity to gravitate towards the most local, and support only the most ad hoc types of regional decision making. They need to become dedicated regionalists committed to what it takes to achieve regional governance excellence — as if their lives depended on it, which they increasingly do. Alvin and Heidi Toffler, in *Creating a New Civilization,* write:

> The responsibility for change, therefore, lies with us. We must begin with ourselves, teaching ourselves not to close our minds prematurely to the novel, the surprising, the seemingly radical. This means fighting off the idea-assassins who rush forward to kill any new suggestion on grounds of its impracticality, while defending whatever now exists as practical, no matter now absurd, oppressive, or unworkable it may be. (Toffler, 1995, 108)

One way to test for and secure commitments of will power is to ask community leaders and citizens, and the organizations they represent, to adopt a "regional renaissance pledge" to support cooperative regional decision making (see Strategic #3, Chapter 4).

In sum, community leaders and citizens need to build the capacity to pursue regional governance excellence in three ways: first, to designate the mechanisms to focus priority attention on achieving regional governance excellence; second, to finance the regional governance initiatives recommended in the SARGEs; and third, to secure community leader and citizen commitments, as well as those of their organizations, to achieving regional governance excellence.

In closing, I hope that these thoughts are useful to pursuing a regional renaissance in which you and your fellow community leaders and citizens:

- appreciate the importance of regional governance,
- participate in developing a SARGE and implementing its priority regional governance initiatives,
- reverse the widening economic, racial and fiscal gaps among communities regionwide,
- become regional citizens in a regional community, and
- establish a network of regional decision making mechanisms to address emerging challenges in a timely manner.

May you achieve the regional excellence to which you aspire!

References

References are organized as follows:

1. Major references cited frequently in the book

2. Other references cited in the book

3. State and national organizations with regional governance agendas

4. Publications addressing regional governance topics

1. Major References

Advisory Commission on Intergovernmental Relations, *Government Functions and Processes: Local and Areawide, Substate Regionalism and the Federal System,* Volume IV, 1974

Berry, Jeffrey, Portnoy, Kent & Thomson, Ken, *The Rebirth of Urban Democracy,* The Brookings Institution, Washington, D.C., 1993

Dodge, William, *Economic Competitiveness Mechanisms: Background Papers,* Montgomery County Leadership Network, Dayton, Ohio, 1992

Dodge, William, "Strategic Intercommunity Partnerships: SIGNETs of Economic Competitiveness in the 1990s," *National Civic Review,* Denver, Colorado, Fall-Winter, 1992

Dodge, William, *Regional Transportation Mechanisms Report,* Interstate Study Commission, Washington, D.C., 1994

Dodge, William & Montgomery, Kim, *Shaping a Region's Future: A Guide to Strategic Decision Making for Regions,* Economic Development Administration/National League of Cities, Washington, D.C., 1995

Downs, Anthony, *New Visions for Metropolitan America,* The Brookings Institution, Washington, D.C., 1994

Kemmis, Daniel, *The Good City and the Good Life,* Houghton Miflin, New York, New York, 1995

National Academy of Public Administration, *Metropolitan Governance: A Handbook for Local Government Study Commissions,* Washington, D.C., 1980

Parr, John, "Civic Infrastructure: A New Approach to Improving Community Life," *National Civic Review,* Denver, Colorado, Spring, 1993

Peirce, Neal, Johnson, Curtis, & Hall, John Stuart, *Citistates: How Urban America Can Prosper in a Competitive World,* Seven Locks Press, Washington, D.C., 1993

Putnam, Robert, *Making Democracy Work: Civic Traditions in Modern Italy,* Princeton University Press, Princeton, New Jersey, 1993

Rusk, David, *Cities Without Suburbs,* Woodrow Wilson Center Press, Washington, D.C., 1993

Sancton, Andrew, *Governing Canada's City-Regions,* Institute for Research on Public Policy, Montreal, Canada, 1994

Wallis, Alan, *Inventing Regionalism,* National Civic League, 1994

2. Other References

Abbott, Carl & Abbott, Margery Post, Historical Development of the Metropolitan Service District, Metro Home Rule Charter Committee, Portland, Oregon, 1991

Abbott, Rebecca, *Schooling That Works,* Connecticut Public Television, Hartford, Connecticut, 1995

Adams, Bruce, *Washington Regional Alliance Project: Phase I Report,* Washington, D.C., 1995

Advisory Commission on Intergovernmental Relations, *The Organization of Local Public Economies,* Washington, D.C., 1987

Advisory Commission on Intergovernmental Relations, *Local Boundary Commissions: Status and Roles in Forming, Adjusting and Dissolving Local Government Boundaries,* Washington, D.C., 1992

Allegheny Conference on Community Development, *The Greater Pittsburgh Region: Working Together to Compete Globally,* Pittsburgh, Pennsylvania, 1994

American Assembly, *Interwoven Destinies: Cities and the Nation,* Eighty-Second American Assembly, Harriman, New York, 1993

Arnstein, Sherry, "A Ladder of Citizen Participation," *The Journal of the American Institute of Planners,* Chicago, Illinois, July 1969

Around the Region, "'Regional Citzenry' Concept to Broaden Participation in Regional Planning Process," Southern California Association of Governments, Los Angeles, California, Spring, Summer 1995

Atkins, Pat, *The Nether Regions: A Typological Classification of Regional Councils,* Dissertation, University of Maryland, College Park, Maryland, 1984

Atkins, Pat & Wilson-Gentry, Laura, "An Etiquette for the 1990s Regional Council," *National Civic Review,* Fall-Winter, 1992

Atkins, Pat, "From the Mauling to the Malling of Regionalism," *Public Administration Review,* Washington, D.C., November/December, 1993

Atkins, Pat & Wilson-Gentry, Laura, "Testing Folklore Assumptions as Determinants of Regional Council State Funding Support and Durability," presented at Urban Affairs Association 23rd Annual Meeting, 1993

Atkins, Pat, "Remakes on Member Remarks," *InterGovernmental Affairs Division Newsletter,* American Planning Association, Chicago, Illinois, June, 1995

Atkins, Pat, "Techniques of Regional Cooperation in the United States," Presented at the American Planning Association Annual Conference, Toronto, Canada, 1995

The Atlanta Project, *Because There Is Hope,* Atlanta, Georgia, 1993

Atlanta Regional Commission, *A Shared Vision for the Atlanta Region*, Atlanta, Georgia, 1993

Atlanta Regional Commission, "ARC Launches Awards to Honor Visionary Leadership," *Vision*, September-October, 1995

Austin, City of, *Strategic Choices*, Austin, Texas, 1994

Axelrod, Robert, *The Evolution of Cooperation*, Basic Books, New York, 1984

Bahl, Roy; Martinez-Vazquez, Jorge; and Sjoquist, David, "Central City-Suburban Disparities," *Public Finance Quarterly*, October, 1992, 420-432

Baltimore Regional Council of Governments, "Establishing a Regional Partnership for Cultural Development," Baltimore, Maryland, 1990

Bank of America et al, *Beyond Growth: New Patterns of Growth to Fit the New California*, San Francisco, California, 1995

Barnes, William, "Whither the Urban Policy Agenda?," *PA Times*, American Society for Public Administration, Washington, D.C., March 1, 1995

Barnes, William & Ledebur, Larry, "Policy Making in the U.S. Common Market of Local Economic Regions," Working Paper, May, 1995

Barringer, Felicity, "Hire Cities' Poor in the Suburbs, Report Advises," *New York Times*, New York, New York, December 4, 1992

Behr, Peter, "In Quest of a 'Greater Washington', *Washington Post*, Washington, D.C., January 13, 1995

Belko, Mark, "Deep snow, poor towns," *Pittsburgh Post Gazette*, Pittsburgh, Pennsylvania, January, 1993

Berke, Arnold, "Striking Back at Sprawl," *Historic Preservation*, Washington, D.C., September/October, 1995

Blais, Pamela, "The Competitive Advantage of City-Regions, *Policy Options*, May, 1994

Blomquist, William & Parks, Roger, "Is Consolidation the Answer for Central Cities in the United States? Some Lessons from Indianapolis-Marion County, Indiana," Working Paper, Indiana University, Indianapolis, Indiana, 1994

Broder, David, "Population Explosion," *Washington Post National Weekly,* Washington, D.C., April 25-May 1, 1994

Brown, Warren & Swoboda, Frank, "Ford's Vision: A Company Without Borders," *Washington Post National Weekly,* Washington, D.C., October 24-30, 1994

California, State of, Governor's Office of Planning and Research, Governor's Interagency Council on Growth Management, "Working Paper on Regional Governance," 1991

Capell, Kerry, "Paying for Public Works," *Governing,* Washington, D.C., August, 1995

Capitol Region Partnership Program, "Description and Long-Range Work Plan," Hartford, Connecticut, 1996

Carter, Steve, "Intergovernmental Strategy," *Public Management,* International City/County Management Association, Washington, D.C., July 1995

Cassidy , John, "Who Killed the Middle Class," *New Yorker,* New York, New York, October 16,1995

CCRC News, "Summary of Preliminary Recommendations," California Constitution Revision Commission, Sacramento, California

Center for Greater Philadelphia, *Regional Network Directory,* University of Pennsylvania, Philadelphia, Pennsylvania, 1994

Center for Greater Philadelphia, "Greater Philadelphia High School Convocation Project," *region*wise,* Philadelphia, Pennsylvania, February 1996

Center for School Study Councils, University of Pennsylvania, Brochure, 1995 Public Policy Institute, Philadelphia, Pennsylvania

Chesnut, Robert, Sermon, East Liberty Presbyterian Church, 1995

Cigler, Beverly, "Regionalism and Intergovernmental Cooperation," Working Paper, Penn State Harrisburg, Middletown, Pennsylvania, 1994

Cisneros, Henry, "Renewing the Bonds of Community," *National Civic Review,* Denver, Colorado, Fall-Winter 1994

Cisneros, Henry, *Regionalism: The New Geography of Opportunity*, U.S. Department of Housing and Urban Development, Washington, D.C., 1995

Citizens League of Greater Cleveland, *Governance: Improving the Effectiveness of Special Purpose Governments*, Cleveland, Ohio, 1989

Citizens League of Greater Cleveland, *Regional Problem Solving in Greater Cleveland: A New Strategy*, Cleveland, Ohio, 1990

Citizens League of Greater Cleveland, *The Performance of Special Purpose Government in Greater Cleveland, 1986-1991*, Cleveland, Ohio, 1992

Citizens League of Greater Cleveland, "What We Think," *Citizen Participation*, Cleveland, Ohio, August, 1992

Citizens League of Southwestern Pennsylvania, *A Citizens Agenda for Strengthening Governance in Southwestern Pennsylvania, An Initial Report*, Pittsburgh, Pennsylvania, 1993

Clark, Charles, "Revitalizing the Cities," *CQ Researcher*, Washington, D.C., October 13, 1995

Clinton, Bill, U.S. President, Inaugural Address, Washington, D.C., January 24, 1995

Coe, Benjamin, "The Tug Hill, New York: Progress Through Cooperation in a Rural Region," *National Civic Review*, Denver, Colorado, Fall–Winter, 1992

Coffey, William, "City-Regions in the New Economy," *Policy Options*, Montreal, Canada, May, 1994

Committee for Economic Development, *Reshaping Government in Metropolitan Areas*, New York, New York, 1970

Committee for Enterprise Development, Symposium on Exploring Regional Solutions, Washington, D.C., 1994

Confluence St. Louis, *Too Many Governments?: A Report on Governmental Structure in St. Louis City and County with Recommendations for Change*, St. Louis, Missouri, 1987

Conner, Desmond, "A New Ladder of Citizen Participation," *National Civic Review*, Denver, Colorado, May/June 1988

Conner, Kevin, "Regional Governance," State of California, Governor's Office of Planning and Research, 1991

Davis, David, "The Zone of Transition as a Political Phenomenon," Working Paper, Annual Meeting of the Midwest Political Science Association, Chicago, Illinois, 1991

Dayton, City of, Division of Neighborhood Affairs, *Community Investment Strategies,* Dayton, Ohio, 1992

Dionne, E. J., Jr., *Why Americans Hate Politics,* Simon & Schuster, New York, New York, 1991

Dodge, William, *Intergovernmental Cooperation Program, A Strategy for Co-operation, Years 2 and 3,* Pittsburgh, Pennsylvania, 1985

Dodge, William, "The Emergence of Intercommunity Partnerships in the 1990s," *Public Management,* International City/County Management Association, Washington, D.C., July, 1988

Dodge, William, *Final Report, Local Government Management Study,* Fort Drum Steering Council, Watertown, New York, 1989

Dodge, William, "Public-Private Partnerships," *Public Management,* International City/County Management Association, Washington, D.C., 1989

Dodge, William, *Final Report, Survey of Regional Civic Organizations,* National Civic League, Denver, Colorado, 1990

Dodge, William, "Regional Problem Solving in the 1990s: Experimentation with Local Governance for the 21st Century," *National Civic Review,* Denver, Colorado, July/August, 1990

Dodge, William, "Regional Civic Organizations: Forums for Strengthening Local Governance in the 1990s," Working Paper, 1991

Dodge, William, "Tax Base Sharing Approaches for Intergovernmental Financing," Working Paper, Greater Baltimore Committee, Baltimore, Maryland, 1991

Dodge, William, "Memorandum to Community Cooperation Task Force," Dayton, Ohio, August 25, 1992

Dodge, William, "The New Intercommunity Governance," *Nation's Cities Weekly*, National League of Cities, Washington, D.C., December 6, 1993

Dodge, William, "Southern Plan a model for saving city's soul," *Tribune-Review*, Pittsburgh, Pennsylvania, December 12, 1993

Dodge, William, *Final Report: Northern Tier Library Services Feasibility Study*, Pittsburgh, Pennsylvania, 1994

Doing Democracy, "Citizens Discover Economic Solutions," Brattleboro, Vermont, Summer, 1995

Doing Democracy, "Interview with an Innovator," Brattleboro, Vermont, Summer, 1995

Doing Democracy, "Interview with an Innovator," Brattleboro, Vermont, Winter 1995

Dreier, Peter, "Why Connecticut's Suburbs Need Healthy Cities," Connecticut Conference on Municipalities, New Haven, Connecticut, 1995

Durning, Dan, "Opinions of Employees and 'Informed Citizens' on the Effects of Consolidating the Governments of Athens and Clark County, Georgia," Working Paper, 1993

Dustin, Jack, *Interlocal Government Cooperation in Cuyahoga and Montgomery Counties*, State and Local Government Commission of Ohio, Columbus, Ohio, 1993

Dustin, Jack, "Bringing the City Back In?," Working Paper, Wright State University, Department of Urban Affairs, Dayton, Ohio, 1994

Eadie, Douglas, *Boards That Work*, American Society of Association Executives, Washington, D.C., 1994

Economic Development/Government Equity Program, Program Guidelines and Working Papers, Montgomery County Government, 1991

Ehrenhalt, Alan, "The Bitter Costs of Municipal Sibling Rivalry," *Governing*, Washington, D.C., May, 1995

Eichler, Mike, "Consensus Organizing Institute: Concept and Background Paper," Working Paper, Boston, Massachusetts, 1994

The Enterprise Corporation, *An Affordable Housing Strategy for Pennsylvania,* Columbia, Maryland, 1991

Erickson, Fanny, Riverside Church, Presentation at East Liberty Presbyterian Church, Pittsburgh, Pennsylvania, 1995

Etzioni, Amitai, *The Spirit of Community,* Crown, New York, New York, 1993

Fosler, Scott, "Governing in the 21st Century," National Academy of Public Administration, Washington, D.C., 1995

Fouhy, Ed, "The Dawn of Public Journalism," *National Civic Review,* Summer-Fall, 1994

Fukuyama, Francis, *Trust,* Free Press, New York, New York, 1995

Gardner, John, *Excellence,* Harper & Brothers, New York, 1961

Gardner, John, *Building Community,* Independent Sector, Washington, D.C., 1991

Gardner, John, "National Renewal," *National Civic Review,* Denver, Colorado, Fall/Winter, 1994

Garreau, Joel, *Edge City: Life on the New Frontier,* Doubleday, New York, New York, 1991

Garreau, Joel, "Shakeout in Progress, But Some Will Be Winners," *The Edge City News,* Broad Run, Virginia, January/February, 1995

German Marshall Fund, *Divided Cities in the Global Economy: The 1992 European-North American State-of-the-Cities Report,* PSARAS Fund, Columbia, South Carolina, 1992

Gerston, Larry & Haas, Peter, "Political Support for Regional Government in the 1990s: Growing in the Suburbs?," *Regionalist,* National Association of Regional Councils, Athens, Georgia, Winter, 1995

Gladwell, Malcolm, "A Plot to Shrink New York City?," *Washington Post National Weekly,* Washington, D.C., March 27-April 2, 1995

Glassman, James, "The Burden of the Rich," *Washington Post National Weekly,* Washington, D.C., July 17-23, 1995

Goodman, Jay, *The Dynamics of Urban Government and Politics,* Second Edition, McMillan Publishing, New York, New York, 1980

Goodwin, Doris Kearns, *No Ordinary Time,* Simon & Schuster, New York, New York, 1994

Government Technology, "Partnership Creates CivicLink," April, 1995

Governors State University, RAP/2000+ Idea Fair, University Park, Illinois, March 11, 1995

Great Britain,, Government of, *The Citizen's Charter: Raising the Standard,* Prime Minister John Major, no date

Greater Baltimore Committee, *Baltimore: Where Science Comes to Life,* Baltimore, Maryland, 1991

Greater Baltimore Committee, *The Strength of Maryland Depends on The State of Baltimore,* Baltimore, Maryland, 1991

Greater Toronto Coordinating Committee, *Shaping Growth in the GTA and GTA 2021: The Challenge of Our Future,* Office of the Greater Toronto Area, Toronto, Canada, 1992

Grossman, Howard, "The Case for National Sub-State Regionalism: Visioning the Future," *Regionalist,* National Association of Regional Councils, Athens, Georgia, Winter, 1995

Gurwitt, Rob, "The Painful Truth About Cities and Suburbs: They Need Each Other," *Governing,* Washington, D.C., February, 1992

Gurwitt, Rob, "A Government That Runs on Citizen Power," *Governing,* Washington, D.C., December, 1992

Gurwitt, Rob, "The Projects Come Down," *Governing,* Washington, D.C., August, 1995

Gutheim, Frederick, *The Potomac,* Rinehart & Company, New York, no date

Hamilton, Nadean L. & Tempero, Richard, "Regional Charter Making in Polk County, Iowa, *National Civic Review,* Denver, Colorado, Fall-Winter, 1992

Harrigan, John, *Political Change in the Metropolis,* Scott Foresman, Glenvill, Illinois, Fourth Edition, 1989

Hartgen, David & McCoy, William, "Uncharted Waters: The Super-Regional Transportation Agency," Working Paper, University of North Carolina At Charlotte, 1989

Hartman, Richard, "Academics look at regional governance," Meeting Summary, Cambridge, Massachusetts, 1993

Henderson, Lenneal, "Metropolitan Governance: Citizen Participation in the Urban Federation," *National Civic Review,* Denver, Colorado, March/April 1990

Hershberg, Theodore, Magidson, Pam & Wernecke, Mary Lou, "Promoting Cooperation in Southeastern Pennsylvania," *National Civic Review,* Denver, Colorado, Fall-Winter, 1992

Hershberg, Ted, "Regionalism," *Philadelphia Inquirer,* September 11, 1994

Hiss, Tony, *The Experience of Place,* Knopf, New York, 1990

Honey, Tim, "It's the Region Stupid.....Your Community," International City/County Management Association, Regionalism Task Force, Washington, D.C., no date

Howitt, Arnold & Altshuler, Alan, "Regional Governance: Challenges of CAAA and ISTEA," *Newsletter, InterGovernmental Affairs Division,* American Planning Association, Chicago, Illinois, October, 1993

Institute of Portland Metropolitan Studies, *Proceedings of the 1995 Annual Leadership Symposium,* Portland State University, Portland, Oregon, 1995

Intergovernmental Cooperation Program, *A Strategy for Cooperation: Years 2 and 3,* Pittsburgh, Pennsylvania, 1985

International City/County Management Association, "Regional Strategies for Local Government Management," *MIS Report,* March, 1992

International City/County Management Association, "ICMA President Participates in Signing of New Executive Order on "Enhancing Intergovernmental Partnerships", *ICMA Newsletter,* Washington, D.C., November 1, 1993

International City/County Management Association, "Interactive Council Meetings," *ICMA Newsletter,* July 10, 1995

Jacksonville Community Council, Inc., *Life in Jacksonville: Quality Indicators for Progress,* Jacksonville, Florida, 1991

Jacobs, Jane, *The Death and Life of Great American Cities,* Vintage, New York, New York, 1961

James, Edmund J., "The Growth of Great Cities in Area and Population," *Annuals of the American Academy of Political and Social Science,* Volume 13, 1899

Jefferson Center for New Democratic Processes, Program Description, January 1994

John, DeWitt, Halley, Alexis & Fosler, Scott, "Remapping Federalism: The Rediscovery of Civic Governance" (unpublished paper), National Academy of Public Administration, Washington, D.C., 1994

Johnson, Haynes, "The Obituary of the American Dream," *Washington Post National Weekly,* April 25-May 1, 1994

Jones, Victor, "Metropolitan Studies," *Public Administration Review,* American Society for Public Administration, Washington, D.C., Volume 13, 129–133

Kanter, Rosabeth, *World Class,* Simon and Schuster, New York, New York, 1995

Keillor, Garrison, Advertisement, Prairie Home Companion, Radio Show, St. Paul, Minneapolis

Kelley, Robert, *The Power of Followership,* Doubleday, New York, New York, 1992

Kemmis, Daniel, *Community and the Politics of Place,* University of Oklahoma Press, Norman, Oklahoma, 1990

King, James, "Model Can Help Governments Work Together," *PA Times,* American Society for Public Administration, Washington, D.C., July 1, 1993

Kirlin, John, "Creating the Conditions for Devising Reasonable and Regional Solutions," *Confronting Regional Challenges,* Lincoln Institute of Land Policy, 1991

Kotkin, Joel, "Beyond White Flight," *Washington Post National Weekly,* Washington, D.C., March 18–24, 1996

Kozul, Jonathan, Presentation at Three Rivers Lecture Series, Pittsburgh, Pennsylvania, 1994

Krupp-Wilmeth, Lisa, "A Look at Mercer Island's Kiosk System," *Public Management,* Washington, D.C., November, 1995

Lang, Richard, "City Problems and Suburban Reactions," *Business Review,* Federal Reserve Bank of Philadelphia, Philadelphia, Pennsylvania, September/October, 1992

Lappé, Frances Moore & DuBois, Paul Martin, *The Quickening of America,* Jossey-Bass, Inc., San Francisco, California, 1994

Larkin, John, "Increased Role for Counties Expected in 90s," *PA Times,* American Society for Public Administration, Washington, D.C., no date

League of Women Voters, Allegheny County Chapter, "2001 The Process Continues," Breakfast Forum, Notes, Pittsburgh, Pennsylvania, 1995

Ledebur, Larry & Barnes, William, *City Distress, Metropolitan Disparities and Economic Growth,* National League of Cities, Washington, D.C., 1992

Ledebur, Larry & Barnes, William, *"All In It Together": Cities, Suburbs and Local Economic Regions,* National League of Cities, Washington, D.C., 1993

Ledebur, Larry & Barnes, William, *The U.S. Common Market,* National League of Cities, Washington, D.C. (publication pending)

Lemov, Penelope, "In Hard Times, Even Governments Must Share," *Governing,* Washington, D.C., September, 1993

Leo, Peter, "Making the news perfectly clear," *Pittsburgh Post Gazette,* Pittsburgh, Pennsylvania, February, 15, 1991

Lewis, Robert, "Citizen Leagues: Free Spaces of Deliberative Democracy," *National Civic Review,* Denver, Colorado, Fall-Winter, 1994

Lewis, Roger, Keynote Speech, *Proceedings, Developing a Vision Plan,* National Capital Region Transportation Planning Board, Washington, D.C., 1994

Lockwood, Charles, "Edge Cities on the Brink," *Wall Street Journal,* New York, New York, December, 1994

Lodge, George, *The New American Ideology,* Knopf, New York, New York, 1980.

Louisville, City of & Jefferson County governments, Compact, Louisville, Kentucky, 1986

Lucchino, Frank, *Reclaiming Hope: Voluntary Disincorporation in Allegheny County,* Allegheny County Government, Pittsburgh, Pennsylvania, 1995

Martin, Roscoe, *Metropolis in Transition: Local Governance Adaption to Changing Urban Needs,* U.S. Housing and Home Finance Agency, Washington, D.C., 1963

McCormack, Ted, "Richmond Metropolitan Government on Hold," *Newsletter, InterGovernmental Affairs Division,* American Planning Association, Chicago, Illinois, February, 1995

McCoy, William, "Building Coalitions for the Future in Charlotte-Mechlenburg," *National Civic Review,* Denver, Colorado, Spring, 1991

Merritt, Davis, "Public Journalism and Public Life," *National Civic Review,* Denver, Colorado, Summer-Fall, 1995

Metro Forum, *Regional Governance in the Denver Metropolitan Area,* Denver, Colorado, 1991

Metropolitan Affairs Nonprofit Corporations, "Regional Productivity," *National Civic Review,* November, 1975

Moore, Carl, "Effective Governance by Cooperation: Negotiated Investment Strategy," *National Civic Review,* Denver, Colorado, July/August, 1988

Moore, Thomas, *Care of the Soul,* Harper, New York, New York, 1992

Morrow, Lance, "Real Points of Life," *Time,* December, 1994

Naftalin, Arthur, *Making One Community Out of Many,* Metropolitan Council, St. Paul, Minnesota, 1986

Nathan, Richard & Adams, Charles, Jr., "Four Perspectives on Urban Hardship," *Political Science Quarterly*, New York, New York, Fall, 1989

National Academy of Public Administration, Spring Meeting, Indianapolis, Indiana, 1993

National Academy of Public Administration, National Association of Regional Councils & National Civic League, Conference on "City-States: Mobilizing Emerging Regional Partnerships," Notes, Washington, D.C., 1993

National Association of Counties, *Introduction to Sustainable Development*, Washington, D.C., 1994

National Association of Regional Councils, *Regional Capital Improvement Programming*, Washington, D.C., 1976

National Association of Regional Councils, *1967-1992, 25 Years of Regionalism: A History of the National Association of Regional Councils*, Washington, D.C., 1992

National Civic League, Metropolitan Governance Statement, Denver, Colorado, 1989

National Civic League, *The Civic Index: A New Approach to Improving Community Life* & *The Civic Index: Profiles in Community Building*, Denver, Colorado, 1993

National Civic League, "Proposal to Establish a Community Building and Collaboration Center," Denver, Colorado, 1993

National Civic League, 1995 Healthy Communities Action Project, Denver, Colorado, 1995

National Council for Urban Economic Development, *Regional Cooperation: Planning and Implementing a Strategy for Economic Prosperity*, Washington, D.C., 1988

National League of Cities, *Global Dollars, Local Sense*, Washington, D.C., 1993

National League of Cities, *Leading Cities in a Global Economy*, Washington, D.C., 1995

Neiman, Jennifer, "Motel/Hotel Taxes For the Arts," *Public Management,* Washington, D.C., January 1996

Nelson, Arthur, "Needed: Efficient Land Use Appeals," *LandLines,* Lincoln Institute of Land Policy, Cambridge, Massachusetts, March, 1994

New York Times, New York, New York, "Governor Weicker's Bully Bugle Call," Editorial, January 8, 1993

Norris, Tyler & Lampe, David, "Healthy Communities, Healthy People: A Challenge of Coordination and Compassion," *National Civic Review,* Denver, Colorado, Summer/Fall, 1994

North Dakota Consensus Council, Inc., *User's Guide to the Tool Chest for North Dakota Governments,* Bismark, North Dakota, 1995

O'Looney, John, "Framing a Social Market For Community Responsibility: Governing in an Age of NIMBYs and LULUs," *National Civic Review,* Denver, Colorado, Winter, 1993

Orfield, Myron, Testimony before the Committee on Local Government and Metropolitan Affairs, Minnesota House of Representatives, Minneapolis, Minnesota, 1993

Osborne, David & Gaebler, Ted, *Reinventing Government,* Addison-Wesley, Reading, Massachusetts, 1992

Pammer, William, Jr. & Dustin, Jack, "Fostering Economic Development through County Tax Sharing," *State and Local Government Review,* University of Georgia, Athens, Georgia, Winter, 1993

Parker, Susan, "Regional Assets?," *Newsletter, American Society for Public Administration,* Pittsburgh, Pennsylvania Chapter, Fall, 1992

Parks, Roger & Oakerson, Ronald, "St. Louis: The ACIR Study," *Intergovernmental Perspective,* Advisory Commission on Intergovernmental Relations, Washington, D.C., Winter, 1989

Parry, David, "A Typology of Intergovernmental Approaches to Service Delivery and Provision," The University of Akron, Center for Urban Studies, Akron, Ohio, 1987

Patrick, Deval, Testimony before U.S. House of Representatives, March 24, 1995

Patterson, James & Kim, Peter, *The Day America Told the Truth,* Prentice Hall, New York, New York, 1991

Pearlstein, Steven, "The Rich Get Richer and...," *Washington Post National Weekly,* Washington, D.C., June 12-18, 1995

Pennsylvania Economy League, *Pressing Regional and Community Problems,* Public Hearing of Citizens League of Southwestern Pennsylvania, 1992

Pennsylvania Economy League, "It's All in the Delivery of Local Governments," *PEL League Newsletter,* June, 1994

Phares, Donald, "Reorganizing the St. Louis Area: The Freeholders' Plan," *Intergovernmental Perspective,* Advisory Commission on Intergovernmental Relations, Washington, D.C., Winter, 1989

Philadelphia Inquirer, Philadelphia, Pennsylvania, "Common Ground," September 11, 1994

Phillips, Kevin, *The Politics of Rich and Poor,* Harper Collins, New York, New York, 1990

Plate, Tom, "Save America: Bowl Together," *Pittsburgh Post Gazette,* October 15, 1995

Popper, Frank, "The Great LULU Trading Game," *Planning,* Chicago, Illinois, May 1992

The Public Innovator, "For the People: Healthy Decision Making," Alliance for Reinventing Government, National Academy of Public Administration, October 27, 1994

The Public Innovator, "The Dawn of CyberPolitics," Alliance for Reinventing Government, National Academy of Public Administration, Washington, D.C., November 10, 1994

The Public Innovator, "Twin Cities Area Seeks 'Livable Communities,'" Alliance for Reinventing Government, National Academy of Public Administration, Washington, D.C., March 28, 1996

Putnam, Robert, "What Makes Democracy Work?," *National Civic Review,* Spring, 1993

Putnam, Robert, Speech, 1995 Annual Leadership Symposium, Institute of Portland Metropolitan Studies, Portland State University, Portland, Oregon, 1995. (Based on "Bowling Alone," Journal of Democracy, Baltimore, Maryland, Jannuary 1995).

Rainbow Research, *Job Opportunity Initiatives: Toward a Better Future for Low-Income Children and Youth,* Annie E. Casey Foundation, Baltimore, Maryland, 1994

Raspberry, William, "The Urban League Union Plan," *Washington Post,* Washington, D.C., July 27, 1994

Reeves, Richard, *American Journey,* Simon and Shuster, New York, New York, 1982

Regional Reporter, "New Leadership council considered," National Association of Regional Councils, Washington, D.C., February, 1993

Reinhardt, William G., "Washington State Picks Six Developers to Help Bust Congestion in Puget Sound," *Public Works Financing,* September, 1994

Rendell, Edward, Mayor, City of Philadelphia, *The New Urban Agenda,* Philadelphia, Pennsylvania, 1994

Richman, Roger & Oliver, James, "Virginia's Urban Partnership: How a Public-Private Coalition Set Out to Improve Virginia's Urban Regions," Working Paper, Norfolk, Virginia, 1995

Richmond, Henry, "Round II: Building Community in America," Presentation to Congress on New Urbanism, San Francisco, California, 1995

Ross, Bernard H. et al, *Urban Politics: Power in Metropolitan America,* F. E. Peacock, Itasca, Illinois, 1991

Rotstein, Gary, "U.S. flight to suburbs must halt, group says," *Pittsburgh Post Gazette,* Pittsburgh, Pennsylvania, November 9, 1993

Rusk, David, Presentation, Atlanta Regional Commission, Atlanta, Georgia, 1995

Sanchez, Rene, "A Required Course in Beating the Freshman Blues," *Washington Post National Weekly,* Washington, D.C., October 23-9, 1995, 31

Sancton, Andrew, "Governing Canada's City-Regions," *Policy Options,* Montreal, Canada, May, 1994

Savitch, H. V. et al, "Ties that Bind; Central Cities, Suburbs, and the New Metropolitan Area," Working Paper, Annual Meeting of the American Political Science Association, Chicago, Illinois, 1992

Savitch, H.V. & Vogel, Ron, "Regional Patterns in a Post City Age," Working Paper, Annual Meeting of the American Political Science Association, Chicago, Illinois, September 1995

Schenking, Ann, "Economic Development/Government Equity Program," *Commentary,* Washington, D.C., Fall 1995

Schwartz, Joe and Exter, Thomas, "The World is Flat," *American Demographics,* April, 1991

Seltzer, Ethan, "Responsibilities to Our Regions," *Newsletter, InterGovernmental Affairs Division,* American Planning Association, Chicago, Illinois, February, 1995

Senge, Peter, *The Fifth Discipline: The Art and Practice of The Learning Organization,* Currency Doubleday, New York, New York, 1990

Shanahan, Eileen, "Going It Jointly: Regional Solutions for Local Problems," *Governing,* Washington, D.C., August, 1991

Shutt, John, "European Exposure: Appraising 'Europe' in the Regions, 1994-1999", Working Paper, Urban Affairs Association Conference, 1994

Skok, James, "Policy Issue Networks and the Public Policy Cycle: A Structured-Functional Framework for Public Administration," *Public Administration Review,* American Society for Public Administration, Washington, D.C., July/August 1995

Sloan, Win, *The Gothic Cathedral,* no date

Smith, David, "Comprehensive Tax Base Sharing," *Economic Development Commentary,* National Council for Urban Economic Development, Summer, 1994

Smith, Roger, "How to Avoid Being Lawyered to Death," *Washington Post National Weekly*, Washington, D.C., October 2-8, 1995

Sorkin, Michael, *Variations on a Theme Park: The New American City and the End of Public Space*, Hill and Wang, New York, New York, 1992

Southern California Association of Governments, *Improved Governance of the Southern California Region*, Los Angeles, California, 1990

The Southwestern Pennsylvania Growth Alliance, *Federal Regional Agenda 1993* and *Regional State Agenda 1994*, Pittsburgh, Pennsylvania

Southwestern Pennsylvania Heritage Preservation Commission, *The Legend of the Allegheny Traveler*, Holidaysburg, Pennsylvania, 1995

Sperling, Susan, *Poplollies and Bellibones: A Celebration of Lost Words*, Penguin, New York, New York, 1977

Sprynczynatyk, Connie, "Shiny New Tools for the Local Government Tool Chest," *NIDR News*, National Institute for Dispute Resolution, May/June, 1995

Stein, David Lewis, "Is There Life After Metro?," *Planning*, Chicago, Illinois, March, 1995

Stouffer, Dale, "Regionalism and Program with Respect to New Orleans," Working Paper, New Orleans, Louisiana, 1995

Strauss, Valerie, "On the Short End of the School Funding Stick," *Washington Post National Weekly*, Washington, D.C., no date

Study Circles Resource Center, *The Study Circle Handbook*, Pomfret, Connecticut

Study Circles Resource Center, *Study Circles in Paired Congregations: Enriching Your Community Through Shared Dialogue on Vital Issues*, Pomfret, Connecticut, 1995

Suhm, Victor, *Regional Unity: Report and Program Recommendations for the North Texas Commission*, Dallas, Texas, 1994

Sulzer, Kenneth & Baldwin, Susan, "All parties included in SANDAG growth strategy," *Regional Reporter*, National Association of Counties, February, 1993

Suplee, Curt, "The Modular Theory of the Mind," *Washington Post National Weekly,* Washington, D.C., December 26, 1994-January 1, 1995

Svara, James, "The Structural Reform Impulse in Local Government," *National Civic Review,* Denver, Colorado, Summer-Fall 1994

Svara, James, *Regionalism in North Carolina,* Working Group on Regions and Regionalism, Raleigh, North Carolina, 1995

Thomas, Clarke, *ISTEA: A Different Kind of Highway Act,* University of Pittsburgh, Institute of Politics, Pittsburgh, Pennsylvania, 1993

Thomas, Clarke, *Fixing What Ain't All Broke: The Governance Dilemma,* University of Pittsburgh, Institute of Politics, 1994

Thomas, Lewis, *The Fragile Species,* Charles Scribner's Sons, New York, New York, 1992

de Tocqueville, Alexis, *Fifth Notebook,* November 30, 1831

Toffler, Alvin, *Future Shock,* Random House, New York, New York, 1970

Toffler, Alvin & Toffler, Heidi, *Creating a New Civilization,* Turner Publishing, Inc., Atlanta, Georgia, 1995

Toms, Michael, "Necessary Guilt," *The Sun,* Chapel Hill, North Carolina, no date

Triangle J Council of Governments, "Strategic Regional Leadership," Research Triangle, North Carolina, no date

United States Department of Housing and Urban Development, *Guidelines for Preparing a Consolidated Strategy and Plan Submission for Housing and Urban Development Programs,* Washington, D.C., 1994

United States Department of Housing and Urban Development, *Empowerment: A New Covenant with America's Communities,* President Clinton's National Urban Policy Report, Washington, D.C., 1995

United Way of America, *United Way's Community Capacity-Building Stories,* Alexandria, Virginia, 1995

University of Oregon, Bureau of Governmental Research and Service, *Current and Emerging Roles for COGs in Oregon,* Eugene, Oregon, 1988

Urban Institute, *Housing Mobility: Promise or Illusion?,* Washington, D.C., 1995

van den Berg, Leo et al, "A Survey of Metropolitan Government in Europe," Working Paper, Erasmus University Rotterdam, The Netherlands, European Institute for Comparative Urban Research, 1994

Vise, David & Henderson, Neil, "Giving People the Keys to Saving Their Cities," *Washington Post National Weekly,* May 16-22, 1994

Vogel, Ronald, *Local Government Reorganization,* League of Women Voters of Louisville and Jefferson County & Department of Political Science, University of Louisville, Kentucky, 1994

Voith, Richard, "City and Suburban Growth, Substitutes and Complements," Federal Reserve Bank of Philadelphia, *Business Review,* September/October, 1992

Wagner, Cynthia, "Challenges for Governance," *Futurist,* Bethesda, Maryland, Sep-Oct 1991

Walker, David, "Snow White and the 17 Dwarfs: From Metro Cooperation to Governance," *National Civic Review,* Denver, Colorado, 1987

Wallis, Allan, "Governance and the Civic Infrastructure of Metropolitan Regions, *National Civic Review,* Denver, Colorado, Spring, 1993

"Washington Regional Network: Citizens Plan for the Future, Surface Transportation Policy Project Resource Guide, Case Studies, no date

West, Harry and Taylor, Zach, "Stimulating Civic Change in Metropolitan Regions," *National Civic Review,* Denver, Colorado, Summer, 1995

Williams, Oliver, *Metropolitan Political Analysis,* Free Press, New York, New York, 1971

Wood, Robert, *Suburbia, Its People and Their Politics,* Houghton Mifflin, Boston, Massachusetts, 1958

Wray, Lyle, "Neighborhood, metro challenges call for new responses," *Minnesota Journal*, Citizens League, Minneapolis/St. Paul, Minnesota, January 25, 1994

Wright, Deil & White, Harvey, *Federalism and Intergovernmental Relations*, American Society for Public Administration, Washington, D.C., 1984

3. State and National Organizations with Regional Governance Agendas

Advisory Commission on Intergovernmental Relations, Washington, D.C., 202-653-5540

Alliance for Redesigning Government, Washington, D.C., 202-466-6887

Alliance for National Renewal, National Civic League, Denver, Colorado, 303-571-4343

American Chamber of Commerce Executives, Alexandria, Virginia, 703-998-0072

American Planning Association, Chicago, Illinois, 312-955-9100

American Society for Public Administration, Washington, D.C., 202-393-7878

Association of Community Organizations for Reform Now (ACORN), Chicago, Illinois, 312-939-7488

Center for Living Democracy, Brattleboro, Vermont, 802-254-4331

Center for the New West, Denver, Colorado, 303-572-5400

Civic Network Television, Washington, D.C., 202-887-5900, 800-746-6286

Coalition of Metropolitan and Urban Universities, c/o University of North Texas, 817-565-2471

Committee for Enterprise Development, Washington, D.C., 202-408-9788

Common Cause, Washington, D.C., 202-833-1200

Corporation for Enterprise Development, Washington, D.C., 202-408-9788

Council of State Governments, Lexington, Kentucky, 606-244-8000

Development District Association of America, Washington, D.C., c/o Robert Sokolowski, 202-884-7701

Industrial Areas Foundation, Chicago, Illinois, 312-245-9211

Institute for Awakening Technology, Lake Oswego, Oregon, 503-635-2615

The Institute for The Regional Community, National Association of Regional Councils, 202-457-0710

Institute for Study of Civic Values, Philadelphia, Pennsylvania, 215-238-1434

International City/County Management Association (ICMA), Washington, D.C., 202-289-ICMA

International Downtown Association, Washington, D.C., 202-783-4963

Jefferson Center for New Democratic Processes, Minneapolis, Minnesota, 612-333-5300

Kettering Foundation, Dayton, Ohio, 513-434-7300, 800-221-3657

League of Women Voters, Washington, D.C., 202-429-1965

Lincoln Institute on Land Policy, Cambridge, Massachusetts, 617-661-3016

National Academy of Public Administration, Washington, D.C., 202-347-3190

National Association for Community Leadership, Indianapolis, Indiana, 317-637-7413

National Association of Counties, Washington, D.C., 202-393-6226

National Association of Development Organizations, Washington, D.C., 202-624-7806

✓ National Association of Regional Councils, Washington, D.C., 202-457-0710

National Association of Regional Planning Councils, Dallas, Texas, 214-342-2638

✓National Civic League, Denver, Colorado, 303-571-4343

National Council for Urban Economic Development, Washington, D.C., 202-223-4735

National Council of State Legislators, Denver, Colorado, 303-830-2200

National Governors Association, Washington, D.C., 202-624-5300

National Growth Management Leadership Project, Portland, Oregon, 503-228-9462

National Institute for Dispute Resolution, Washington, D.C., 202-466-4764

✓National League of Cities, Washington, D.C., 202-626-3000

North American Institute for Comparative Urban Research, University of Missouri-St. Louis, St. Louis, Missouri, 314-516-5273

The North Dakota Consensus Council, Inc., Bismark, North Dakota, 701-224-0588

Program for Community Problem Solving, Washington, D.C., 202-783-2961

Public Education Fund Network, Washington, D.C., 202-628-7460

Sister Cities International, Washington, D.C., 202-466-8000

Study Circles Resource Center, Pomfret, Connecticut, 203-928-2616

United Way of America, Alexandria, Virginia, 202-836-7100

Urban Affairs Association, Newark, Delaware, 302-831-1681

4. Publications Addressing Regional Governance Topics

Cityscape, Office of Policy Development and Research, U.S. Department of Housing and Urban Development, Washington, D.C., 202-708-0544

Community Link, Civic Network Television, Washington, D.C., 202-887-5900, 800-746-6286

Economic Development Digest, National Association of Development Organizations, Washington, D.C., 202-624-8813

The Edge City News, Broad Run, Virginia, 703-347-1414

Focus on Study Circles, Newsletter, Study Circles Resource Center, 203-928-2616

Governing, Congressional Quarterly, Inc., Washington, D.C., 202-862-8802

Intergovernmental Perspective, Advisory Commission on Intergovernmental Relations, Washington, D.C., 202-653-5540

Journal of Urban Affairs, Urban Affairs Association, Newark, Delaware, 302-831-1681

Kitchen Table, Newsletter, Alliance for National Renewal, Denver, Colorado, 303-571-4343

LandLines, Lincoln Institute on Land Policy, Cambridge, Massachusetts, 702-347-3190

Metropolitan Universities, Transaction Publishers, Rutgers - The State University, New Brunswick, New Jersey, 201-932-2280

Nation's Cities Weekly, National League of Cities, Washington, D.C., 202-626-3000

National Civic Review, National Civic League, Denver, Colorado, 303-571-4343

Newsletter, InterGovernmental Affairs Division, American Planning Association, 312-955-9100

NIDR News, Newsletter, National Institute for Dispute Resolution, Washington, D.C., 202-466-4764

Partnership Spotlight, Piedmont Triad Partnership, Greensboro, North Carolina, 910-669-4556

Planning, American Planning Association, Chicago, Illinois, 312-955-9100

The Public Innovator, Alliance for Redesigning Government, National Academy of Public Administration, Washington, D.C., 202-466-6887

Public Management, International City/County Management Association (ICMA), Washington, D.C., 202-289-ICMA

Publius, Center for the Study of Federalism, Temple University and Center for State and Local Government, Lafayette University, 610-250-5598

Regional Reporter, Newsletter, National Association of Regional Councils, 202-457-0710

The Regionalist, Journal, National Association of Regional Councils and Institute for Community and Area Development, Athens, Georgia, 706-542-3350

Urban Affairs Review, Sage Publications, Thousand Oaks, California, 805-499-9774

Index